Jessica James, Michael Leister, and Christoph Rieger

Random Walks in Fixed Income and Foreign Exchange

The Moorad Choudhry Global Banking Series

Series Editor
Professor Moorad Choudhry

Jessica James, Michael Leister,
and Christoph Rieger

Random Walks in Fixed Income and Foreign Exchange

Unexpected Discoveries in Issuance,
Investment and Hedging of Yield Curve Instruments

DE GRUYTER

ISBN 978-3-11-068868-9
E-ISBN (PDF) 978-3-11-068873-3
E-ISBN (EPUB) 978-3-11-068879-5
ISSN 2627-8847

Library of Congress Control Number: 2021933285

Bibliographic information published by the Deutsche Nationalbibliothek
The Deutsche Nationalbibliothek lists this publication in the Deutsche Nationalbibliografie; detailed bibliographic data are available on the Internet at http://dnb.dnb.de.

Cover image: Nikada/E+/Getty Images
Typesetting: Integra Software Services Pvt. Ltd.
Printing and binding: CPI books GmbH, Leck

www.degruyter.com

Advance Praise for *Random Walks in Fixed Income and Foreign Exchange*

This collection is beautifully written by practitioners at the forefront of "actually useful research". I highly recommend it for enhancing knowledge of the cross-currency basis, how to hedge fixed income securities and understanding yield-curve behaviour in the low-interest world . . . all key to successful employment as the global economy transforms through the conduit of financial markets.

Professor Carol Alexander
Professor of Finance, University of Sussex

This book covers some important material in a way that makes it accessible to a wide range of practitioners and academics. The first part of the book looks at the cross-currency basis. It explains why it has existed since 2008 and discusses whether traders can profit from it. The second part of the book considers the impact of low interest rates on the way we should analyze yield curves. It carefully considers the term premium, duration, and convexity. The whole book is a "must-read" for everyone concerned with FX or fixed income markets.

John Hull
Maple Financial Professor of Derivatives and Risk Management,
Joseph L. Rotman School of Management, University of Toronto

Random Walks in Fixed Income and Foreign Exchange reminds us that while there are fundamental principles of finance, nothing in the field stays the same. Markets evolve constantly, with changes in one quickly rippling through to others. But that doesn't mean the relationship between assets stays the same. All this makes for new risks, and new opportunities. This book does a great job in helping you understand the latest market factors and relationships.

Peter Eisenehardt
Secretary General, International Council of Securities Associations, London,
and Faculty Member, The BTRM

https://doi.org/10.1515/9783110688733-202

Foreword

It is sometimes said, not least by me, that there appears to be something of a divide between academia and practice in finance and banking. Those who publish in academia on finance topics have little or no experience in banking, and those who practise in finance only rarely, if ever, read academic journal articles on the subject. If this is indeed the case, it is a pity. That's because both sides would benefit from closer involvement with the other: academics from focusing their research on areas of direct relevance to practitioners, who would be interested to read practical recommendations on how they should direct their operations; and practitioners, by being able to apply an academic rigour to their analysis and drawing of conclusions. Thus, any activity that results in both sides coming closer together is a positive development for society.

This book reduces slightly the level of clear blue water between academia and practice in finance. But before I expound on its many virtues, I must declare an interest. One of the authors is a personal friend of mine, but I was aware of Professor James and the quality of her work many years before I met her, as I was a big fan of her co-authored book *Interest Rate Modelling* (John Wiley & Sons Ltd) which I purchased over 20 years ago. I still have that very well-thumbed copy. It is an excellent read. But then again yield curves and yield curve analysis was my first love in finance and banking, so perhaps I was pre-disposed to be appreciative of a book with such a title? Not a bit of it. This topic is one of the most well-researched subjects in finance-related academia, but from my own personal observations I would suggest that over 80% of the output in this space has virtually zero practical relevance for the employee of a bank. What made Jessica's book stand out was its accessibility and genuine value for the practitioner.

And this is exactly what stands out in this latest offering from Professor James and her co-authors Michael Leister and Christoph Rieger. It helps to bridge the divide between academia and practice, and the result is a genuinely worthwhile addition to the financial economics literature.

The Foreign Exchange (FX) markets are a multi-trillion dollar vital segment of the global economy, and the basics of it are generally well understood – there is, after all, a large number of publications and websites in this space. But for corporate entities using FX markets for hedging, and that covers very many entities around the world, there are aspects of the market that are less well understood, such as the cross-currency "basis". Banks who provide these products to their corporate customers also will want to know about some of the more arcane aspects of the market. This book addresses these issues with elan. Another technical topic that is presented accessibly with a minimum of mathematics (we are adherents to the late Professor Stephen Hawking's dictum that for each equation in a book, the readership is cut by one-half!) is the FX conversion factor, something that can be of material significance to those issuing or investing in a non-domestic currency.

https://doi.org/10.1515/9783110688733-203

The authors cover these subjects with exceptional clarity and precision in this book. They also discuss at length that most favourite topic of mine, the yield curve and the term premium. The term premium is an aspect of yield curve analysis that is, again, not as well understood by practitioners as it should be. They will benefit immediately from a reading of the relevant chapters herein.

I can honestly say that I am more excited about this book than I have been about any other financial markets texts I have come across in a long time. It is great to see a work that has value for both the academic and the practitioner, from writers who are clearly at the top of their game. I do hope you enjoy reading it.

Professor Moorad Choudhry
Surrey, England
31 January 2021

Contents

Preface

The title of this book is taken from a delightful book called *A Random Walk in Science* by Robert Weber. It's a collection of stories about how science fits into society and manages to combine rigour, humanity and humour. When we were asked if there was any way that our somewhat eclectic set of papers would combine into a single book, it immediately came to mind as a unifying theme.

It will probably not raise as many laughs as its namesake, but what links the different elements in this book is the spirit of pure curiosity which led to their creation. It has been the greatest pleasure to be able to investigate the interactions between the areas of fixed income and FX and find that there is much to learn and discover.

The first section examines the rise of the cross-currency basis in the post-crisis world, digs into its origins and applications, and investigates the implication of the new credit-sensitive world for issuance, investment and hedging. In Chapter 1, we define and dig into the origins of the basis, which before 2008 would have represented a juicy arbitrage opportunity. Understanding why this is not so today leads us to the discussion in Chapter 2 about the drivers and sustainers of the basis, and in Chapter 3 we show that it is possible to derive and create many cross-currency bases which are not usually quoted in the market but which can represent very real opportunities for issuers and investors. Chapter 4 derives a new way of looking at FX hedging of fixed income assets, followed by Chapter 5, which shows how to analyse these hedged assets and understand the linked effects of the basis and the two yield curves which underly their valuation.

The second section examines the impact of the new world on the yield curve, and vice versa. Term premium, duration and convexity all take on new importance in this new state of ultra-low rates and flat term structures. The search for yield in this brave new world has driven issuers to issue, and investors to buy, century-long bonds, in a world where only a scant handful of currencies have ever survived that long. Convexity has been a driver of this process – whether for good or bad, time will tell. We show how to derive a closed-form solution for both duration and convexity, and show how implied convexity at the start of the life of a bond can be compared to its realised value through its lifetime.

We have updated all graphs and charts, where possible, to the current day, and have adjusted the text appropriately. This was not possible for Chapter 6 on Term Premium, which is reprinted with kind permission from Taylor & Francis in the form it originally appeared, but it is followed by an update in Chapter 7 which incorporates additional models and compares their recent evolution.

We hope you enjoy reading this book as much as we enjoyed the research.

https://doi.org/10.1515/9783110688733-205

Chapter 1
What Really is the Cross-Currency Basis?

The cross-currency basis – often just called the 'basis' – is a strange creature.[1] It is referred to often enough in the financial markets that most participants think that they probably ought to know what it is. I was certainly one of them. 'Some credit adjustment to currency hedging' was how I vaguely thought of it. However, the more one studies and understands it, the stranger and more important it becomes. It is nothing less than a violation of the arbitrage conditions governing the relationships between interest rates and foreign exchange rates, and before it was observed, it would have been thought of as impossible. This paper describes how to calculate the basis, discusses some potential drivers, and ends with some unexpected applications.

The story of cross-currency basis swaps originates with the start of the floating currency market regime in the late 1970s and early 1980s, as corporations and investors with global reach sought methods of insuring themselves against sharp currency movements. Forward FX rate contracts became popular. The forward rate calculation is trivial (see equation (1)), and any deviation in the market from the calculated rate implied by interest rate differentials gives traders a chance to do arbitrage trades, which made such deviations unlikely.

And yet, since 2008, such deviations have persistently emerged. It is these deviations, expressed in a spread to one of the Libor interest rates used to calculate the forward FX rate, which are known as the cross-currency bases. We plot the basis for EURUSD in Figure 1.1; it is remarkable how large and persistent it can be, given that before 2008, arbitrage activity maintained it at almost zero.

The Calculation Underlying the Cross-Currency Basis Swap

A Quick Note on Terminology

An FX forward is a contract that locks in the price at which a counterparty can buy or sell a currency on a future date. The exchange rate is typically today's rate, adjusted for the interest rate differential in the two currencies. If the interest rate in the local currency is higher than that of the USD (or whatever the reference currency is), the FX forward will include a devaluation expectation.

1 This chapter was first published as Commerzbank's Rates Radar, 'More "interest" in cross-currency basis swaps', March 2017.

https://doi.org/10.1515/9783110688733-001

Figure 1.1: 1y EURUSD xccy basis.
Source: Commerzbank Research, Bloomberg

In a cross-currency swap, the parties exchange a stream of cashflows in one currency for a stream of cashflows in another. The typical cross-currency swap involves the exchange of both recurring interest and principal (usually at the end of the swap), and thus can fully cover the currency risk of a loan transaction. Conceptually, cross-currency swaps can be viewed as a series of forward contracts packaged together. For much more detail on more of these, see Appendix 1.B.

Perhaps the Simplest Formula in Financial Mathematics

The calculation to discover the forward rate is trivial. It is found using the following expression:

$$\frac{F}{S}=\frac{1+r_f}{1+r_d} \tag{1}$$

where F is the forward FX rate, S is the spot (current) FX rate, r_f is the foreign interest rate and r_d is the domestic interest rate. The FX rate must be quoted as units of foreign currency per domestic currency – for example, 1.1 USD (US dollar) per EUR (Euro). EURUSD is the conventional way of naming this rate in the market.

This calculation arises very simply. There are two ways of getting from holding the domestic currency now, to holding the foreign currency in the future, illustrated in Figure 1.2.

Method 1. Invest now for the period in question, at the domestic interest rate, then exchange at the end of the period.

Method 2. Exchange now so that you hold the foreign currency, and invest at the foreign currency rate for the period.

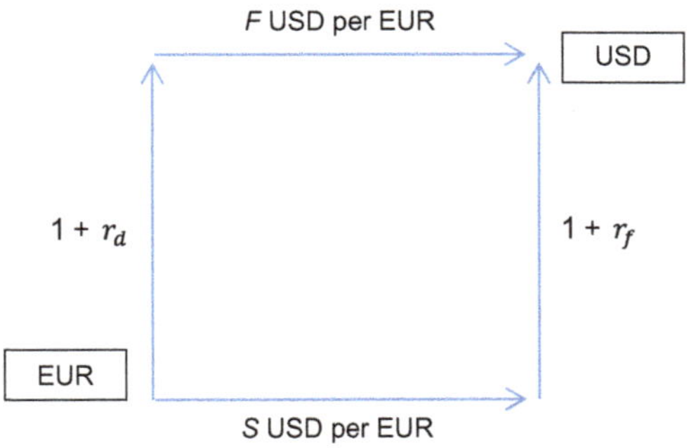

Figure 1.2: Forward FX rate calculation.

Arbitrage pricing would tell us that Method 1 and Method 2 must be exactly the same, apart from perhaps some small trading spread effects, or there will be a chance to 'round trip' the system and make some risk-free money (arbitrage). Conventionally, and in the pre-crisis world, this will only occur in a small and transient manner, as sharp-eyed traders look out for the chance and thus keep pressure on the forward rate to comply with equation (1).

This type of situation has traditionally (pre-crisis) arisen in small and temporary forms, quickly eliminated by arbitrage trading. Thus this method of calculating the forward rate was thought to be completely robust. How could it possibly be incorrect in any substantial way?

But as we will see, even this apparently unbreakable piece of mathematics is vulnerable to unforeseen market effects. The existence of a non-zero cross-currency basis 'breaks' equation (1).

How the Calculation Distorts No-Arbitrage Pricing

The relationship in equation (1) is protected by arbitrage constraints, which one would think, in this era where both humans and machines comb the market for strategies and opportunities, would be sufficient to ensure its integrity. However, market size and liquidity are not enough to ensure perfect efficiency. In Appendix 1.A, we show that the FX market has by some definitions been markedly inefficient since its origins as a floating rate, by allowing a profitable carry trade to persist. And we can present simple evidence that an acute distortion of equation (1) has occurred and moreover persists to this day.

Let us go back to the equation.

$$\frac{F}{S} = \frac{1 + r_f}{1 + r_d} \tag{1}$$

If EUR is the domestic currency, and USD the foreign currency, then a quick rearrangement gives us the following equation:

$$r_d = \frac{S}{F} \times (1 + r_f) - 1 \tag{2}$$

Now, all of these rates are readily observable in the market. To check it out precisely, we calculated r_d using equation (2), and compared it to the market rate since 2000. Before about 2008, the calculated value of r_d matches the value of r_d obtained from the time series EUSW1V3 Curncy (on Bloomberg), the EUR 1-year swap rate. But after that date, they vary considerably, sometimes by up to 1%. If we plot the difference in Figure 1.3, calculated using $r_{d\text{-theoretical}} - r_{d\text{-market}}$, then we obtain the grey line. We have added to the graph the quoted xccy (shorthand for cross-currency) EURUSD 1y basis swap (black line).

The degree to which the arbitrage pricing is violated is almost exactly equal to the market quantity known as the cross-currency basis swap.

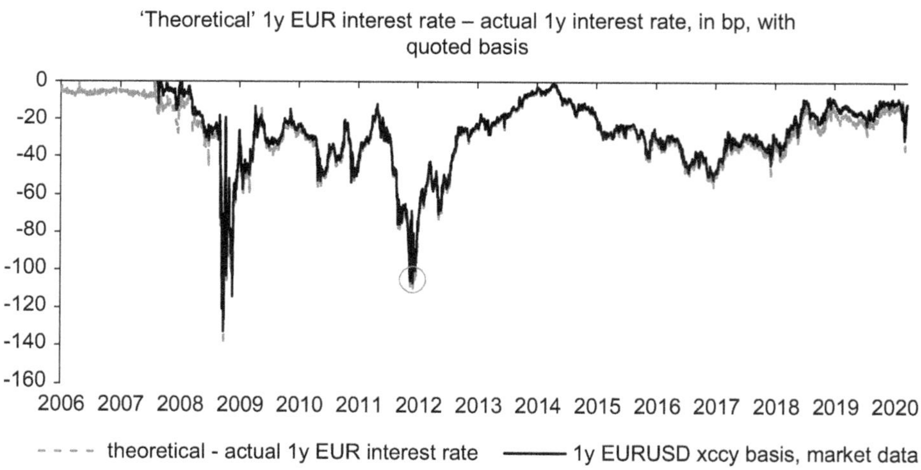

Figure 1.3: Theoretical and actual EUR interest rate difference.
Source: Commerzbank Research, Bloomberg

It's clear to see that apart from a few not-so-good data points, they are essentially the same. So what is going on?

Essentially, equation (1) is no longer holding, and has not held since 2008, even between EUR and USD, the world's largest currencies. This degree of violation is called the 'basis' or 'basis swap' and it is expressed as the difference between the non-USD interest rate (in this case, the 1-year EUR swap rate) implied by the FX forward, and the actual market value of this rate.

Here's a quick example taken from one of the more extreme recent periods (grey circle in the graph in Figure 1.3). The codes are the Bloomberg tickers for the rates, so that the interested reader can check the calculation.

On 29th December 2011

EUR-USD xccy basis	= 101.9bp	(EUBS1 Curncy)
EURUSD spot FX rate	= 1.296	(EURUSD Curncy)
EUR 1y swap rate	= 1.094%	(EUSW1V3 Curncy)
USD 1y swap rate	= 0.691%	(USSA1 Curncy)
EURUSD 1y FX forward	= 1.304	(EUR12m Index)

Using equation (2), we calculate the 'theoretical' EUR 1y swap rate as follows:
EUR 1y swap rate (theoretical) = $r_d = \frac{S}{F} \times (1 + r_f) - 1 = 1.296/1.304 \times (1{+}0.691\%) - 1$
EUR 1y swap rate (theoretical) = 0.073%
But the actual swap rate is not 0.0733%, it is 1.094%. The difference is
0.073% – 1.094% = –1.021% = –102.1bp
And this is almost exactly equal to the quoted basis in the market, –1.019%.

Of course, that is not the only way to express the inequality. We could equally well plot the difference between the theoretical FX forward rate, derived from the spot rate and the interest rates available in the market, and the actual quoted rate, $F_{theoretical} - F_{market}$. Then we would create the following graph, as shown in Figure 1.4.

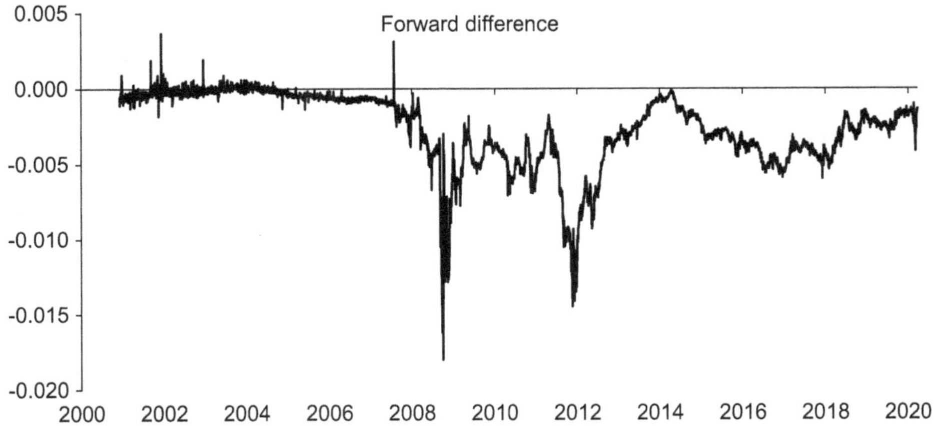

Figure 1.4: Forward difference.
Source: Commerzbank Research, Bloomberg

And if we wanted, we could rotate the whole situation once more and arrive at a spot FX rate difference. Though this is probably not the best way to view the issue, a shift to the spot rate would be just as valid to explain the market mismatch.

We have illustrated the situation using the 1-year rates, only because they involve the least amount of arithmetic. But one may exactly repeat this analysis for tenors from 3m to 30y, and the same relationships will hold. So however we look at it, the forward rate calculation is broken, and not even in a transient way – the basis seems to have moved in and is here to stay!

So, What Actually is a 'Cross-Currency Basis Swap'?

It's worth explaining exactly what this means, and also what is meant when folks refer simply to 'the basis'. A cross-currency basis swap (often abbreviated to 'xccy basis swap') can formally be set out as in Figure 1.5. Here, we assume that an institution starts off with EUR funding, which it converts with a basis swap to USD funding. This could be a EUR-based issuer that has sold a EUR bond locally, and so already has EUR bond cashflows such as coupon and redemption, but would rather convert them to USD. Practically, most sub-1-year hedging is done using currency forwards (a single exchange at the final date), whereas longer term hedging tends to be done using swaps (final exchange plus interim interest rate exchanges).

The central figure is the contract known as the cross-currency basis swap, where there are initial and final exchanges of capital (both at the spot exchange rate at the start of the deal) and interim floating rate interest rate exchanges. At the start of the deal, both currency legs will have the same value, but of course as FX rates vary, the value of the deal can change. Variations in interest rates will have only a small effect as the interest rate cashflows are all floating; the 'next' coupon is the only one which is known and fixed.

The quantity often somewhat confusingly referred to as the 'basis' is an adjustment to the central basis swap agreement. The basis is the result of supply and demand for USD cashflows. Strong demand for USD cashflows means that the EURIBOR interest rate available for the deal is not the one which will make the PV of the EUR and the USD legs equal; it is a little less, and *this difference is the basis*. It is exactly what we calculated in equation (2). The reader can already see that a basis which can be larger than 1% will be highly significant to issuers and investors.

Conversion Factor

Before we go on to discuss the various drivers of the cross-currency basis, it is worth introducing one more effect that is often neglected. When we discuss the motivations of issuers and investors, the cost of issuance is strongly influenced by one

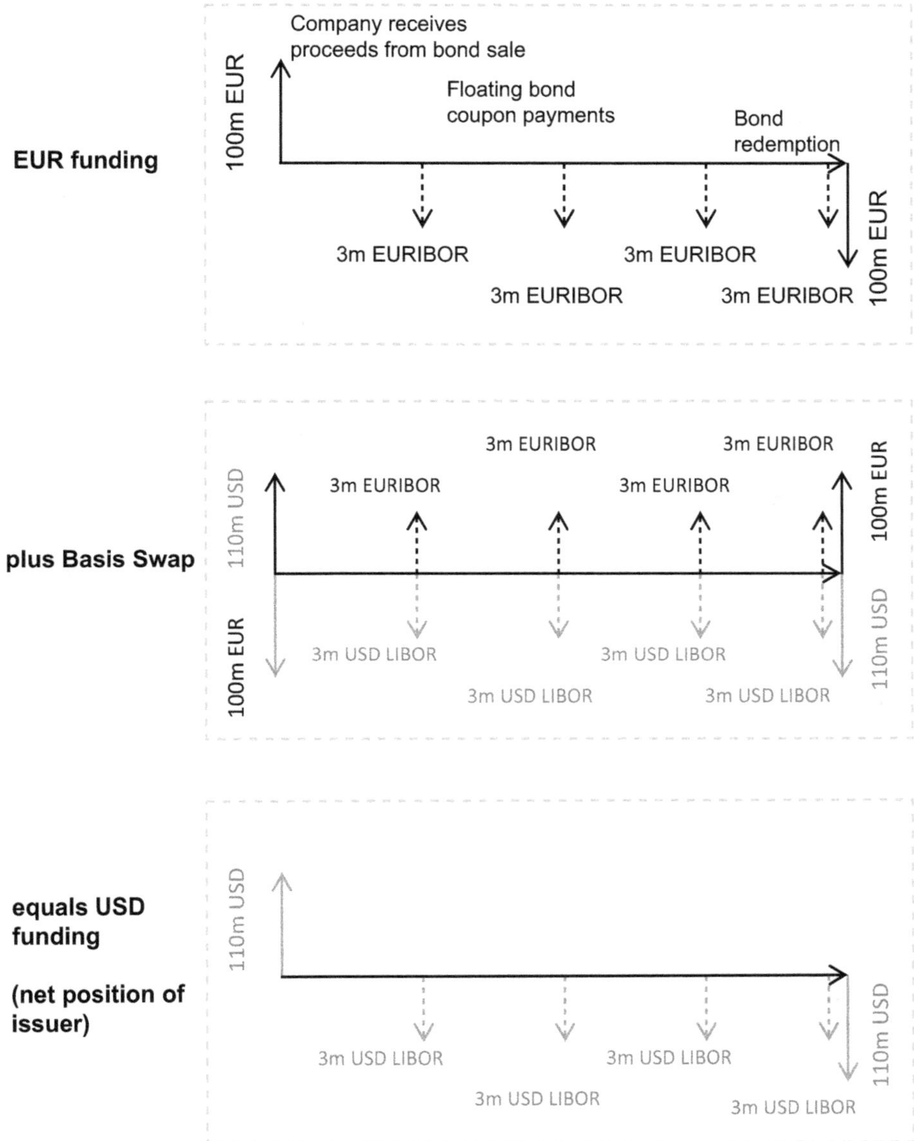

Figure 1.5: Cross-currency basis swap.
Source: Commerzbank Research

additional item: the conversion factor. The conversion factor is the number of basis points per annum in one currency that equates to 1 basis point per annum in another currency – thus it varies with the tenor and structure of the interest rate curves of the two currencies. It is important to remember that it does not depend upon the FX rate, where 1 basis point in one currency is 1 basis point in the other, at all times.

Another way of thinking about the conversion factor is that it comes from different convexities, or yield curve shapes, in the two currencies and is thus dependent both on interest rate curves and spread levels.

Where interest rate differentials are small, the conversion factor will make only a small difference to the rates – typically just 1 or 2 basis points – but where the differentials are large, the difference may be quite significant.

To convert from basis points in a non-EUR currency into basis points in EUR:

- If the non-EUR rates < EUR rates, then EUR conversion factor > 1
- If the non-EUR rates > EUR rates, then EUR conversion factor < 1

Or vs the USD,

- If the non-USD rates < USD rates, then USD conversion factor > 1
- If the non-USD rates > USD rates, then USD conversion factor < 1

The conversion factor of a particular tenor is given by the ratio of the sum of the discount factors up to that point of the different currencies – so for the 10-year point, it is the sum of all the EUR discount factors divided by the sum of all the USD discount factors. This tells us that the 10y EUR-to-USD conversion factor was 1.091 basis points on 20 February 2017, as in Table 1.1. Hence, a credit spread of 400bp over the EUR IRS swap curve translates into 400 x 1.091 = 436bp in USD. In order to swap the EUR instrument into USD, you would need to further add the EUR/USD currency swap costs as well as the EUR basis swap cost of 39.5 bp (as of 20 February 2017). Finally, you might have to consider the Libor frequency of the EUR and USD legs. If the EUR leg is 6m, as is market standard, and the USD leg is 3m, as is also often the case, then the 3/6 EUR swap costs will also need to be added. If the two legs are the same, then this cost is zero.

Table 1.1: Example of conversion factor calculation as of 20 February 2017.

Interest rates as of 20 Feb 2017										
Tenor	1y	2y	3y	4y	5y	6y	7y	8y	9y	10y
USD	1.30%	1.56%	1.75%	1.90%	2.01%	2.09%	2.18%	2.26%	2.32%	2.38%
EUR	−0.21%	−0.15%	−0.07%	0.02%	0.13%	0.26%	0.38%	0.51%	0.64%	0.75%
Discount Factors										
USD	0.991	0.976	0.959	0.940	0.920	0.900	0.879	0.859	0.838	0.818
EUR	1.004	1.007	1.008	1.008	1.005	0.999	0.990	0.978	0.964	0.948
Conversion Factors										
	1.013	1.022	1.032	1.042	1.051	1.061	1.069	1.077	1.085	1.091

Source: Commerzbank Research

This example shows that the conversion factor element in cross-currency swaps made around 48% (or 36bp) of the overall swap costs of 76.0bp if the credit spread of the instrument is 400bp in February 2017.

We note that an advantage for an issuer is a disadvantage for an investor, and vice versa. Thus, investors looking to buy bonds can apply exactly the same analysis to find where they may get the best value.

For a detailed discussion of the conversion factor, see Chapter 5.

Where does the Cross-Currency Basis Come from?

In brief, the basis arises because issuers prefer to match the currency mix they have on the asset side with the currency mix on the liability side, while investors prefer to hedge their FX risk. If an issuer cannot obtain sufficient foreign currency funding (as during the 2008 financial crisis when European banks had to fund lots of dollar assets but had lost access to the dollar funding market), they can create synthetic foreign funding via domestic funding in combination with FX forwards (in the FX market) or basis swaps (which belong more to the rates market). This can create a mismatch in the supply/demand for foreign funding and the hedging instruments. As long as the access to foreign funding remains distorted between domestic and foreign issuers and market participants lack balance sheets or credit lines to arbitrage away the distortion, there will be pressure for the basis to exist. In general, this hedging need translates to demand for certain currencies, often the USD. For a good explanation of these causes and effects, see Borio et al. (2016).

In Figure 1.6 is a rough illustration of the different potential sources of the basis. It centres on issuance of debt in different countries and currencies. Note that the top boxes and the bottom boxes 'balance' each other – if the top boxes dominate, the basis becomes more negative; if the bottom box effects grow, the basis becomes less negative.

Some explanation of these terms is useful.

- USD (EUR) payer swap: the owner of a cross-currency basis swap, which changes their net position from paying USD (EUR) floating rates to paying EUR (USD) floating rates.
- Credit spread: the difference between rates which a company pays on its own curve (in USD, respectively EUR) and the IRS curve for the same currency. When we hear that 'credit spreads are tight' it means that demand for corporate debt in that currency is high, so the cost of debt is relatively low.
- Negative basis: the difference between the actual interest rate for a currency and the theoretical interest rate calculated using the FX forward rate, FX spot rate and (usually) the USD interest rate. When the actual rate is less than the theoretical rate, the basis is negative.

Issuers and the xccy basis
Situations where issuers would be USD payers

USD Payer swap: USD funded, wish to raise EUR

Why? Tight EUR credit spreads relative to USD

Result: **More negative basis**

Investors and the xccy basis
Situations where investors would be USD payers

USD Payer swap: EUR based, EUR synthetic investment

Why? Asset diversification, capture higher yields abroad

Result: **More negative basis**

Issuers and the xccy basis
Situations where issuers would be EUR payers

EUR Payer swap: EUR funded, wish to raise USD

Why? For some products and tenors, it is cheaper to issue in USD

Result: **Less negative basis**

Investors and the xccy basis
Situations where investors would be EUR payers

EUR Payer swap: USD funded, but EUR investment

Why? Asset diversification

Result: **Less negative basis**

Figure 1.6: Potential sources of the xccy basis.
Source: Commerzbank

Let's think of a situation in which an issuer finds themselves when they need to issue debt. They want to do it in the most economical way. For a USD issuer, the 'ground zero' or best possible level could be considered to be the IRS curve in USD (although some highly rated entities like GE can even trade inside the swap rate at the short end). The cost above that level is the credit spread due to their own issuer quality, or USD_{spread}. Similarly, the cost of issuance to a Euro-area issuer is EUR_{spread}.

The cost of issuing in another currency, and then hedging the FX risk of the issue, will depend on the credit spread in the other country for companies of similar quality, the cross-currency basis, and the conversion factor.

So, now we have the full rationale, which companies must bear in mind when making their issuance choice:

For the USD entity, they will issue in EUR (and buy USD payer xccy basis swaps) if

$$\mathbf{USD_{spread} > EUR_{spread} * Conversion\ Factor + xccy\ basis}$$

This is the case for entities like SSSAs where the ECB PSPP is active.

For the EUR entity, they will issue in USD (and buy EUR payer xccy basis swaps) if

$$\mathbf{EUR_{spread} > USD_{spread} * Conversion\ Factor + xccy\ basis}$$

This would most frequently be the case for higher-spread products (AT1 and T2, high-yield issuers) where the ECB is not active, and where for longer tenors the conversion factors are very favourable.

As an example, consider a US firm on 20 February 2017 whose bonds have a 200bp credit spread over the US swap rate. The subsidiary of the firm in Europe can issue bonds which have 100bp credit spread over the EUR swap rate. The basis is 39.5bp, and the conversion factor is 1.091.

$$\mathbf{USD_{spread} = 200bp}$$

$$\mathbf{EUR_{spread} = 100bp * 1.091 + 39.5bp}$$

$$\mathbf{= 148.6bp}$$

Thus, they'll be about 50bp better off if they issue in Europe.

The effect of this long-term behaviour is to skew the effective USD interest rate higher. However, this skew will differ from one currency pair to the next as credit spread and other effects persist to different extents in different markets – thus the market 'expression' of this USD demand as a spread to the non-USD interest rate. Another way of putting it is that counterparties impose increasingly large spreads on the trade, which only ever seems to go one way!

Euro-area supras and agencies are the prominent counterexample, as they actively cover their EUR funding needs in the USD market and hence take advantage of the basis.

Another significant reason is currency mismatches on the balance sheets of large financial institutions. As yields change, balance sheets may be structurally biased towards or against specific currencies. FX derivatives like swaps will have to be used to cover any currency gaps between assets and liabilities, which will place pressure on equation (1) again. So here again, imbalances in the supply and demand for currency hedging result in a non-zero basis, as these institutions are usually fully FX-hedged.

Additionally, strategic hedging on the part of investors with foreign currency holdings can also apply pressure to widen (that is, make more negative) the basis. Once more, the hunt for yield sends the market into foreign territory. But portfolio allocation ratios, once established and prevalent, move slowly, and thus another persistent currency hedge position can exist.

The desirability of a currency is closely connected with yield, and one good indicator of this is the FX carry trade. The G10 FX carry trade is the result of allocating funds to higher-yielding currencies by borrowing in the lower-yielding currencies. In Figure 1.7 we can see that this trade correlates closely with the EURUSD basis swap, showing that the basis is strongly influenced by yield – and thus ultimately central bank policies. However, as can be seen in the chart, during stress periods such as 2008 and 2011/12, the basis is highly volatile and can significantly decouple from the carry/yield proxies.

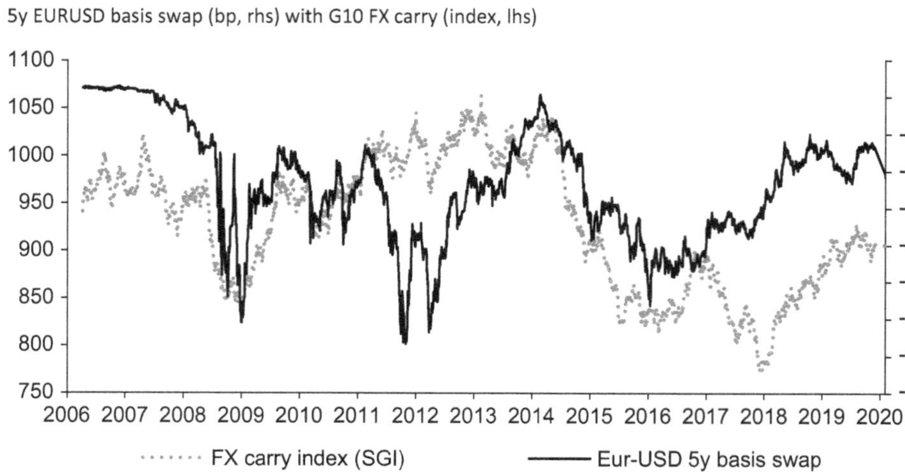

Figure 1.7: Cross-currency basis swap with FX carry.
Source: Bloomberg, Commerzbank Research

What Keeps the Basis Swap from Being Arbitraged Away?

We can see why there might be one-way pressure on the forward rate or Libor rates, but traditionally, an equal and opposite pressure would be provided by arbitrage activity which would bring rates back in line with equation (1). Perhaps the important question is not 'Why does the basis swap exist?' because we know that pressures and temporary dislocations often occur in financial markets. The true question is, 'Why does it stay?'

There are quite a few reasons as to why it persists, and they all have to do with the more stringent regulatory regime governing the markets since the crisis, which ultimately prevents markets from balancing supply and demand for FX hedges. We list the more significant ones in the following section.

Capital Cost of FX Derivatives

The regulatory burden of holding different deal types on books has changed. Derivatives like cross-currency swaps, which are used to arbitrage the currency imbalances described in the previous section, all involve capital flows – often substantial – at the end date. These will require large amounts of risk capital to be held against them. Thus, there will be a limit to how many may be done, and there may be a cost to doing them, as the risk capital used to protect them will be in safe, low-yielding instruments. Arbitraging will thus entail a cost and will have a limited extent for most institutions.

Counterparty Risks and Credit Limits

Arbitrage activities require counterparties and the credit quality of the counterparties limits the exposure that one institution can have to others. Thus, large-leverage and high-risk deals can only occur with a limited set of counterparties and to a limited degree. In that regard, the varying cost and availability of repo funding across jurisdictions limit the extent to which leveraged investors can arbitrage the basis away.

Clearing

Cross-currency swaps are not eligible for clearing with many of the world's larger exchanges. Non-cleared derivatives tend to attract a higher cost of funding, and the introduction of bilateral variation margining for uncleared trades makes it difficult to execute trades, as numerous legal CSA amendments have not yet been signed. Though there are currently some exceptions made for the currency market, generally the delays to implement clearing for these deal types impose yet another limit on their number and extent.

Horses for Courses

Of course, there are a few institutions that can do the arbitrage to a degree. But that degree will vary. For a highly rated cash rich organisation, which could issue bonds in USD and take advantage of the basis to do a swap to the end date to deliver value in a different currency, the cost of placing bonds is important. For a large hedge fund, the price and availability of funding to provide the large arbitrage cashflows will be paramount.

For a useful discussion of the causes of the basis, see Du, Tepper and Verdelhan (2016), which also argues that the dominant reason for its persistence are regulation-driven balance sheet costs.

How Could an Institution Make Money from the Cross-Currency Basis Swap?

This is the burning question! There is no definitive answer, as different institutions will have very different situations, needs and relative advantages. But the graph in Figure 1.9 suggests that at least for some folks, for some of the time, there is money to be made.

We have calculated a 'yield pickup' for 1y government bonds. We assume that the investor is based in Germany and can hold (and short via repo if necessary) bonds in Germany, the USA, Japan, the UK and Australia, with a similar rating or perceived credit risk. The yield pickup is the bond interest rate differential hedged for the 1y period via the cross-currency swap market, including the basis. Thus the pickup is given by

$$\Delta_{\mathbf{bond}} - \Delta_{\mathbf{swap}} + \mathbf{basis}$$

where Δ_{bond} and Δ_{swap} are the 1y yield differentials for the relevant instruments in each currency. Writing it in this way clearly illustrates where the dislocations arise. If the spread of bond yield to swap was the same in both currencies, the first two terms would cancel out. If then the basis were zero, there would be no pickup at all. So it is due to differential market views on credit and to the basis. Figures 1.8 and 1.9 are the time series of this yield pickup since the end of 2008 for the different currencies. The second graph focuses on the EURUSD case, showing Δ_{bond} and Δ_{swap} and the basis separately.

We see that the time series contain different correlation 'zones'. The start of the series in sees both JPY and USD with a negative basis from the EUR investor's point of view; in 2008, clearly both were seen as safe havens from the crisis storm. In 2011, however, the JPY correlates more strongly with AUD than USD, and only the USD is seen as the true safe haven in the first of the Greek debt crises. More recently, both USD and JPY maintain a negative basis, but short-range movement of the JPY basis can correlate with more risky currencies. Finally, we see that all four currency bases are going lower vs the EUR, quite possibly indicating a general nervousness about the Euro area in a time of multiple elections, where political surprises and reversals are becoming the norm.

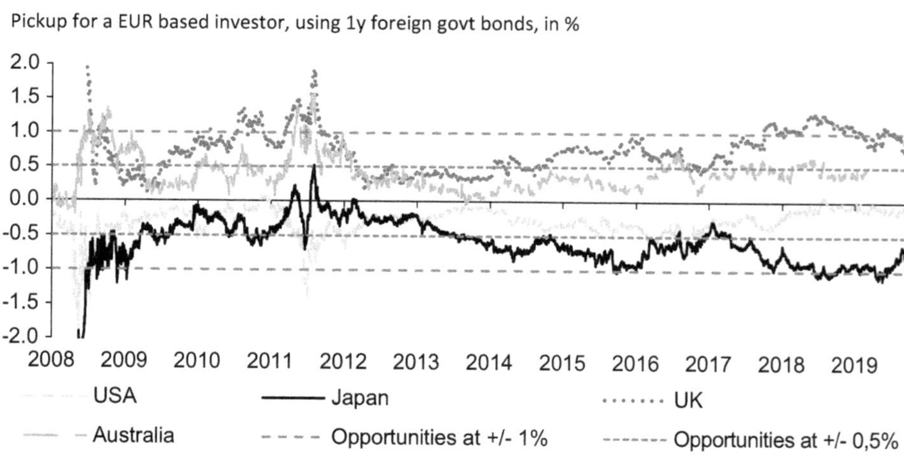

Figure 1.8: Yield pickup, with potential arbitrage opportunity levels.
Source: Commerzbank, Bloomberg

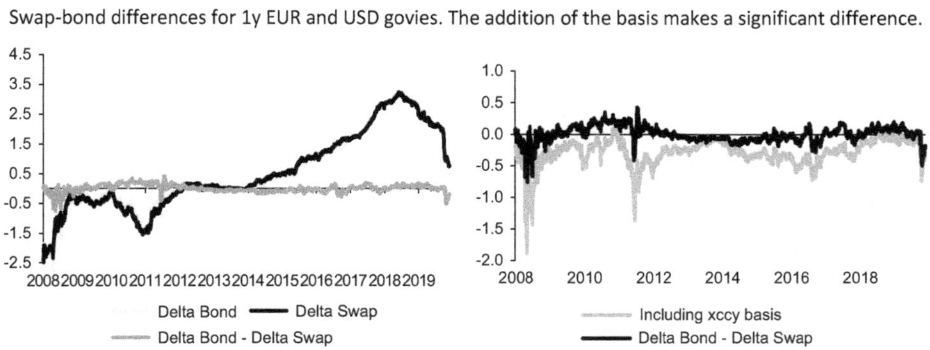

Figure 1.9: EURUSD yield pickup components (%).
Source: Bloomberg, Commerzbank Research

Is this pickup really available in the market? Not entirely – this assumes no repo costs and ignores credit issues and the cost of capital. But nevertheless, it is rarely lower than 30bp for any currency and is often greater than 50bp. For different institutions, there could be opportunities at some level.

Appendix 1.A: The FX carry trade

A Historical View – UIP and CIP

UIP – The First to Fall

The first way in which the FX market declined to obey market expectation was Uncovered Interest Rate Parity (UIP). In the early days of the floating FX rate regime, it was assumed that spot rates would, on average, follow the path laid out by the forward rates. The forward rate path predicts (from equation (1)) that the higher nominal interest-bearing currency will depreciate relative to the lower interest-bearing currency. This does not on the face of it seem unreasonable – investors in higher-yielding (higher inflation) currencies are compensated for the currency weakening by higher interest rate income. Put differently, higher interest rates exist due to higher levels of risk (regarding inflation and central bank expectations, for example), thus, it is plausible to assume that more risky currencies will depreciate relative to less risky ones. Uncovered Interest Rate Parity is said to hold if currencies follow, on average, the forward rate path.

It is useful for market participants, risk managers and quants if UIP does hold. This means that the arbitrage pricing is correct on average and does not allow for systematic trading strategies to deliver profit, and it means that the middle office risk management of long-term positions within financial institutions can use the same valuation models as the front office traders.

But this does not hold. The devaluation of currencies implied by their interest rate regimes does not, on average, occur. As the evidence mounted that UIP is violated – this was first pointed out in 1984 (see Fama [1984]) – and that forward rates have no predictive power over the path of spot rates, the market and various academic institutions reluctantly had to admit that this particular assumption was invalid. We summarise the evidence in Figure 1.10, which was taken from James, Fullwood and Billington (2015) and has since been updated.

This is the result of pursuing a systematic rules-based, quarterly carry-trading strategy in all liquid G10 currency crosses (heavy black line). A carry trade is where the trader takes a position against the forward rate (same as doing a short forward trade), borrowing in the lower-yielding currency to lend in the higher-yielding one. If the spot rate does move to the forward rate, then the trader will make no profit. If the spot rate stays the same and does not move over the course of the deal, the trader will make exactly the forward interest rate differential (known as forward points) – this 'perfect carry trade' is represented by the fine grey dashed line. The central heavy grey dashed line is the actual average path of the spot FX rates.

As can be clearly seen, the actual carry trade has almost identical results (with some noise) to the 'perfect' carry trade. This is the same as saying that on average,

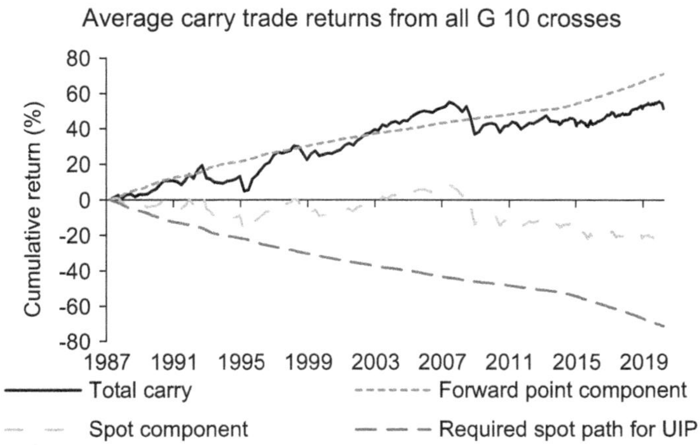

Figure 1.10: Carry trade returns.

FX rates do not move toward the forward rates – they are more likely to be the same as the spot rate at the start of the deal.

So UIP bites the dust. What about CIP?

CIP – Surely Invulnerable?

Covered Interest Rate Parity (CIP) was thought to be a much harder nut to crack. Covered Interest Rate Parity is said to hold if equation (1) holds. However, as we have shown, the existence and persistence of the non-zero cross-currency basis clearly shows that indeed, CIP has fallen as well.

Appendix 1.B: The Cross-Currency Toolkit

The Three Elements

There are different financial products available to allow investors and issuers to adjust their currency exposures. The most liquid and widely used are:

- FX swaps
- FX outrights (or forward outrights)
- Cross-currency basis swaps

Each serves different sections of the market and is useful in different ways. In the following section, we explain the mechanics of each and their major uses.

FX Swap

Figure 1.11 is a schematic of the cashflows involved in an FX swap between parties A and B. We assume we have a principal amount *P* in EUR, and that the current spot FX rate is *S* USD per EUR, with a forward rate *F*.

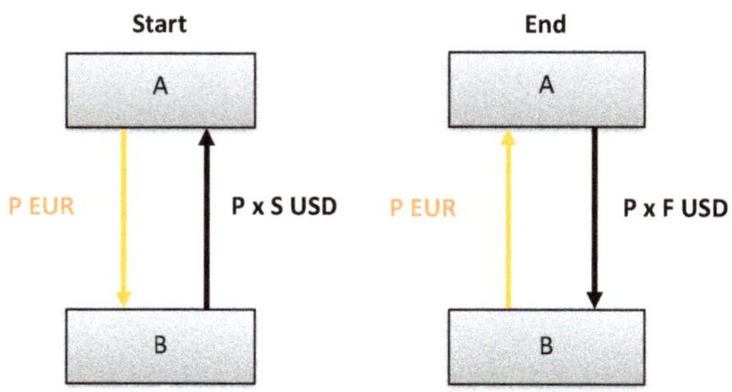

Figure 1.11: FX swap.
Definition of FX swap: Party A borrows Currency 1 to lend Currency 2

Usual Maturity: up to 1y

Uses: FX swaps are mostly a liquidity and treasury management tool. Users are:

- Asset Managers: investors in overseas markets who don't want currency risk. Lenders of domestic currency vs the foreign currency they need to fund
- Bank Treasurers: wish to lower their cost of funding and liquidity in different currencies
- Central Banks: manage their liquidity profiles
- Corporate Treasurers: act like banks for their own short-term funding, and manage their treasury position in different currencies

Note that the basis is embedded into the forward rate, so though it is not explicit in the diagram, it is certainly included.

FX Outright (Forward Outright)

In Figure 1.12, we show the cashflows involved in an FX Outright (often called Forward Outright) between parties A and B. We again assume we have a principal amount *P* in EUR, and that the current spot FX rate is *S* USD per EUR, with a forward rate *F*. Though simple in concept, in execution this tends to be done as a swap plus a spot transaction.

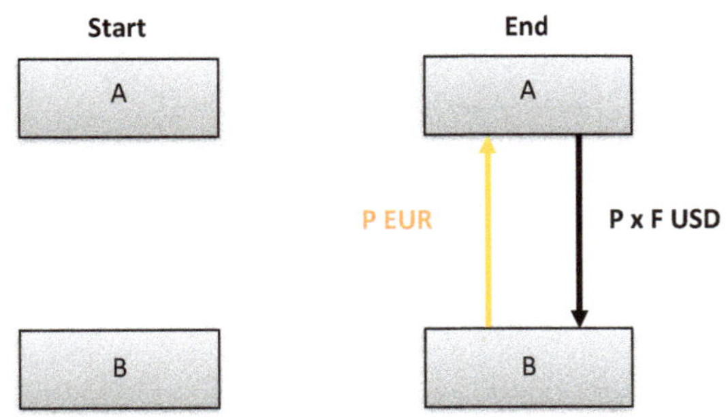

Figure 1.12: FX outright.

Definition of FX swap: Party A and Party B exchange Currency 1 for Currency 2 at a future date.

In fact, it is usually done as a spot trade plus a swap, as in Figure 1.13.

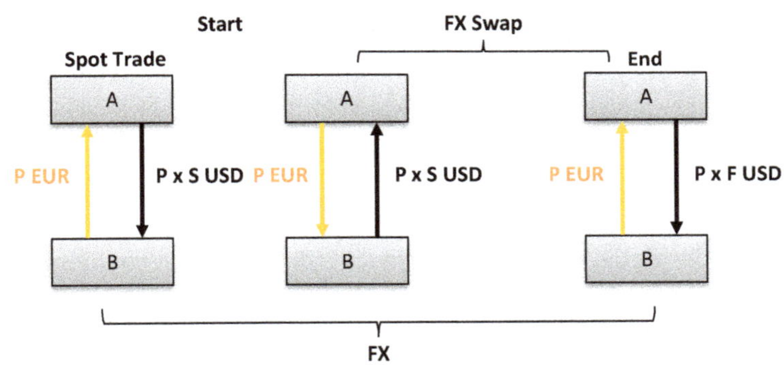

Figure 1.13: Spot trade plus swap.

Usual Maturity: below 1y or 2y

Uses: This market tends to be extensively used by corporates and exporters, to cover trade and repatriation flows.

As before, the basis is embedded in the forward rate.

Cross-Currency Basis Swap

In Figure 1.14, we now include the interim interest payments included in a cross-currency basis swap.

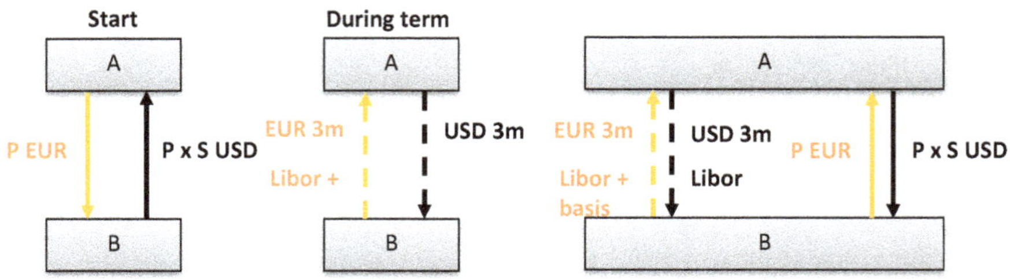

Figure 1.14: Cross-currency basis swap.

Definition of FX cross-currency basis swap: where two parties borrow from, and simultaneously lend to, each other an equivalent amount of money denominated in two different currencies for a predefined period of time, including floating interim interest payments, usually 3m.

Usual Maturity: up to 30y in some cases, though up to 10y is more usual

Uses: Primarily used by debt issuers

- SSAs: natural multi-currency users. Different locations will have different currency mixes.
- Corporates: Some large corporates can act like SSAs. Others may use EUR or USD as funding currencies, swapping back to USD.
- Banks: Treasuries minimise cost of funding and liquidity. They vary according to location. Some derivative desks manage the currency risk of different counterparties with xccy swaps.
- Asset managers hardly ever use this market due to the high cost of capital and regulatory constraints. As they would be the natural arbitrageurs in this space, the non-zero basis can persist.

The basis is explicit in the EUR Libor flows.

Chapter 2
XVA and the Cross-Currency Basis

The financial world changed in 2008.[1] Before the crisis, there was only one 'yield curve', and markets were relatively arbitrage-free. In the post-crisis world, credit concerns cause curves to multiply, and various regulations designed to protect end up delivering unintended consequences, allowing previously impossible 'arbitrage' situations to persist.

A contributing factor to the persistence of these apparent 'arbitrages' is the XVA costs of certain deal types to those market participants who might normally take advantage of the arbitrage. In this chapter, we introduce the concepts underpinning XVA and estimate these costs to show their probable effect on the cross-currency (xccy) basis.

Finally, we drill into the mechanics of attempting to use the xccy basis as an arbitrage and show why it is simply impossible for many market participants, though for others it may at some level be profitable. These variable profit opportunities place limits and pressure on the basis, which we attempt to quantify.

XVA – What is It?

A Brief Summary of Counterparty Risk

The quantities grouped under the perhaps unintuitive acronym of 'XVA' are various credit-derived costs of doing deals. The acronym XVA had its origins in Credit Valuation Adjustment (CVA), which evolved into XVA as the various valuation adjustments grew. These adjustments derive from the older-style management of loan portfolios, where companies wished to avoid excessive or concentrated exposure to individual counterparties or closely correlated counterparties. For a single loan, the traditional calculation would look something like this:

$$\text{Expected loss} = (\text{Exposure at default}) \times (\text{probability of default}) \times (\text{loss given default})$$

Here, 'exposure' is the amount of the loan outstanding at the time of default (some may have been partially paid back). To value a loan, the bank will consider its expected income, the difference between the interest received on the loan and the cost of borrowing the money to lend on to the customer, against the expected loss. Those earnings are set against the amount of capital that the bank is required to hold for the

1 This chapter was first published as Commerzbank's Rates Radar, 'XVA and funding derived market dislocations', November 2017.

https://doi.org/10.1515/9783110688733-002

risk. The capital requirement for a loan is a calculation depending on a variety of factors, such as the credit risk of the borrower and the maturity of the exposure.

The complexities involved in taking this concept from the simple loan to a derivatives portfolio are many, but the basic building block – that of exposure to a counterparty – remains the same. They can be qualitatively outlined as follows.

Multiple transactions. Once more than one transaction is on the books, the interaction between them must be considered. Does one offset the other? Do they add up? Are the counterparties in similar areas, meaning that they are more likely to default at the same time?

Positive and negative values. A simple loan has a tenor and a principal amount and only creates an exposure for the lender. But even a simple derivative product like a swap introduces an additional layer of complexity, as it can create exposure for either counterparty; depending upon market conditions, it can have a positive or negative value.

Probability of different exposures. A complex deal can take on a range of values and neither of the counterparties can be sure what it will be worth at different points in time. Thus, instead of a single value it has a range of values which have a range of probabilities attached to them at different times in the future.

Exposure profiles. Different contracts have different risks throughout their lifetimes. Thus, an interest rate swap has a low exposure (meaning that its overall value will not have moved far from its start value) at the beginning of its life. It will have a low exposure near the end of its life, as there is little uncertainty left about its ultimate value. In the middle of its life, its exposure will be highest, as it has plenty of payments left to run, and rates may have moved far from the start values by that time. So its exposure profile is 'humped' as a function of time. A cross-currency swap, on the other hand, has its highest exposure right at the end of its life, as at that point, it exchanges principle amounts whose values depend on exchange rates and are not fixed until the end point, so its exposure profile rises towards the final date.

Mitigation measures. To reduce exposure, many counterparties began to take mitigation measures such as netting agreements or posting collateral. In a netting agreement, two counterparties agree that in the event of a default by one of them, any payments made will be calculated by netting offsetting deals. This is designed to avoid a situation in which the defaulting counterparty does not pay what they owe but still claims what they are owed. Collateral posting occurs when a deal accrues a positive value to one counterparty (they are owed money), and thus a negative value to the other (who owes money). The latter counterparty sends collateral in the form of high-quality assets to the former counterparty. In the event of a default, this counterparty may retain the collateral, meaning that their effective exposure is much lower. Collateral has become a hugely popular mitigation measure – ISDA (2010) estimates that 63% of all FX derivative trades are covered by collateral arrangements.

Netting set. The use of netting agreements leads to the interesting situation where the risk of a deal depends upon the portfolio or netting set it will be added to. If it is largely offsetting, its additional risk can be low or even negative. Thus, deal risk and cost can be determined and can be unique to the counterparties involved, as well as their current portfolio and legal position.

Risk vs Cost

The risk of a deal and the cost of a deal are different but related quantities, and it is interesting to note that over the years the focus has somewhat shifted from risk to cost. All the various complexities described here serve to reduce the risk of a deal to the holder. If we assume that the cost is a function of holding capital to support the deal risk, then to an extent, reducing risk will reduce cost. But what if a particular deal turns out to reduce risk overall? Or what if, perhaps, a risky but profitable deal can only be justified if it is hedged – but the hedge is expensive?

Additionally, a decision made on risk grounds is complex. Imagine a risky deal that is profitable. The client perhaps also does a lot of other business with the bank, so there is a degree of offset. However, this deal adds risk in a currency where the bank is already highly exposed. This is a decision that would take time and would involve multiple people.

While it may be argued that some decisions are inherently complex and should not be oversimplified, it is surely the case that for most deals, if all the various complexities described here could be reduced to a simple cost, then oh, how much easier it would be! As long as the following is the case:

$$\text{Profit of deal} > \text{cost of doing deal}$$

then the deal should be done. How easy, how efficient! No need to worry about exposures, netting, correlations or collateral. The growing complexity of managing the risk of a portfolio of deals paved the way for the introduction of CVA.

CVA – The First Horse in the XVA Stable

Credit Value Adjustment (CVA) seems like a beautifully simple solution to this set of complexities, but it has its own problems. CVA is the change in value of the deal due to the possibility of counterparty default. If the counterparty will never default, CVA is zero. It is useful and convenient to express CVA as a running annualised spread.

There are many methods, varying in complexity, which are used to calculate CVA. In the following section, we list the most common.

(1) Full Calculation

For a complete and exact value, CVA is given by

$$CVA = (1-\delta)\sum_{j=1}^{m} DF(t_j)EE(t_j)q(t_{j-1}, t_j)$$

Here,

δ is the recovery fraction, so $(1-\delta)$ is the percentage of the deal value lost in the event of a default. This is largely dependent upon legal and relationship factors.

$DF(t_j)$ is the discount factor for time t_j. This is relatively simply determined from risk-free rates.

$EE(t_j)$ is the expected exposure at time t_j. This is the idiosyncratic calculation which involves all exposure, netting and collateral considerations, and can vary considerably from one institution to another. It will be obtained from the desk or team in charge of these calculations.

$q(t_{j-1}, t_j)$ is the default probability from time t_j to t_{j-1}. One would usually use default probabilities implied from historical data, though there are occasions where it may be preferred to use market implied figures (though this can become a somewhat circular issue).

(2) Cost of Hedging

However, there are other ways of looking at the CVA calculation. If CVA is just the change in value which comes from credit risk, shouldn't it simply be the cost of hedging away this credit risk? For many large institutions, one may effectively hedge away the risk of default using a Credit Default Swap (CDS), as shown in Figure 2.1.

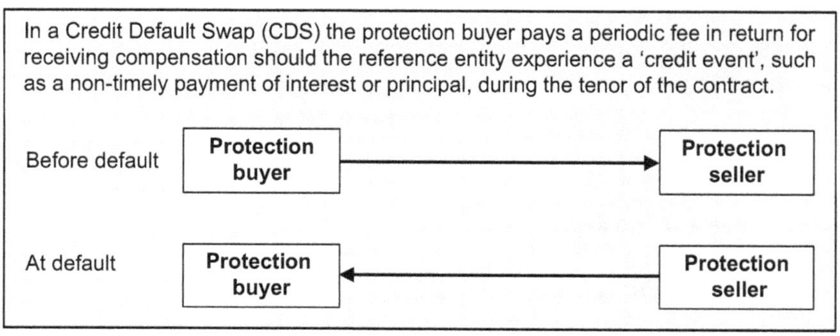

Figure 2.1: Credit Default Swap.

If we use this method, then we have the following:

$$CVA = \sum_{t=1}^{T} PV_{cashflow}(CDS_t)$$

This is the sum of the CDS to protect each of the future cashflows of the deal.

It is perhaps worth a quick aside on the relationship of CDS to credit spreads. In theory, they arise from exactly the same source – the perceived default risk of a company and its effect on the cost it must pay to borrow. Thus, the total value of the spread between the company bond yields and the risk-free rate should mirror the value of the CDS payments. However, in reality these two prices can diverge substantially and create a 'basis' between CDS and bonds (defined as the difference between the CDS' and the bond's spread). Credit-specific factors such as documentation can be important, and generally, supply-demand dynamics in the bond market are an important factor behind this basis. In practice, however, the CDS-bond basis is dominated by diverging liquidity dynamics and segmentation between markets. Before the financial crisis, the creation of synthetic CDO products meant that CDS-bond basis contracted significantly. In Europe, since 2015, the ECB's € QE program has created a force in the opposite direction, causing the basis to become wider. Last but not least, the rise of CVA desks during the last decade has introduced another important factor as they tend to be buyers of protection.

While all of these factors have contributed to a structurally wider CDS-bond basis since the crisis, it is interesting to note that the CDS-bond basis is correlated with the xccy basis – although no direct relationship exists between the two (see Figure 2.2 for an example from Italy). It is possible that this underscores that relative scarcity conditions are exerting similar influences on both bases and that regulatory XVA costs are also inhibiting arbitrage opportunities in similar ways on both instruments.

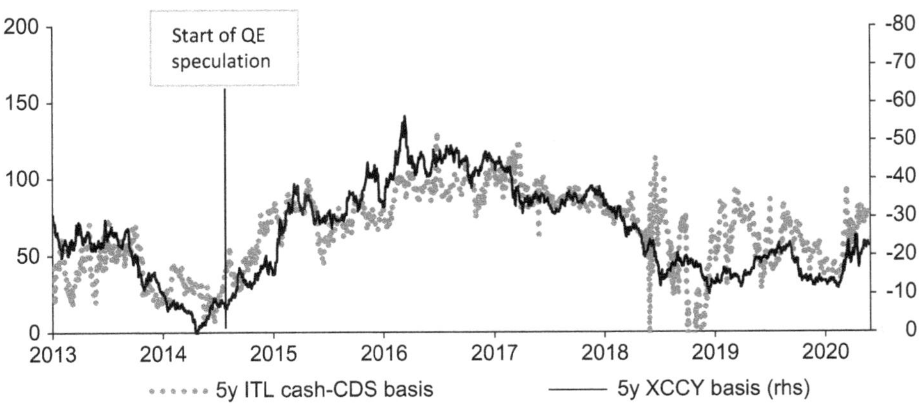

Figure 2.2: 5y cash-CDS and cross EURUSD currency bases, in bp.
Source: Commerzbank, Bloomberg

(3) Discounted Cashflow Approach

In this case, the CVA is assumed to be the difference between the future cashflows discounted by the risk-free rate and the future cashflows discounted by the credit-adjusted rate.

$$CVA = FV_{risk\,free} - FV_{credit\,adjusted}$$

While in theory this ought to come out with very similar results to the other calculations, it has a degree of flexibility in that the credit adjustment spread can be credit spread of either counterparty, depending on which way round the exposure is.

(4) Duration Approach

This is perhaps the crudest method, but is very quick and easy to use. In this case,

$$CVA = MTM \times Credit\,Spread \times Duration$$

This uses the duration to measure how much the fair value of the deal changes by applying the credit spread to the risk-free valuation. It's certainly the 'quick and dirty' method of the bunch, but is fairly well correlated to the other methods.

DVA – The Next Calculation

CVA was the first universally recognised attempt to apply a simple cost to cut through the various problems of counterparty credit risk and exposure. But it was very soon realised that it was not the whole story. For every transaction, each counterparty will calculate CVA with respect to the other(s). Debit value adjustment (DVA) is the CVA from the perspective of a company's counterparty looking back at the company. When this was first introduced, it was controversial. Why should a company include its own credit risk in a calculation? When the credit quality of a company goes down, its DVA goes up, meaning that deals may be 'cheaper' to do.

However, there are some strong arguments for DVA calculations to be included in the 'cost' of a deal to a trading desk. The main ones are listed as follows.

- DVA is needed to arrive at a mid-market value of the deal from both counterparties' points of view (although this must be tempered by the realisation that the DVA that one counterparty calculates is probably not exactly the same as the CVA calculated by the other).
- In one way, DVA has always been included when valuing transactions like bonds – lower-credit issuers have to pay a higher credit spread when selling bonds (i.e. make them more valuable).

- Finally, in case of a default, a lower credit counterparty would repay only the recovery amount, which is lower for lower credits, so it can be viewed as a benefit to the issuer.

Bilateral valuation adjustment (BVA) is sometimes used to refer to CVA+DVA.

FVA – Funding Impact

Funding valuation adjustment (FVA) attempts to capture the cost or benefit to the funding situation, though this calculation does tend to overlap with DVA and there is variability in its calculation method among different institutions. It is strongly dependent upon documentation and is generally a function of the nature of the business relationship between the two counterparties. It may in some cases be thought of as the expected loss that the funding company would incur if the counterparty were to default.

Finally, collateral valuation adjustment (COLVA) attempts to calculate the impact of any posted collateral. This impact is sometimes included in the CVA/DVA calculation.

As these different adjustment quantities arose and were incorporated into valuation frameworks, the catch-all 'acronym' which became used to refer to them as a group was XVA. The X, it must be supposed, just stands for 'anything'. For a useful discussion of the calculation methods behind the XVA suite, see Ruiz (2015), Gregory (2011) and Ernst and Young (2014).

How XVA Costs Could Affect the Cross-Currency Basis

All of these various costs mean that some deals, with some counterparties, are more expensive to do than they used to be. Cross-currency swaps are of particular interest. We also examined the post-crisis dislocations in the xccy basis in Chapter 1. Due to their large notional exchange at expiry, they tend to have high risk and therefore XVA costs. However, these are the exact trades which would be used to quickly take advantage of and monetise the arbitrage that is the cross-currency basis. While there are many other factors driving its generation, the XVA costs are likely to be a large part of the reason it persists in the market.

In Figures 2.3 and 2.4, we show the 5y cross-currency basis for EURUSD and USDJPY. Recall that in the days before the crisis when there was only one valuation curve and no XVA, this would have been seen as a pure arbitrage to be quickly traded on. At current levels, there are about 30 basis points per year available for the 10y trade – something substantial must be in the way of doing these deals.

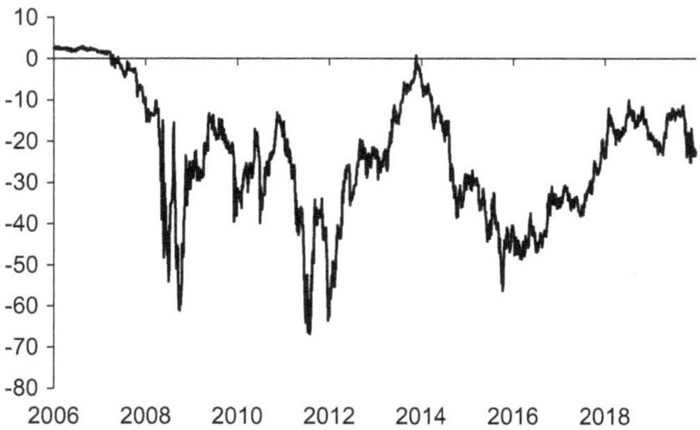

Figure 2.3: 5y xccy basis for EURUSD in bp.
Source: Bloomberg, Commerzbank Research

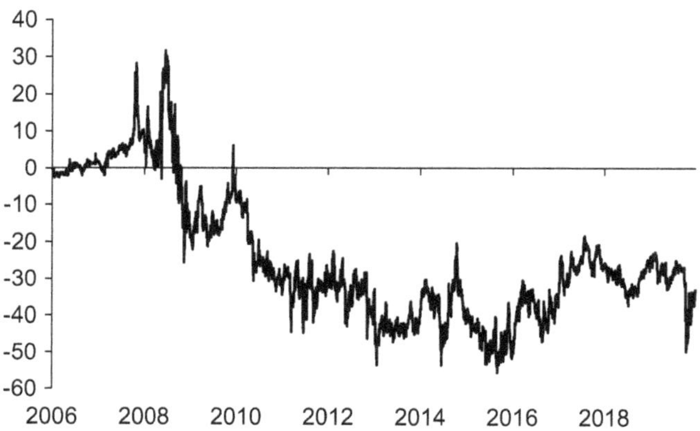

Figure 2.4: 5y xccy basis for USDJPY in bp.
Source: Bloomberg, Commerzbank Research

Sample XVA Calculation Using Market Standard Calculation Approach

In Table 2.1, we give a set of sample calculations for the cost of doing EURUSD cross-currency deals from the point of view of a standard market maker, taken from 20 November 2017. The calculations are done assuming a 'standard' counterparty of A(collateralised), BBB(collateralised) and BBB(uncollateralised) credit quality with no particular degree of offset to other parts of the trading book. The costs are all annualised in basis points. Note that the total deal cost is calculated as max(A, B+C) + D + E, where A = Net CVA, B = Rating CVA, C = Cost of Capital, D = FVA, E = EU Bank Levy.

Table 2.1: Sample XVA calculations from 20 November 2017, in bp annually.

EURUSD xccy XVA charges	A(c) 10y	A(c) 5y	A(c) 2y	BBB(c) 10y	BBB(c) 5y	BBB(c) 2y	BBB(u) 10y	BBB(u) 5y	BBB(u) 2y
Net CVA	0.4	0.2	0.1	1.3	1.3	0.9	17.0	6.6	1.1
Rating CVA	0.0	0.0	0.0	0.3	0.3	0.3	3.1	2.0	1.1
FVA	0.0	0.0	0.0	0.0	0.1	0.1	4.1	2.4	1.1
Cost of Capital	1.2	1.0	0.8	1.2	1.6	2.0	7.8	6.2	3.3
EU Bank Levy	0.0	0.0	0.0	0.0	0.0	0.0	0.1	0.1	0.0
Total Deal Cost	1.3	1.1	0.8	1.5	1.9	2.5	21.1	10.7	5.5

Source: Bloomberg, Commerzbank Research

What can we take from this table?

- CVA is higher for longer-term deals.
- CVA and FVA are higher for lower-credit counterparties.
- Collateral makes a large difference – the total cost of uncollateralised deals is many times that of the same deal with posted collateral.

Let us take the 10y xccy swap as a benchmark. The table tells us that the XVA cost of doing this deal with an AA, BBB(c) or BBB(c) counterparty would be 1.3, 1.5 or 21 bp. On that day (20 February 2017), the EURUSD 10y basis swap traded at –38 bp. Thus, on the surface, Commerzbank would be delighted to do this deal! Even most conservatively, there would have been about 20 bp of profit to be made – and it is likely that our counterparties to this trade would be better credits than BBB, and that we would use collateral, so 30 bp is a more realistic figure.

This seems odd. Much has been made of the impact of regulatory capital and XVA on the cross-currency basis. But our own, fairly conservative calculations indicate that these charges are not nearly large enough to cause the substantial basis we see in the market. We are not alone in our calculations of these costs – in EBA (2014), we see that the European Banking Authority has made similar estimates of CVA and regulatory costs.

Can we gain an indication of whether 20 November 2017 is an outlier? Although there is nothing very precise available, we can 'scale' the CVA part of the trade costs, assuming that the other costs stay approximately constant. A reasonable index to use when scaling CVA might be the Markit ITraxx Europe Senior Financial Index (SNRFIN 5Y on Bloomberg), which comprises 30 equally weighted CDS spreads on investment grade European financial entities. If we look back at all the equations for the CVA calculations, it's clear that it should roughly scale with CDS spreads in all cases. Thus, we take the value of this index on 20 November, and scale other CVA values in the time series by the ratio of the index value on that date to the value on other dates.

The following chart in Figure 2.5 perhaps raises more questions than it answers. We have used the BBB uncollateralised credit 10y CVA charge as a benchmark.

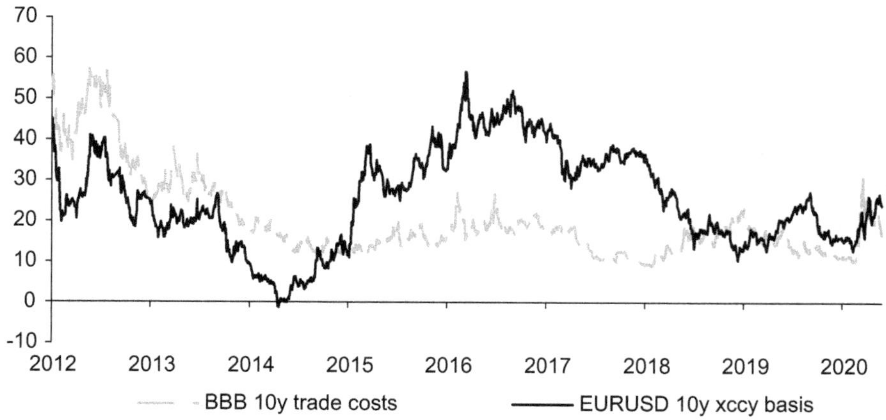

Figure 2.5: 10y BBB xccy basis and uncollateralised trade cost, in bp.
Source: Bloomberg, Commerzbank Research

Xccy basis is plotted as positive number, though usually it would be negative.

Prior to 2014, we could have made a case that XVA charges and the xccy basis were strongly related, and that the basis was to some extent limited by the charges. We would expect the conservative uncollateralised BBB costs to provide a safe upper bound, which does indeed seem to be the case. The two were highly correlated and the basis did not seem to move too far away. But from 2014 to 2019, this useful relationship breaks down, with the basis rising sharply while the XVA costs are low and fairly stable. After that point, the two series maintain similar lower levels but with little apparent correlation. It is difficult to believe, from this evidence, that XVA costs and the basis are strongly connected.

Funding Constraints

To finally understand what stops market participants from taking advantage of the cross-currency basis, we turned to the trading desk and the mechanics of doing such a deal. Let us assume that a rookie trader decides that he or she is going to trade the xccy basis and make some money on it.

The following data is taken from trading screens on 6 July 2017, for deals with start date 10 July 2017 and end date 10 July 2018 (interest rates are 1y IRS/3M).

EUR interest rate	–0.30%
USD interest rate	1.48%
Spot FX Rate	1.1423
Market FX Forward Rate	1.1660 (forward points are 237)
Implied FX Forward	1.1626 (implied from interest rates)

The implied forward is calculated using the expression

$$\frac{FX2}{FX1} = \frac{1+r_2}{1+r_1}$$

where

FX1= Spot FX rate

FX2 = 1y implied forward FX rate

r_2 = USD 1y interest rate

r_1 = EUR 1y interest rate

This expression is famously 'broken' by the existence of the xccy basis – prior to 2008, the implied forward rate was always very close to the actual market rate. The xccy basis here is often quoted as a spread to the implied forward, so in this case it would be 33 'forward pips'. This translates back to an interest rate spread of –28 basis points – so one could also imply a USD 1y interest rate of 1.48% + 0.28% = 1.76%. The negative sign attached to the basis is due to the fact that the xccy basis is quoted as a spread to the non-USD interest rate. Thus, if one applied the 'correction' to the EUR interest rate, it would come out as –0.58%.

What does our hypothetical rookie trader think? This is what might be going through his or her head: 'The difference between the interest rate derived FX forward and the actual traded forward is 33 forward pips, or –28 basis points. So, I will do the two interest rate contracts, and the actual traded forward, to lock in the basis.'

But now, reality begins to bite. These interest rates are NOT depo rates. They are 1y swap rates vs 3m Libor. The USD depo rate is about 28 basis points higher, at 1.77%. This is one way of appreciating that the basis (expressed like this) is due to credit. With a swap, the principal is never at risk, only the differences between fixed and floating rates. With a deposit, the principal is at risk, and the rate is higher. So our hopeful trader cannot borrow and lend at these rates at all. This is part of the 'multiplication of curves' which we mentioned right at the start – the yield curve for swaps (less credit risk) and for deposits (more credit risk) are not the same, whereas before the crisis, they were almost the same.[2]

2 Another reason for the discrepancy between swap and deposit rates is the inconsistency of the panel-based Libor fixings that are derived from 'expert judgement' with no real interbank volumes taking place, especially for longer terms.

Ok, says the still-hopeful trader. Let's do the two interest rate components of this set of deals with two fixed-floating IRS. Fine, we can now access these interest rates.

But because the trader is not doing the deposit contracts, he or she will have to fund the cashflows, so he or she will need to hold the principal amount on the books until the deal expiry. This needs to be funded. Oh no! That means accessing the deposit market once more – and the deposit rates include the basis. There is no escape – the poor trader will have to borrow at an effective rate close to that available in the deposit market. Even though a trading desk usually funds by rolling overnight or short-term, the implied forward cost of the accumulated overnight funding will still add up not to the 1y swap rate, but to something like the 1y depo rate.[3] So, though there is uncertainty, as the overnight rate may of course change over the course of the deal, it is not possible to lock in a profit, and the implied P/L is flat.

Before the crisis, the trader would have funded at Libor, and the depo and swap rates would have been very little different, so if a basis had existed, it would have been a good opportunity for arbitrage.

In Figure 2.6, we show the 1y US swap rate and deposit rate since 2000, and the spread between them together with the xccy basis is shown in Figure 2.7. It's clear that they are closely connected though not identical, as the basis also responds to pressure from the EUR side.

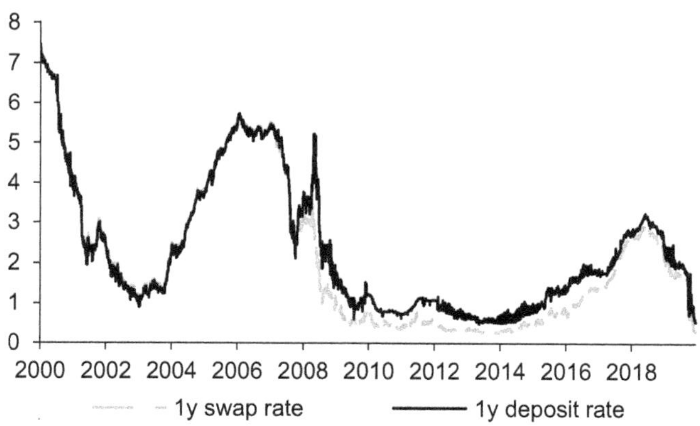

Figure 2.6: 1y USD swap rate and deposit rate.
Source: Bloomberg, Commerzbank Research

3 Why can the trading desk not fund cheaply at the OIS rates? The answer is that in most desks, they can get funding from the bank Treasury, but this will have a spread added on reflecting the Treasury's current position and risk perception. The resulting funding available to the desk is often close to (or sometimes worse than) levels available in the market.

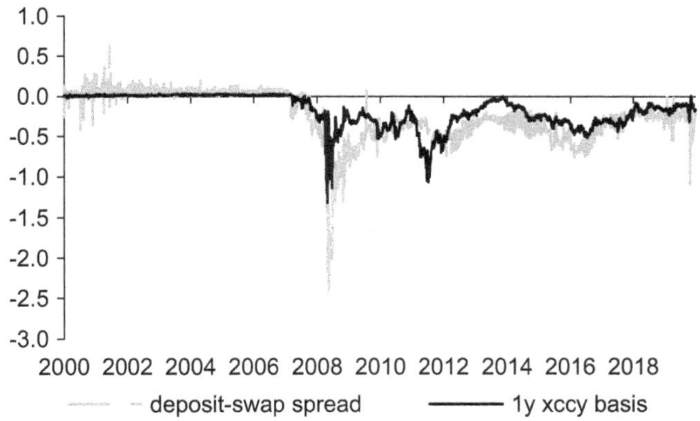

Figure 2.7: 1y USD swap-deposit spread, with 1y xccy EURUSD basis.
Source: Bloomberg, Commerzbank Research

Now, as our young trader, now a little older and wiser, sadly abandons plans to make money on the basis, is there anyone who *can* do the trade? Yes! Under some circumstances, bank Treasuries can borrow at close to the swap rates from the central banks. This is one way that central banks inject liquidity. So these desks can make a profit from this situation. Similarly, some high-quality credits can do it or can come close. Our previous paper shows in detail how some entities (for example, large investors or insurance companies) can at times lock in at least part of the basis when hedging fixed income investments.[4] There is an excellent analysis in Rime, Schrimpf and Syrstad (2017), which shows that the very top-tier banks in some markets have, at some points in the past, been able to fund at levels that allow them to treat the xccy basis as at least a partial arbitrage. The current situation is such that the arbitrage may still be available, though it is narrower than it has been at other times. Thus, there is pressure on the basis not to widen too far, but not the kind of old-style risk-free arbitrage pressure.

Would it ever make sense for our trader to do this trade? Yes, indeed. If the basis widened too far, he or she might put on the trade believing that the actual funding (as opposed to the implied) would not stay at these elevated levels. But it would be a trade with risk attached, and not a traditional arbitrage.

Thus, pressure on the basis not to widen has no 'hard' level at which it comes in. Those who can make risk-free money on the basis do so only because they can access cheap USD funding. Those who make money on the basis with a risk-based trade do so because they correctly judge when it is too extended. The basis is a natural consequence of greater sensitivity to credit risk, and demand for and access to USD. For a useful discussion of forces operating on the basis, see Rime, Schrimpf

4 For an in-depth discussion, see Chapter 1.

and Syrstad (2017) and Borio et al. (2016), and for an excellent explanation of multiple curve discounting, see Hull (2014).

Detail on Daily Funding/Rollover Process

In the previous section, we described how a trader might 'attempt' to capture the xccy basis – and fail. In fact, though this broad-brush description is correct, it may be of interest to go into some detail about how the actuality of the daily rolling and funding occurs. A detailed diagram of the process may be found in the online appendix of Rime, Schrimpf and Syrstad (2017), but it may be useful to add some numbers in.

Rather than funding the future cashflow for the whole tenor of the deal, the desk operates on a shorter-term basis. They will fund the future cashflow for short periods, often overnight (O/N). It is important to realise that the funding of the cashflow is like a miniature of the larger deal; both an interest rate component and a forward FX component are involved. Thus the O/N funding cost is usually measured in forward points, which are the overnight levels for the FX forward. These are usually not annualised.

We have said that the cost of funding the cashflow ends up adding to the xccy basis. This is true but is more complex for the O/N case. Essentially, the implied curve of the O/N forward rates incorporates both the OIS currency rates and the FX forward. Figure 2.8 is the graph of the entire 1-day forward-forward implied curve, as calculated by Commerzbank's STIRT desk, for 6 July 2017. It is derived from various averages over different number of days – from 2 to 15 – with the greater granularity around points of interest like the turn of the year. Thus, we would expect it to look smoother than the actual historical forward in Figure 2.9, but otherwise should show similar features.

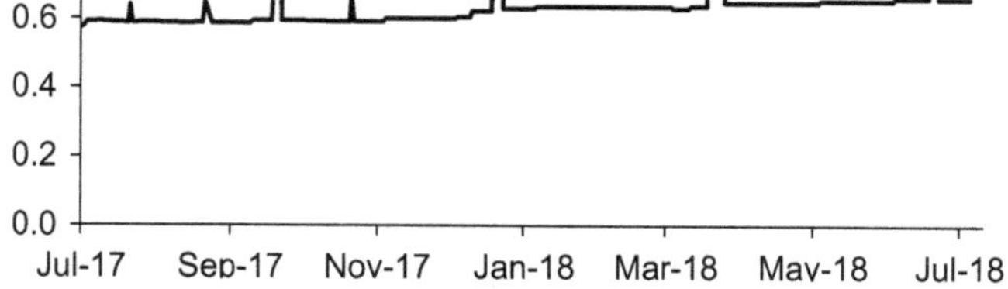

Figure 2.8: 1-day EURUSD forward-forward curve in forward points.
Source: Bloomberg, Commerzbank Research

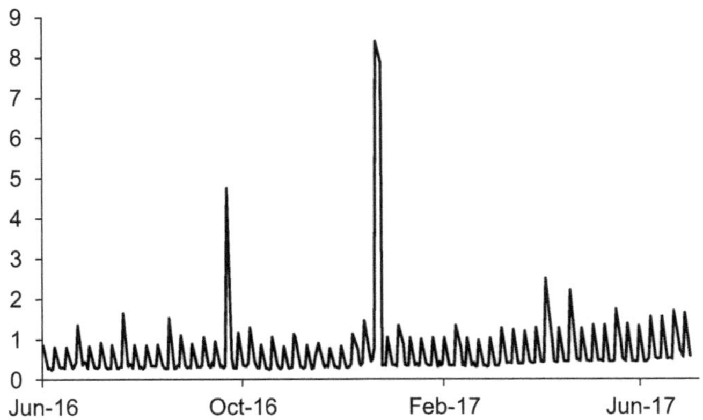

Figure 2.9: 1-day historical FX forward.
Source: Bloomberg, Commerzbank Research

These two graphs are informative. On 6 July 2017, the forward points are 0.55. This is the difference between the market forward FX rate for 1 day and the spot rate. Harking back to our earlier calculation, this looks very optimistic for the arbitrage trade. If we can fund at this level for the whole deal, then 0.55 x 365 = 201. But the actual forward points for a 1-year deal are 237. To get to this number, the difference between the 1y forward (1.166) and the spot (1.142) is 0.0237; multiply this by 10,000 to get the forward points as they are quoted by the market. We can make this money (which comes out to about 0.28% of notional) if these points remain stable!

But they don't. From the Commerzbank STIRT desk, we obtained the implied curve for that day, going out to 1 year. As seen in Figure 2.9, various spikes at times of high USD demand are priced in. This means that we need to look at the average for the year – and it comes out at 0.63 forward points, which is 230 forward points over the year, which leaves us with very nearly nothing!

But has it been correct? Well, we can also look at historical O/N rates – and they say the same thing. Figure 2.10 shows the actual historical levels of these over the last year. It is more active than the desk-supplied forward curve, as it includes the change in levels over each weekend, which the forward curve from the desk smooths out with averaging. But in fact, it averages out to exactly 0.63 forward points as well – though this is in the past, it is certainly consistent with the idea that it has not been possible to make money.

Historical Funding Data

We have shown that for an 'average' trading desk, it's unlikely that they will be able to lock in a profit from trading the cross-currency basis. It seems likely, however, that some institutions may have occasional situations which will enable them to lock in a profit. It is important to note that for the situation of a trading desk, with a daily roll and funding process, profits will be made only over these short periods; a brief arbitrage may well exist if the desk can borrow or lend for a day or two at better than market rates.

Very fortunately, we have access to the internal Commerzbank funding levels available from late 2008 to 2017. Specifically, we have access to Treasury rates made available to the internal trading desks for different currencies. This is not quite the same as the rates the desks dealt at, since they also had the option of trading outside of the bank, but it is an excellent indication of supply and demand as seen by a large German commercial bank. We use this to calculate the forward points available to the desk.

The forward points are the difference between the forward FX rate and the spot FX rate. Using the previous notation, we can say:

$$\text{Forward Points} = FX2 - FX1$$

But we know:

$$\frac{FX2}{FX1} = \frac{1+r_2}{1+r_1}$$

So, we can say:

$$\text{Forward Points} = FX1\left(\frac{1+r_2}{1+r_1} - 1\right)$$

$$\text{Forward Points} = FX1\left(\frac{r_2 - r_1}{1+r_1}\right) \times 10{,}000$$

The additional factor of 10,000 is usually applied to make the number easier to handle.

As we have the internal time series for r_1 and r_2 available (in this case for EUR and USD), plus the spot FX rate FX1, this allows us to create Figures 2.10 and 2.11, where we compare the effective forward points available to the desk with the overnight and Tom/Next forward points available in the market. We show both cases, as the tenor of the internal rate varies between them.

First of all, it's clear that at some points in time some desks can lock in a short-dated profit. There are clearly days where the internal rates differ somewhat from market rates – for a trader with the right positioning, this is good news.

This is perhaps to be expected – part of the job of a trading desk is to pick up on short-term discrepancies. But we can learn something from the overall pattern of the discrepancies, which may probably be generalised to most substantial investment banks.

Let's first summarise how a trading desk will see things.

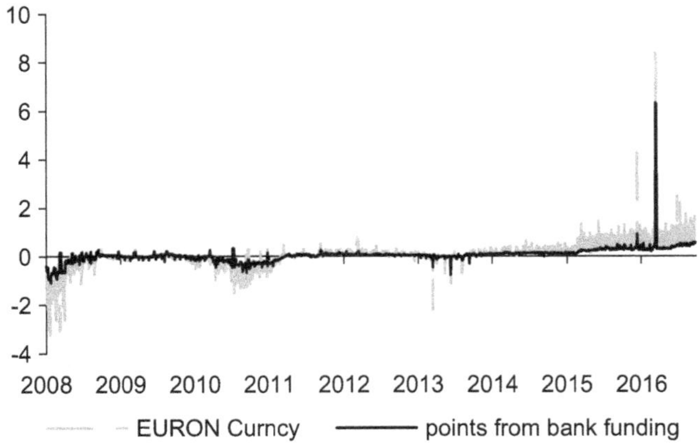

Figure 2.10: Internal forward points vs market O/N in %.
Source: Bloomberg, Commerzbank Research

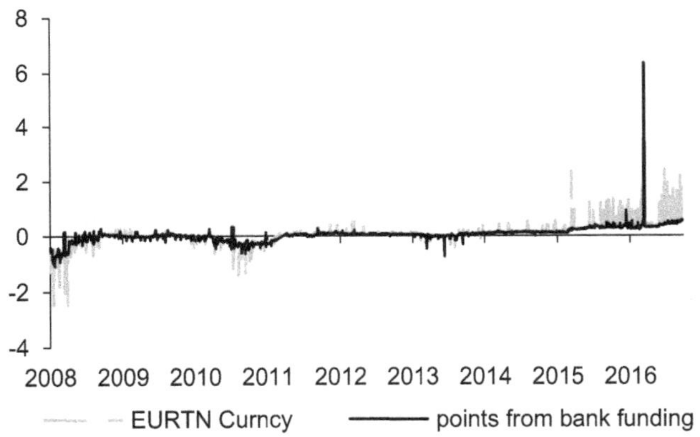

Figure 2.11: Internal forward points vs market T/N in %.
Source: Bloomberg, Commerzbank Research

- If you are LONG USD/SHORT EUR, you want the points to be higher – i.e. 55 rather than 50 (you need to lend out the USD and get the EUR in for as many pips as you can).
- If you are SHORT USD/LONG EUR, you want the points to be lower – i.e. 50 rather than 55.
- The points are currently positive, as EUR rates are below USD.
- in the case where EUR rates are higher, the points will be negative, but the same rationale applies – with LONG USD/SHORT EUR, you want a bigger NEGATIVE number (you want to lend out the USD at as big a number as you can ie –45 not –40), and with SHORT USD/LONG EUR, you want a less negative number (–40 not –45).

What do we see in the graphs? When USD rates are higher than EUR, generally the internal points are less positive. When USD rates are lower than EUR, the internal points are less negative. This is a disadvantage to those who are overall long of USD.

This can be seen as part of an internal redistribution process, as on average, most of the trading desks will tend to be long of USD – for example, oil and many other commodities are valued in USD, and it is one of the most important tactical and strategic risk currencies. Conversely, the Treasury is likely to be long of EUR overall. This means that it can generate interest income when the EUR has positive interest rates, but it is costly when there are negative rates. Thus, as the Treasury needs to manage its own position, it will offer a higher spread to the internal trading desks in positive periods (flow from desk to Treasury) and a lower spread to the desks in negative periods (flow from Treasury to desk). The desks in turn will hope to make money by short-term management of positions, often including short-dated carry.

Trading the xccy Basis

With a last look at our trader, let's see when the risk-based trade would have been profitable over time. If the trader puts on the trade assuming that the basis is too large and will close up, then there's an easy way to approximate the P/L that the trade would make – look at the average levels of the basis over the next year. Figure 2.12 is a chart of the xccy basis vs its average level for the following year, and the difference between them. Note that this is only an indication of the profit of the trade, as we ought to strictly look at trades whose tenor shortens towards the end of the deal, but it will be good enough to give us an indication.

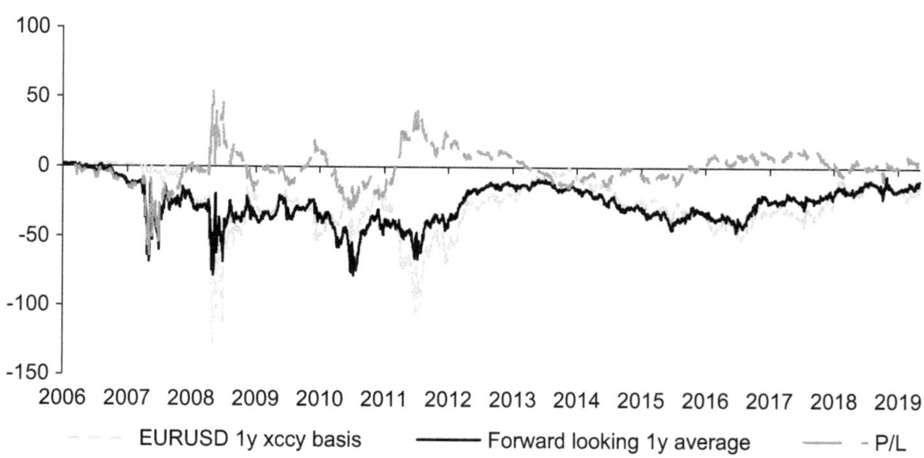

Figure 2.12: Indication of profitability of xccy basis trade. 1y tenor, all in bp.
Source: Bloomberg, Commerzbank Research

It can be seen that positioning for the transient nature of large basis spikes has been generally beneficial. In Table 2.2, we also tabulate the average profit per trade if it is entered at different levels.

Table 2.2: Average profit per trade.

Level where trade is entered (bp)	−10	−20	−30	−40	−50	−60	−70	−80
Average profit per trade in bp	0.97	2.20	6.51	14.54	22.48	26.40	30.21	35.00
Number of trades	1959	1612	884	491	289	182	106	56

Source: Bloomberg, Commerzbank Research

Though the trade has been profitable overall, this has varied with the time period. But its substantial profitability at entry levels of 40 or greater mean that we might expect trading pressure to close up the basis being strongly felt at that point.

Chapter 3
Calculating Novel Cross-Currency Bases and FX Hedged Pickups

The cross-currency (xccy) basis is, in the post-crisis world, an essential part of any overseas investment or funding decision.[1] Sensitivity to credit risk and quality mean that relationships among interest rates, FX rates and FX forwards have become far more complex, with opportunities arising and disappearing as the markets evolve. Chapter 1 and Chapter 2 have illustrated how some investors can discover opportunities in overseas bond markets which can even be fully FX hedged, the so-called 'hedged pickups', when rate differentials and the xccy basis align to deliver a positive return.

However, not all liquid crosses have a corresponding quoted xccy basis. Almost all quoted xccy bases are to the USD, with just a few to the EUR. So if an opportunity arises in, say, GBPJPY, it is more difficult to spot and may go unnoticed by market participants who could take advantage of it.

Fortunately, it is possible to calculate almost all of these cross rate xccy bases, and from them, their hedged pickups. These calculations, while not the same as market quotes, are excellent indicators of where opportunities may be found in these liquid but less explored crosses.

What is the FX Hedged Pickup?

The FX hedged pickup is the gain (or loss) which may be secured by shorting one bond, going long of another, and hedging the FX risk. Here we consider government bonds and two hedge types: (1) the full hedge for the tenor of the bonds, and (2) a short 3m or 6m hedge after it is assumed that the bonds would be sold. It's important to remember that (2) entails more risk, as changes in the value of the bonds are not hedged in this case. In the pre-crisis days, when there was in essence only one 'yield curve' and no xccy basis, there would have been little or no pickup available. In the post-crisis world, the curve has split into many, depending on credit levels, and the xccy basis is often substantial, and so these pickups can be significant.

In essence, the FX hedged pickup is found using the following expression:

$$\text{Pickup} = \text{Delta Bond} - \text{Delta Swap} +/- \text{Basis}$$

1 This chapter was first published in Commerzbank's Rates Radar 'Calculating novel cross-currency bases and FX hedged pickups', October 2018.

https://doi.org/10.1515/9783110688733-003

For example, for a EU investor who would like to short their own government debt and buy US government debt instead due to higher yields:

$$\text{Delta Bond} = \text{US bond yield} - \text{EU bond yield}$$

$$\text{Delta Swap} = \text{USA swap rate} - \text{EUR swap rate}$$

Finally, the xccy basis must be included. This is always quoted as a spread to the non-USD (or if USD is absent from the pair, the non-base currency), so it may be added or subtracted depending on the currency quote convention.

For the short-dated 'rolling pickup', the interest rate and the xccy basis will be 3m or 6m. The bond yields may be any liquid tenor. For the more complete 'maturity matched' hedge, the tenor of all the instruments must match. This latter transaction is inherently more of a true hedge, as the rolling hedge is short-term and may be derailed by changes in the underlying value of the bonds.

Finding xccy Bases

Which xccy bases are already easily available as quotes and time series? Tables 3.1–3.3 show which tenors and crosses are available to USD, EUR and JPY.

Table 3.1: Available series for xccy basis swaps to the USD.

	EUR	USD	GBP	JPY	AUD	CAD	CHF	SEK
3M	✓		✓	✓	✓	✓	✓	✗
6M	✓		✓	✓	✓	✓	✓	✗
1Y	✓		✓	✓	✓	✓	✓	✓
2Y	✓		✓	✓	✓	✓	✓	✓
3Y	✓		✓	✓	✓	✓	✓	✓
4Y	✓		✓	✓	✓	✓	✓	✓
5Y	✓		✓	✓	✓	✓	✓	✓
6Y	✓		✓	✓	✓	✓	✓	✓
7Y	✓		✓	✓	✓	✓	✓	✓
8Y	✓		✓	✓	✓	✓	✓	✓
9Y	✓		✓	✓	✓	✓	✓	✓
10Y	✓		✓	✓	✓	✓	✓	✓

Table 3.1 (continued)

	EUR	USD	GBP	JPY	AUD	CAD	CHF	SEK
15Y	✓		✓	✓	✓	✓	✓	✓
20y	✓		✓	✓	✓	✓	✓	✓
30Y	✓		✓	✓	✓	✓	✓	✓

Source: Bloomberg, Commerzbank Research

Table 3.2: Available series for xccy basis swaps to the EUR.

	EUR	USD	GBP	JPY	AUD	CAD	CHF	SEK
3M		✓	✗	✗	✗	✗	✗	✗
6M		✓	✗	✗	✗	✗	✗	✗
1Y		✓	✓	✓	✓	✓	✓	✓
2Y		✓	✓	✓	✓	✓	✓	✓
3Y		✓	✓	✓	✓	✓	✓	✓
4Y		✓	✓	✓	✓	✓	✓	✓
5Y		✓	✓	✓	✓	✓	✓	✓
6Y		✓	✓	✓	✓	✓	✓	✗
7Y		✓	✓	✓	✓	✓	✓	✓
8Y		✓	✓	✓	✓	✓	✓	✗
9Y		✓	✓	✓	✓	✓	✓	✗
10Y		✓	✓	✓	✓	✓	✓	✓
15Y		✓	✓	✓	✓	✓	✓	✓
20y		✓	✓	✓	✓	✓	✓	✓
30Y		✓	✗	✓	✗	✗	✓	✗

Source: Bloomberg, Commerzbank Research

It's clear that the data vs the USD is a more complete set than that vs the EUR, and that the short-dated (3m and 6m) xccy basis swaps are very poorly represented for anything except the USD. Thus the short-dated 'rolling' FX hedged pickups to anything except the USD would be impossible to calculate unless there were some other way of deriving the 3m and 6m xccy bases. The data for JPY investors is very sparse indeed – and as deals involving, for example, AUD or GBP vs JPY are hardly uncommon, this makes it potentially useful to investigate.

Table 3.3: Available series for xccy basis swaps to the JPY.

	EUR	USD	GBP	JPY	AUD	CAD	CHF	SEK
3M	✗	✓	✗		✗	✗	✗	✗
6M	✗	✓	✗		✗	✗	✗	✗
1Y	✓	✓	✗		✗	✗	✗	✗
2Y	✓	✓	✗		✗	✗	✗	✗
3Y	✓	✓	✗		✗	✗	✗	✗
4Y	✓	✓	✗		✗	✗	✗	✗
5Y	✓	✓	✗		✗	✗	✗	✗
6Y	✓	✓	✗		✗	✗	✗	✗
7Y	✓	✓	✗		✗	✗	✗	✗
8Y	✓	✓	✗		✗	✗	✗	✗
9Y	✓	✓	✗		✗	✗	✗	✗
10Y	✓	✓	✗		✗	✗	✗	✗
15Y	✓	✓	✗		✗	✗	✗	✗
20y	✓	✓	✗		✗	✗	✗	✗
30Y	✓	✓	✗		✗	✗	✗	✗

Source: Bloomberg, Commerzbank Research

How can we fill in some of these data series? First of all, there is a useful additive property of basis swaps. We may say that

$$XCCY_{AB} = XCCY_{CA} - XCCY_{CB}$$

where A, B and C are currencies, and XCCY is the basis swap. So for USD, EUR and JPY, we have

$$XCCY_{JPY-GBP} = XCCY_{USD-JPY} - XCCY_{USD-GBP}$$

Thus we can use the USD basis swaps to construct many of the missing JPY ones. We can see that the relationship holds well in the case of EUR, USD and JPY, where the EURJPY basis swap is available both by construction and quoted in the market. In Figure 3.1, we graph the quoted and the constructed rates for the 10y case.

How many of the currency crosses can we fill in now with this new technique? Tables 3.4 and 3.5 are the 'new' versions of the available series for the EUR and the JPY.

This is much better – for EUR we have a complete set, but we still lack the important short-dated basis swaps for the JPY crosses. But all is not lost. These can be

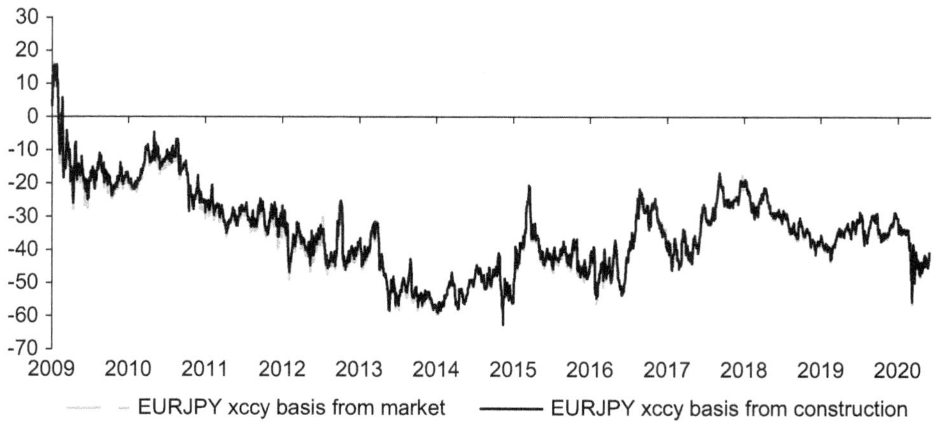

Figure 3.1: Constructed and quoted EURJPY 10y xccy basis in bp.
Source: Bloomberg, Commerzbank Research

Table 3.4: Available series for xccy basis swaps to the EUR, with basis series reconstruction from other bases.

	EUR	USD	GBP	JPY	AUD	CAD	CHF	SEK
3M		✓	✓	✓	✓	✓	✓	✓
6M		✓	✓	✓	✓	✓	✓	✓
1Y		✓	✓	✓	✓	✓	✓	✓
2Y		✓	✓	✓	✓	✓	✓	✓
3Y		✓	✓	✓	✓	✓	✓	✓
4Y		✓	✓	✓	✓	✓	✓	✓
5Y		✓	✓	✓	✓	✓	✓	✓
6Y		✓	✓	✓	✓	✓	✓	✓
7Y		✓	✓	✓	✓	✓	✓	✓
8Y		✓	✓	✓	✓	✓	✓	✓
9Y		✓	✓	✓	✓	✓	✓	✓
10Y		✓	✓	✓	✓	✓	✓	✓
15Y		✓	✓	✓	✓	✓	✓	✓
20y		✓	✓	✓	✓	✓	✓	✓
30Y		✓	✓	✓	✓	✓	✓	✓

Source: Bloomberg, Commerzbank

Table 3.5: Available series for xccy basis swaps to the JPY, with basis series reconstruction from other bases.

	EUR	USD	GBP	JPY	AUD	CAD	CHF	SEK
3M	✗	✓	✗		✗	✗	✗	✗
6M	✗	✓	✗		✗	✗	✗	✗
1Y	✓	✓	✓		✓	✓	✓	✓
2Y	✓	✓	✓		✓	✓	✓	✓
3Y	✓	✓	✓		✓	✓	✓	✓
4Y	✓	✓	✓		✓	✓	✓	✓
5Y	✓	✓	✓		✓	✓	✓	✓
6Y	✓	✓	✓		✓	✓	✓	✓
7Y	✓	✓	✓		✓	✓	✓	✓
8Y	✓	✓	✓		✓	✓	✓	✓
9Y	✓	✓	✓		✓	✓	✓	✓
10Y	✓	✓	✓		✓	✓	✓	✓
15Y	✓	✓	✓		✓	✓	✓	✓
20y	✓	✓	✓		✓	✓	✓	✓
30Y	✓	✓	✓		✓	✓	✓	✓

Source: Bloomberg, Commerzbank

derived from spot FX rates, forward FX rates and short-dated interest rates. As an example, to find the EURJPY 3m basis, we can do the following:

$$\text{EURJPY basis} = 100 \times \left[\left(\frac{F}{S} \times \left(1 + \frac{r_d}{400}\right) - 1\right) \times 400 - r_f\right]$$

where

F = 3m forward FX rate for EURJPY
S = spot rate for EURJPY
r_d = domestic interest rate (EUR)
r_f = foreign interest rate (JPY)

Finally, now we can fill in the last lines on the JPY table of data availability.

Now we can graph xccy bases that are not usually quoted. As an example, we give GBPJPY 10y and 3m xccy bases in Figure 3.2, and CHFJPY in Figure 3.3. These are certainly rates used in international trade, but there is usually no time series data available.

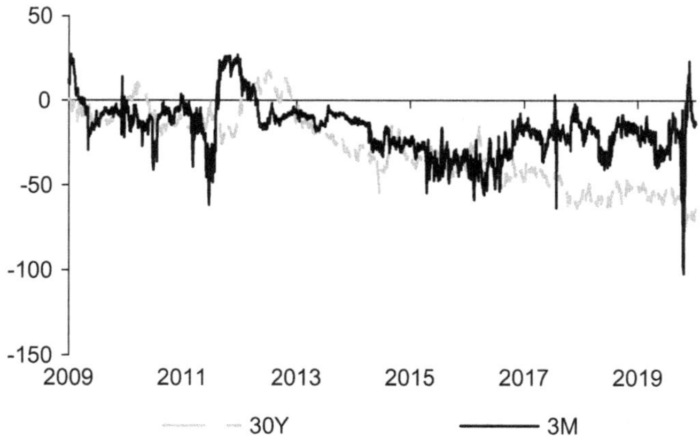

Figure 3.2: Xccy basis for GBPJPY in bp.
Source: Commerzbank, Bloomberg

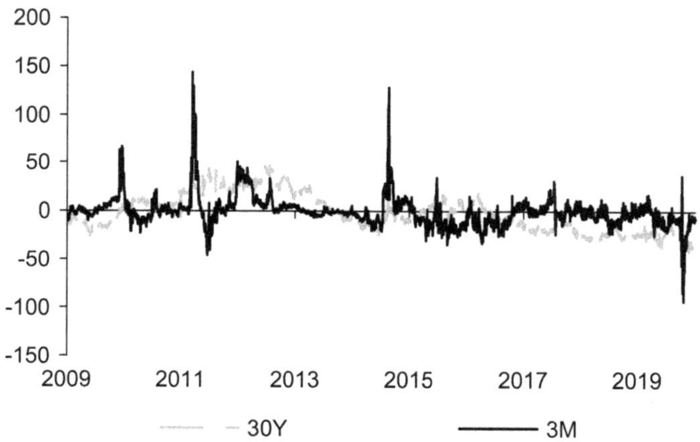

Figure 3.3: Xccy basis for CHFJPY in bp.
Source: Commerzbank, Bloomberg

What is remarkable about both these graphs is that the basis can be pretty large – over a per cent in the case of the 3m CHFJPY. While, with these reconstructed rates, one needs to bear in mind that they may be noisy, the excessions do seem to mirror market events – for example, one of the largest spikes in the CHFJPY 3m basis occurs early in 2015 when the SNB ceased to maintain the pegged FX rate.

For other examples of these unusual xccy basis time series, see Appendix 3.A, where we have graphed a selection of tenors for the EUR and JPY crosses. Please note that as some rates are reconstructed from others, particularly the 3m rates, they can be rather noisy, but the levels and dynamics will contain useful information. For completeness, we also include the USD bases, which are available in the market but are interesting for comparison purposes.

Calculating FX Hedged Pickup

Now that we have the full set of xccy bases, perhaps we can generate a similar set of FX hedged pickups – which may represent opportunities for some investors. In Figures 3.4 to 3.7, we graph the FX hedged pickups, both rolling and matched maturity, for some JPY crosses (assuming from JPY based entity, so going short the JPY bond). It can be seen that some are at significant levels.

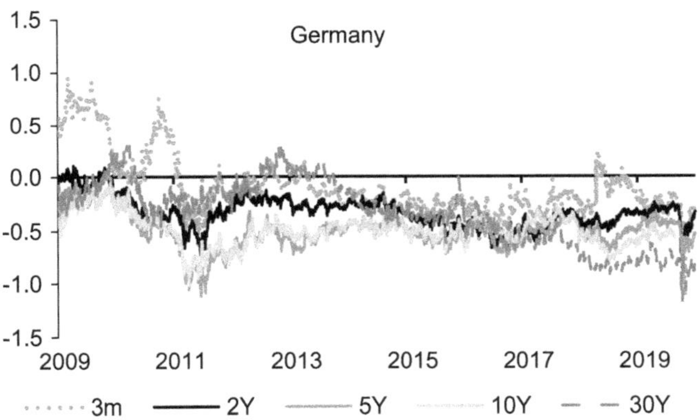

Figure 3.4: FX hedged pickup for EURJPY in %.
Source: Bloomberg, Commerzbank Research

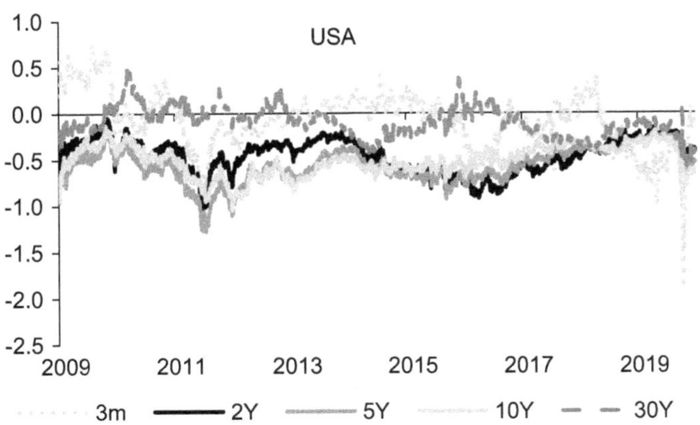

Figure 3.5: FX hedged pickup for USDJPY in %.
Source: Bloomberg, Commerzbank Research

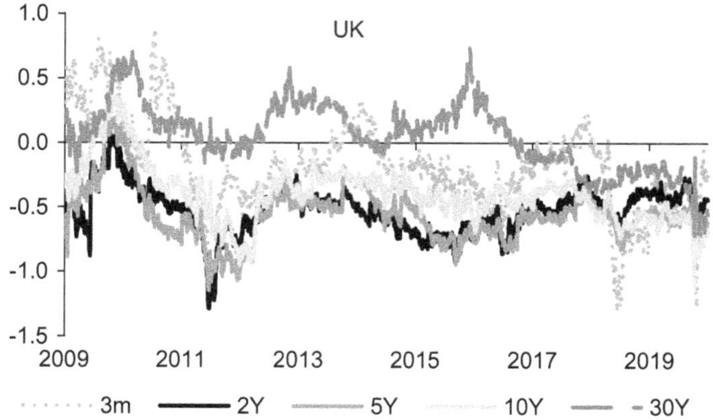

Figure 3.6: FX hedged pickup for GBPJPY in %.
Source: Bloomberg, Commerzbank Research

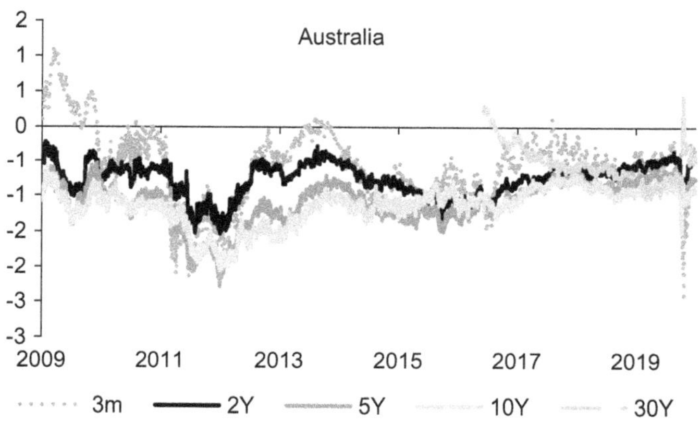

Figure 3.7: FX hedged pickup for AUDJPY in %.
Source: Bloomberg, Commerzbank Research

The potential value in some of these pickups is considerable. All values are annualised and thus, for example, the 30y EURJPY pickup is currently at almost −1% – indicating that one could short EUR government bonds, buy JPY government bonds, lock in a 30y FX hedge, and generate nearly 1% of pickup per year. It's important to remember that this would be dependent on multiple factors – only an entity with good enough market access and credit would be able to attempt this, and the various rates are calculated rather than market quotes, so it would be advisable to check them carefully in the market. But as indications of potential value, these results are extremely interesting. In Appendix 3.B, we have graphed FX hedged pickups to the EUR, USD and JPY. These are not the only possible crosses; in theory, all others within the currency set are obtainable.

Appendix 3.A: Xccy Bases

To the EUR

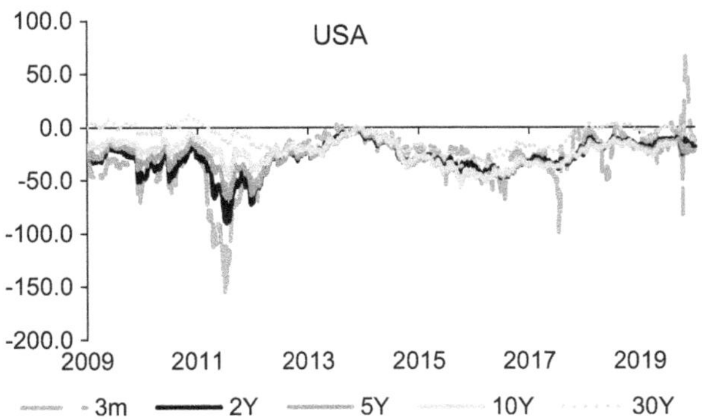

Figure 3.8: Xccy basis for EURUSD in bp (to the EUR).

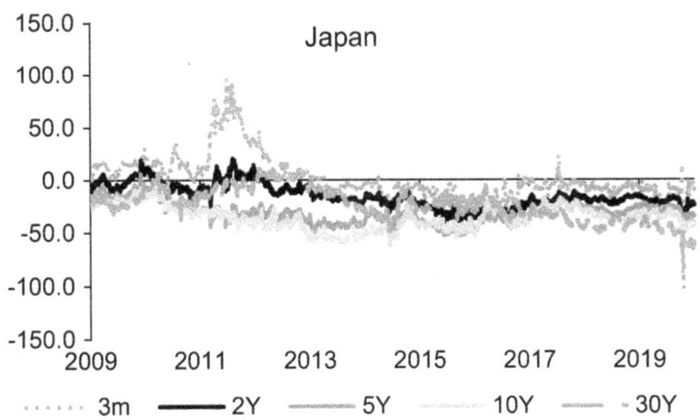

Figure 3.9: Xccy basis for EURJPY in bp (to the EUR).

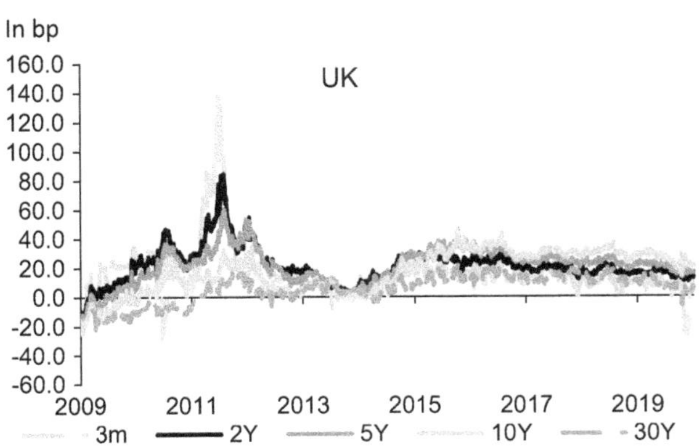

Figure 3.10: Xccy basis for EURGBP (to the EUR).

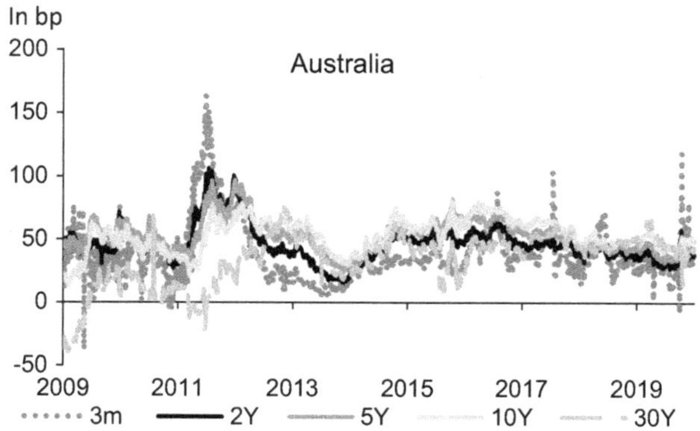

Figure 3.11: Xccy basis for EURAUD (to the EUR).

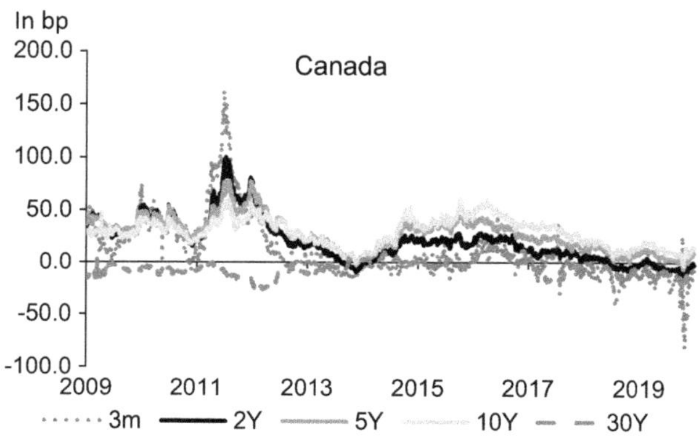

Figure 3.12: Xccy basis for EURCAD (to the EUR).

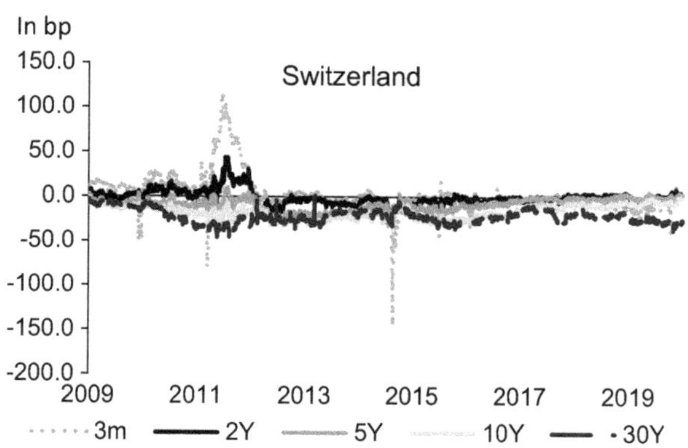

Figure 3.13: Xccy basis for EURCHF (to the EUR).

To the USD

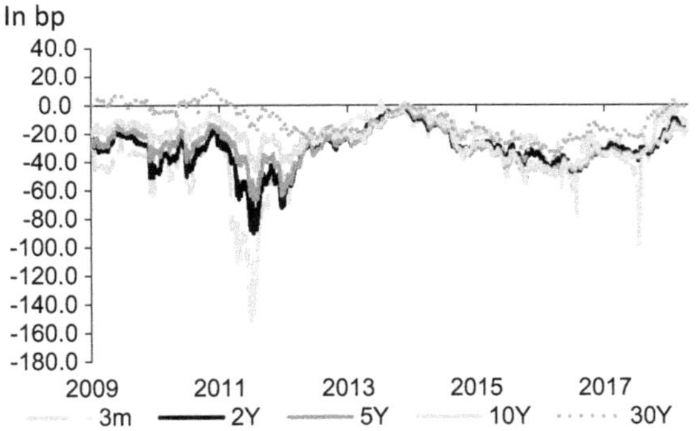

Figure 3.14: Xccy basis for EURUSD (to the USD).
Source: Bloomberg, Commerzbank Research

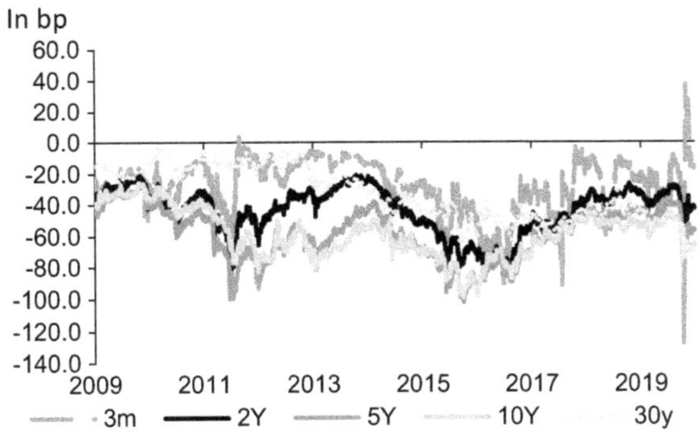

Figure 3.15: Xccy basis for USDJPY (to the USD).
Source: Bloomberg, Commerzbank Research

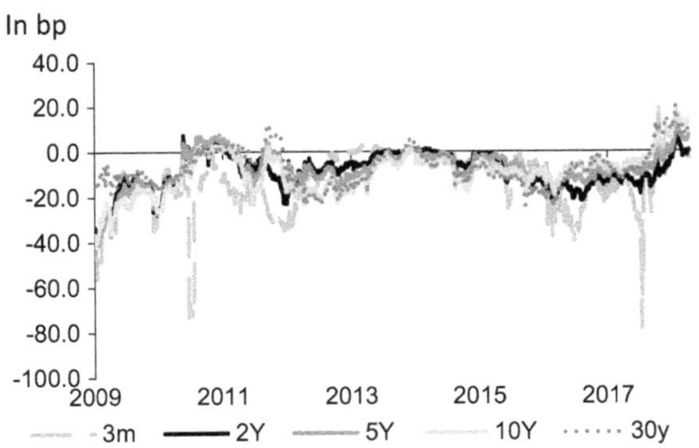

Figure 3.16: Xccy basis for USDGBP (to the USD).
Source: Bloomberg, Commerzbank Research

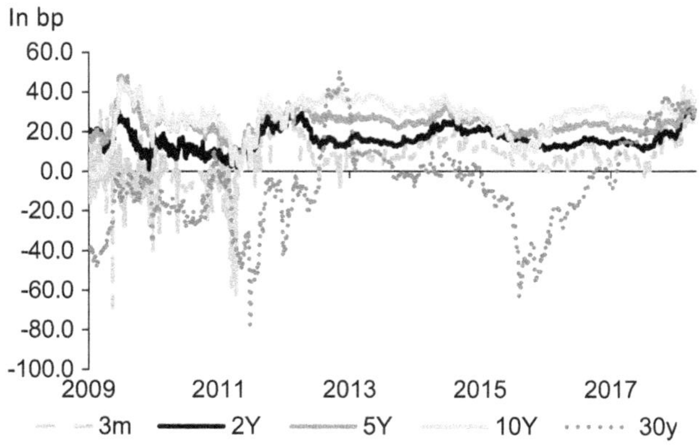

Figure 3.17: Xccy basis for USDAUD (to the USD).
Source: Bloomberg, Commerzbank Research

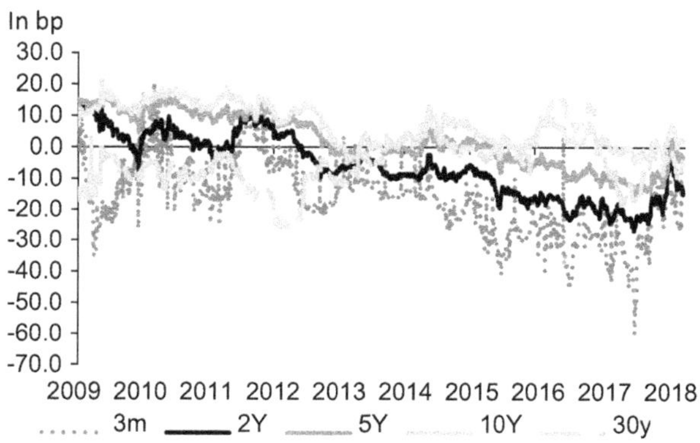

Figure 3.18: Xccy basis for USDCAD (to the USD).
Source: Bloomberg, Commerzbank Research

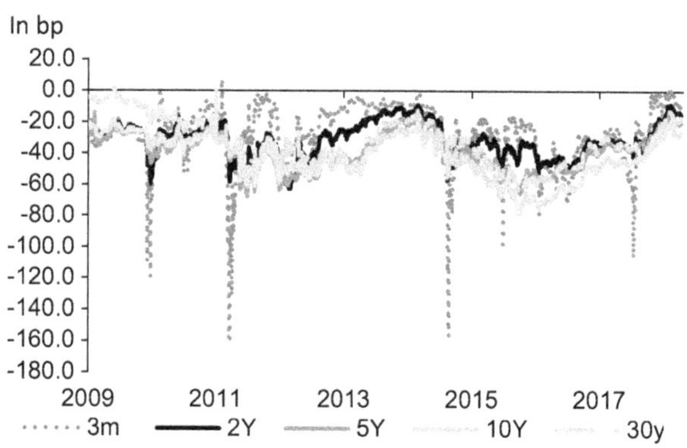

Figure 3.19: Xccy basis for USDCHF (to the USD).
Source: Bloomberg, Commerzbank Research

To the JPY

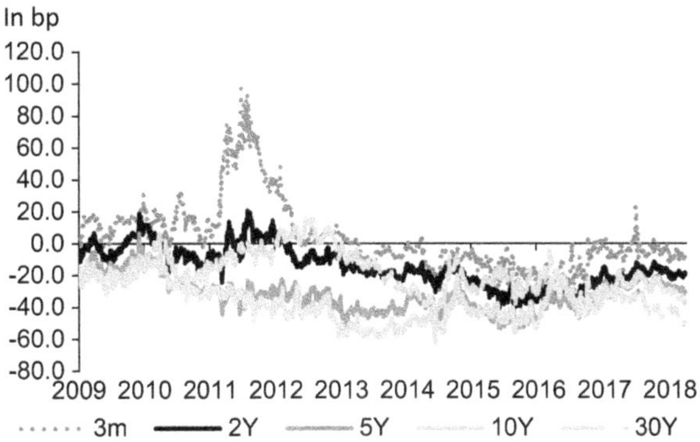

Figure 3.20: Xccy basis for EURJPY (to the JPY).
Source: Bloomberg, Commerzbank Research

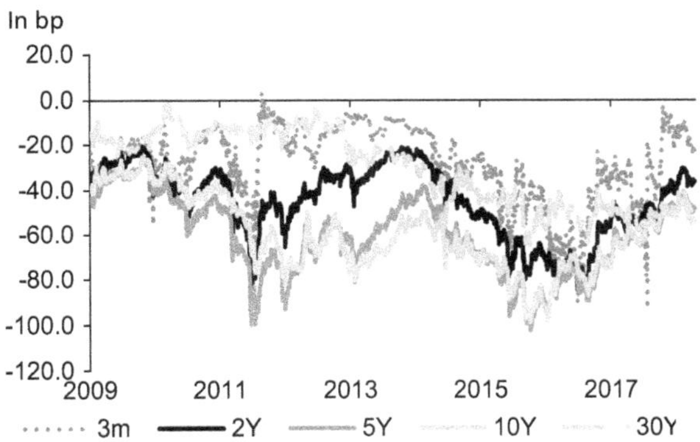

Figure 3.21: Xccy basis for USDJPY (to the JPY).
Source: Bloomberg, Commerzbank Research

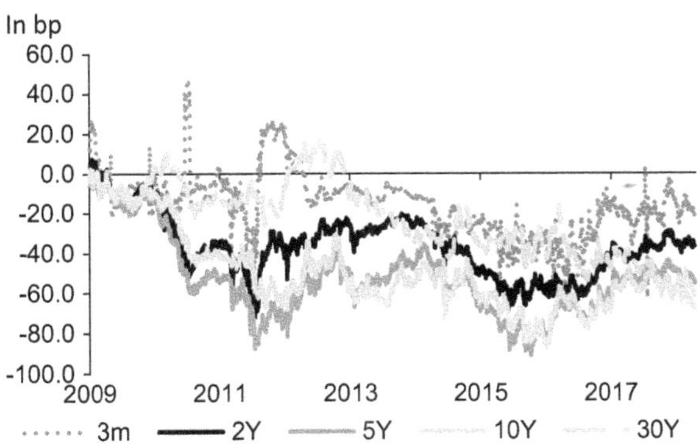

Figure 3.22: Xccy basis for GBPJPY (to the JPY).
Source: Bloomberg, Commerzbank Research

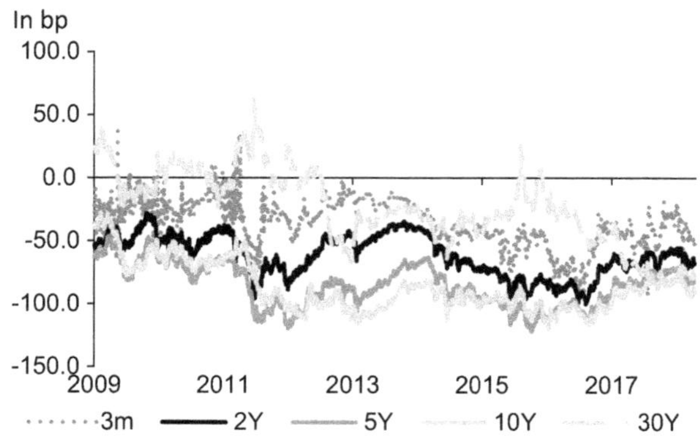

Figure 3.23: Xccy basis for AUDJPY (to the JPY).
Source: Bloomberg, Commerzbank Research

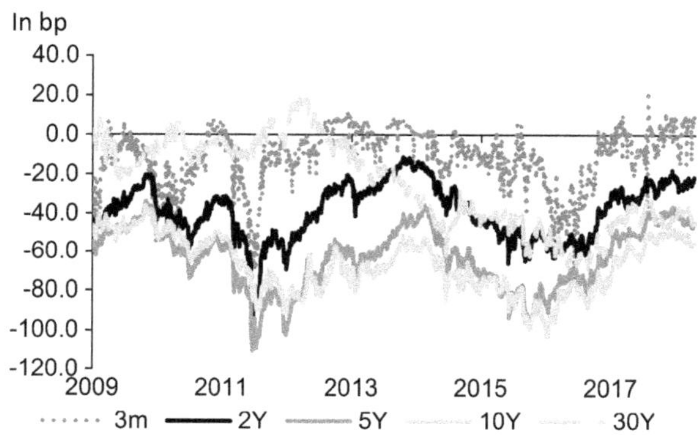

Figure 3.24: Xccy basis for CADJPY (to the JPY).
Source: Bloomberg, Commerzbank Research

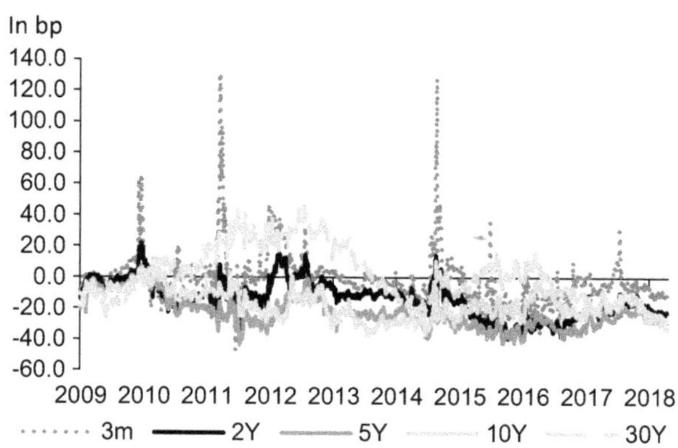

Figure 3.25: Xccy basis for CHFJPY (to the JPY).
Source: Bloomberg, Commerzbank Research

Appendix 3.B: FX Hedged Pickups

To the EUR

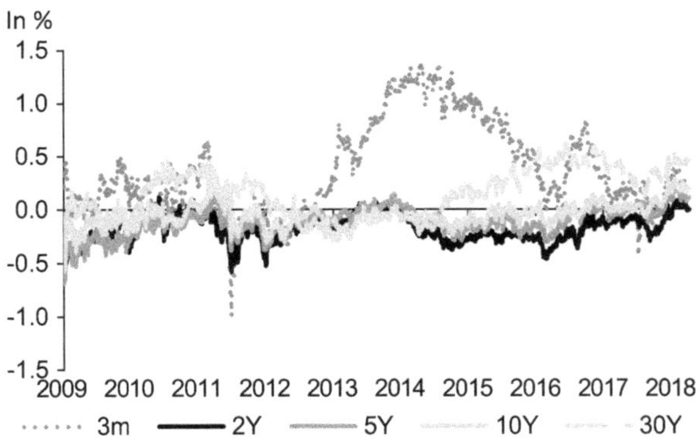

Figure 3.26: FX hedged pickup for EURUSD (to the EUR).
Source: Bloomberg, Commerzbank Research

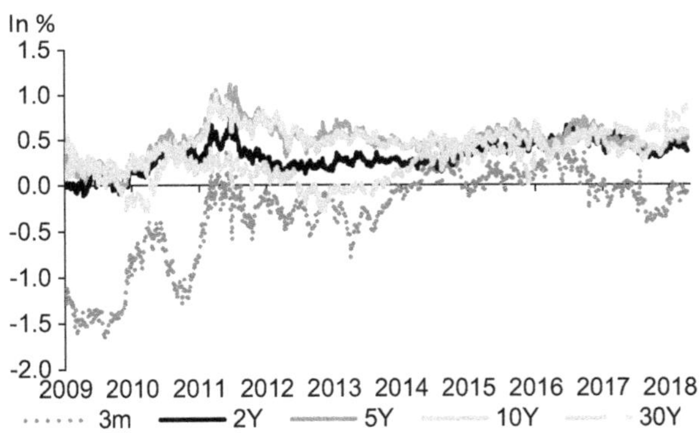

Figure 3.27: FX hedged pickup for EURJPY (to the EUR).
Source: Bloomberg, Commerzbank Research

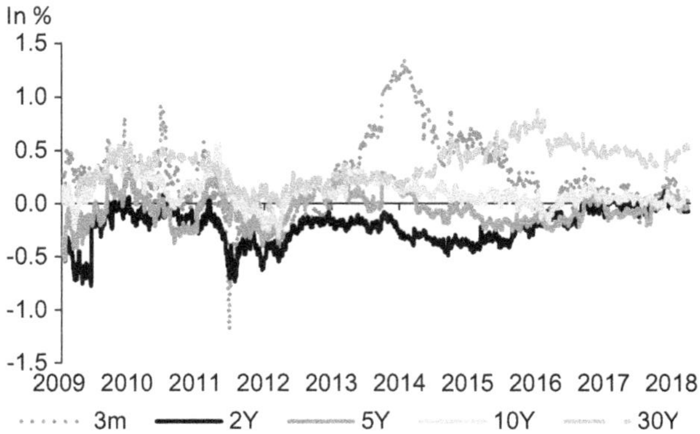

Figure 3.28: FX hedged pickup for EURGBP (to the EUR).
Source: Bloomberg, Commerzbank Research

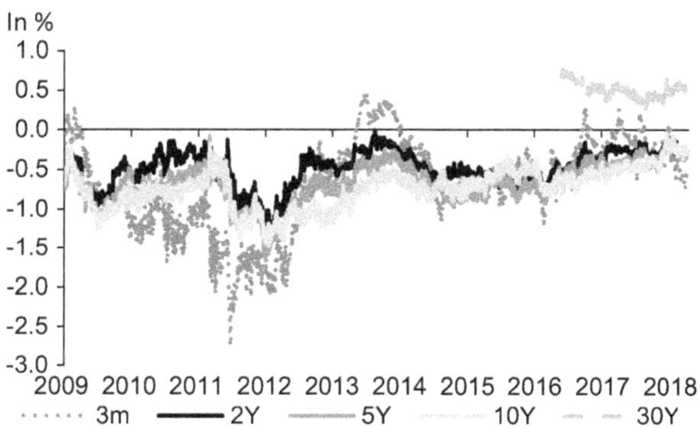

Figure 3.29: FX hedged pickup for EURAUD (to the EUR).
Source: Bloomberg, Commerzbank Research

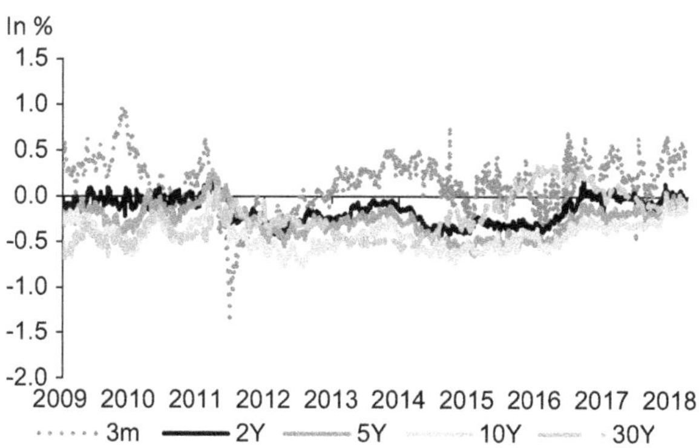

Figure 3.30: FX hedged pickup for EURCAD (to the EUR).
Source: Bloomberg, Commerzbank Research

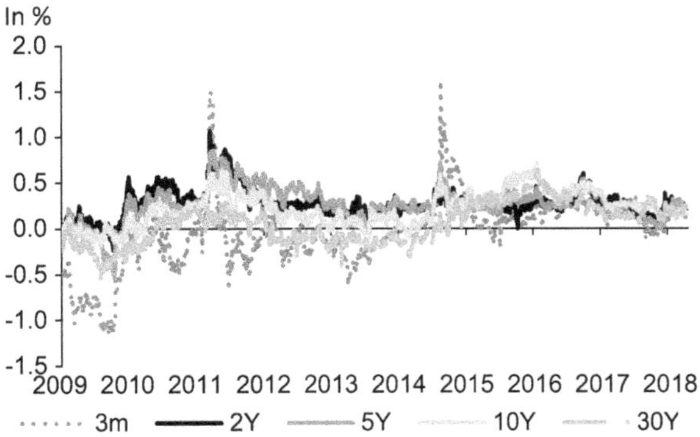

Figure 3.31: FX hedged pickup for EURCHF (to the EUR).
Source: Bloomberg, Commerzbank Research

To the USD

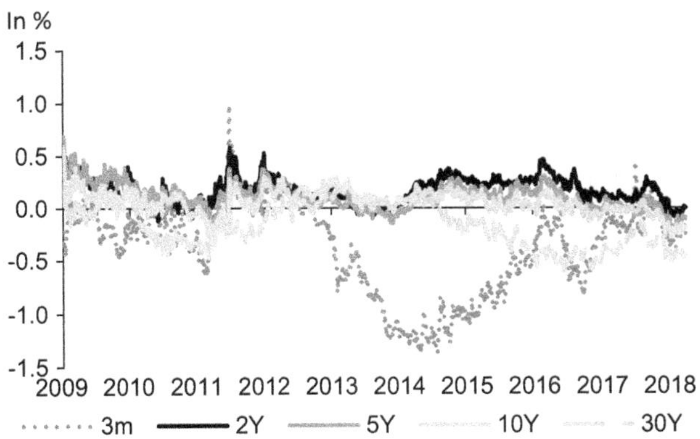

Figure 3.32: FX hedged pickup for EURUSD (to the USD).
Source: Bloomberg, Commerzbank Research

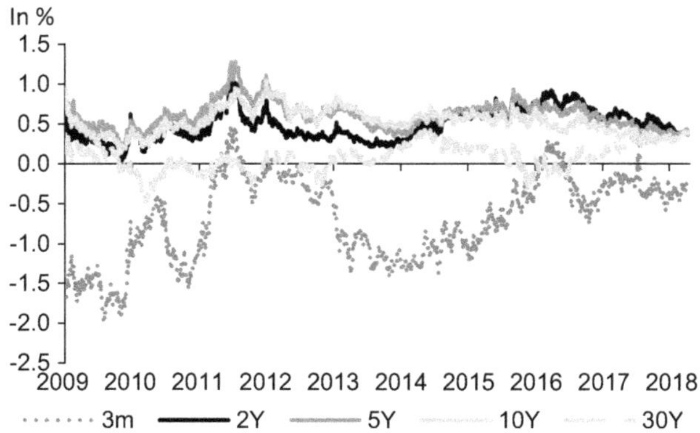

Figure 3.33: FX hedged pickup for USDJPY (to the USD).
Source: Bloomberg, Commerzbank Research

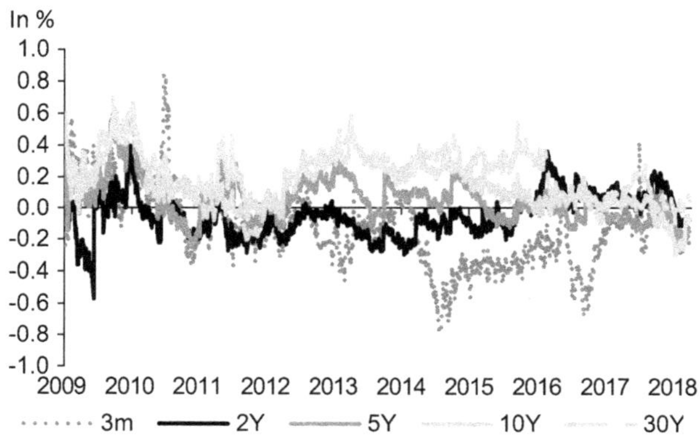

Figure 3.34: FX hedged pickup for USDGBP (to the USD).
Source: Bloomberg, Commerzbank Research

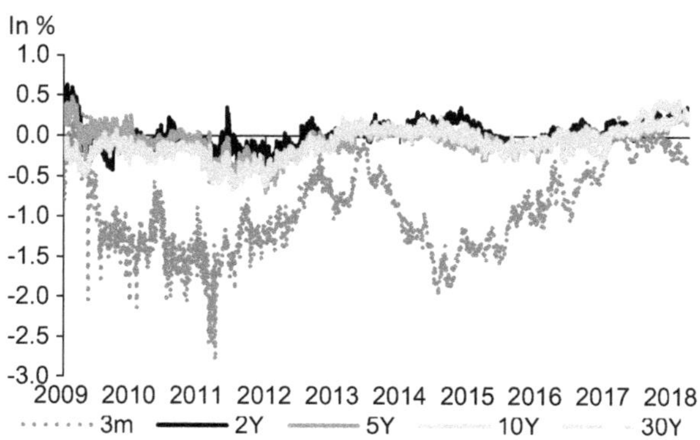

Figure 3.35: FX hedged pickup for USDAUD (to the USD).
Source: Bloomberg, Commerzbank Research

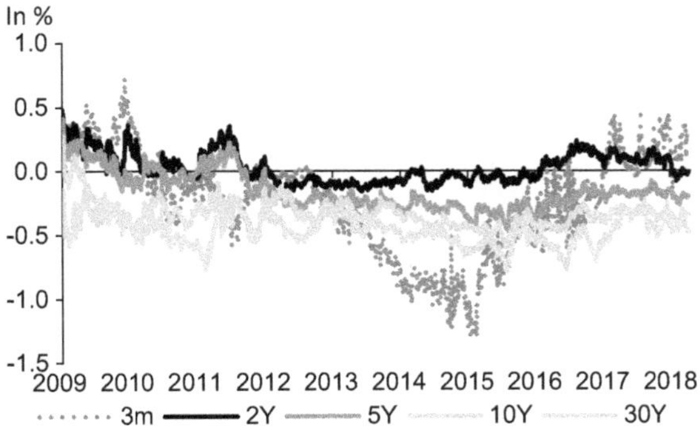

Figure 3.36: FX hedged pickup for USDCAD (to the USD).
Source: Bloomberg, Commerzbank Research

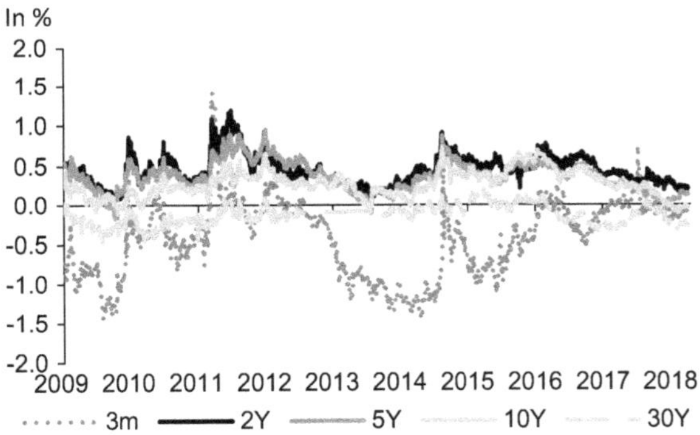

Figure 3.37: FX hedged pickup for USDCHF (to the USD).
Source: Bloomberg, Commerzbank Research

To the JPY

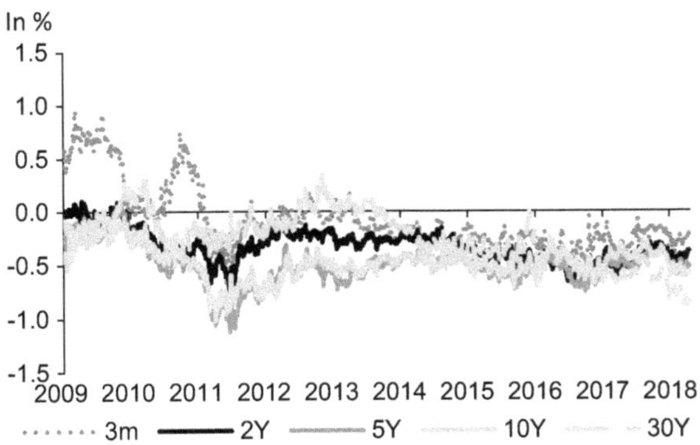

Figure 3.38: FX hedged pickup for EURJPY (to the JPY).
Source: Bloomberg, Commerzbank Research

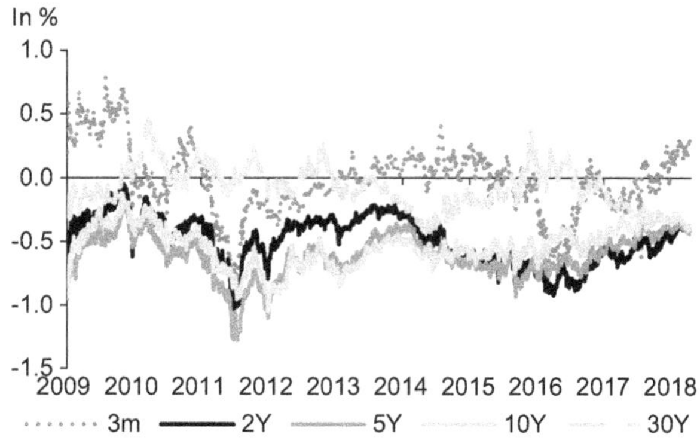

Figure 3.39: FX hedged pickup for USDJPY (to the JPY).
Source: Bloomberg, Commerzbank Research

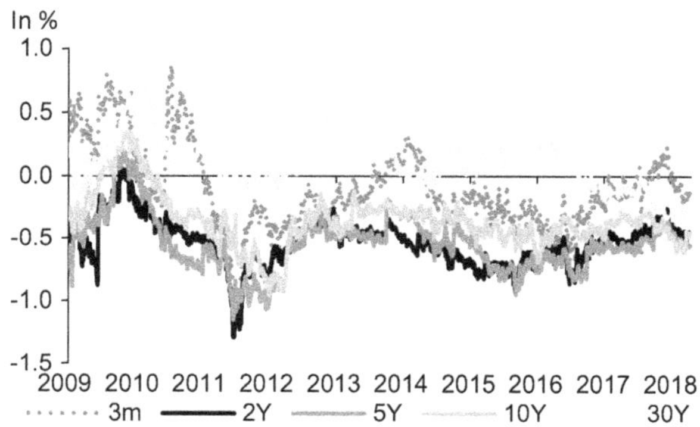

Figure 3.40: FX hedged pickup for GBPJPY (to the JPY).
Source: Bloomberg, Commerzbank Research

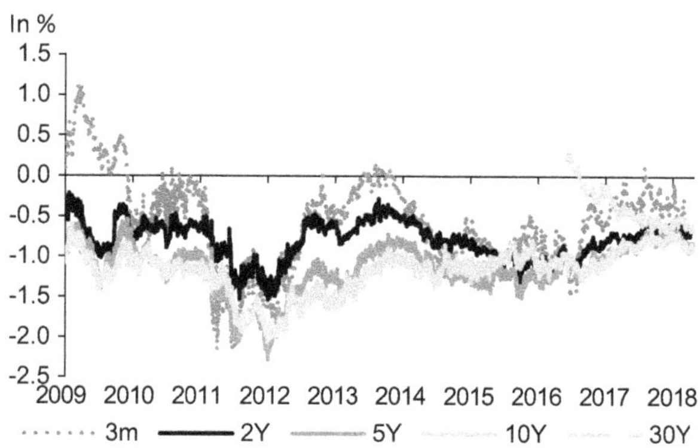

Figure 3.41: FX hedged pickup for AUDJPY (to the JPY).
Source: Bloomberg, Commerzbank Research

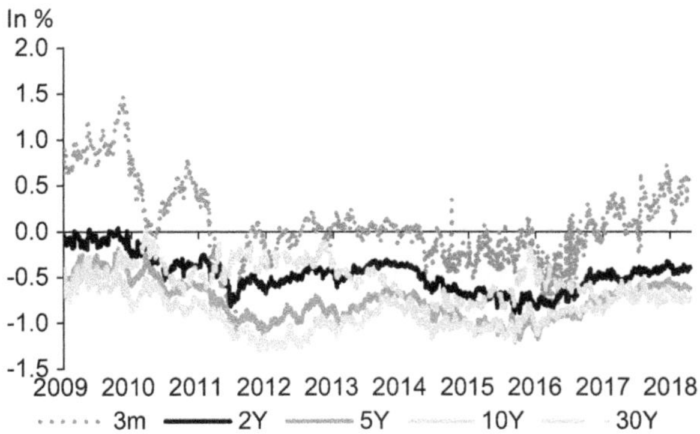

Figure 3.42: FX hedged pickup for CADJPY (to the JPY).
Source: Bloomberg, Commerzbank Research

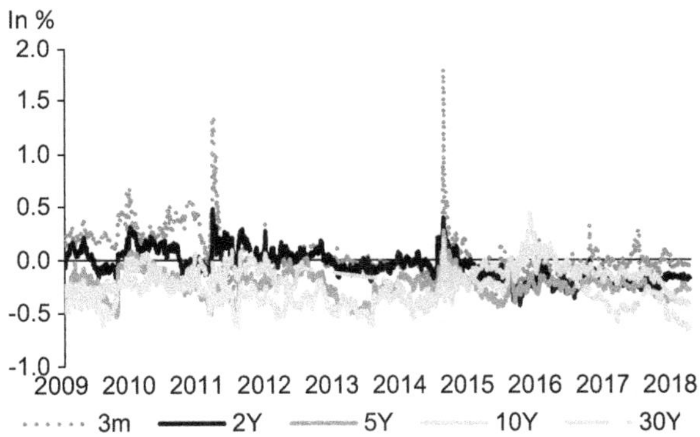

Figure 3.43: FX hedged pickup for CHFJPY (to the JPY).
Source: Bloomberg, Commerzbank Research

Chapter 4
FX Hedging of Fixed Income – What is the Best Way?

In Chapter 1 and Chapter 3, we showed that in some cases, it may be possible to hedge the FX risk of some fixed income instruments and lock in a gain, for institutions with access to the right markets and credit ratings.[1] However, the science of hedging FX risk for fixed income instruments was not designed purely to take advantage of this type of opportunity, but rather to reduce risk on the overseas fixed income assets. In this chapter, we examine alternative ways of hedging these assets and show that it is possible to express the various alternatives in a coherent mathematical framework. We will also illustrate the risks of some popular partial hedge methods that are not all that they seem.

FX Hedge Strategies

Before going into detail about the results of different hedge strategies and pickups, it is worth defining exactly what they are:

- The **maturity-matched** pickup is equal to the cross-currency basis minus the swap spread differential of the assets minus the 3s/6s basis (as the EUR asset swap is usually quoted versus 6m). When holding the position to maturity, one already knows the return when entering into the trade (i.e. it is a full hedge). We have defined this case as 'maturity-matched' but it could also be called 'cash-flow matched' or 'cross currency swap hedged' – the important thing is that it is a complete hedge whose pickup is known and locked in from the start.
- The pickup from **rolling hedges** via a short-dated FX swap derives from the steepness of the foreign yield curve relative to the domestic curve, but it is not a full hedge. For example, a large increase in funding rates of the foreign currency over the term of the trade would generate negative returns. In this sense, it is related to an interest rate carry trade.
- **Unhedged positions** – where the investor buys a higher-yielding instrument funded by borrowing in a lower yielding one – are fully exposed to FX swings. In effect, they are an FX carry trade and thus are highly volatile.

1 This chapter was first published as Commerzbank's Rates Radar, 'Hedging currency risk on fixed income instruments', June 2017.

https://doi.org/10.1515/9783110688733-004

Maturity-Matched Hedges

Reducing Uncertainty to the Minimum Level for the Whole Tenor

As a EUR-based (or JPY-based) investor, the higher yields currently available for US bonds across the tenor range are attractive. How could the EUR-based investor take advantage of this?

In a financial market with no capital charges or regulatory and XVA issues, it would not be possible to preserve any kind of yield pickup by investing in a foreign bond and then hedging the FX risk. The 'theoretical' forward FX rate would, in the pre-2008 crisis days, have almost exactly cancelled out the yield pickup, though there might have been some credit spread available. But even this was small.

Now, however, there exists in general a substantial cross-currency basis, meaning that the arbitrage relationship between FX spot and forward, and interest rates, has broken down to an extent, partly due to the demand for different currencies and partly due to regulatory activity that restricts arbitrage trades. The actual cross currency basis is usually expressed as a difference to the non-USD interest rate of the currency pair, though it could equally be expressed as a spread to the USD rate or to the FX spot or theoretical forward rate. Additionally, credit spread differentials have become far more significant since the crisis, and may provide additional pickup in different industries and tenors.

We would execute the hedge in the swap market, which has slightly different rates from the government bonds (though they are correlated), and we would include the basis swap. The (US) basis swap is the extra cost of borrowing US dollars via a currency swap compared to what it should be purely according to interest rate differentials.

What, then, will the cost of hedging be? The mechanics of the package are thus: the EUR-based investor exchanges EUR for USD, buys the USD bond, and puts on a maturity-matched FX hedge. Simplistically, assuming a 1-year period, and without worrying about coupon payments, we can write this as the following.

FX is the FX rate at the start of the deal

FR_1 is the 1-year forward FX rate for the bond maturity

$$P = \text{EUR principal amount at start of deal}$$

$$P \times FX = \text{USD principal amount at start of deal}$$

$$P \times \frac{FX}{FR_1} = \text{EUR principal amount at end of deal}$$

As stated, we are not worrying about hedging the interest rate risk.

Thus

$$\text{EUR hedge cost} = P - P \times \frac{FX}{FR_1} \tag{1}$$

But from the arbitrage-based construction of the forward rate FR, we know that

$$FX = FR_1 \frac{1+R_1}{1+R_2}$$

Where R_1 is the EUR interest rate, and R_2 is the USD interest rate for the bond tenor.

Thus, the EUR hedge cost is given by

$$\text{EUR hedge cost} = P - \left[\frac{P}{FR_1}\right]\left[FR_1 \frac{1+R_1}{1+R_2}\right]$$

$$\text{EUR hedge cost} = P\left[1 - \frac{1+R_1}{1+R_2}\right] = P\left[\frac{R_2 - R_1}{1+R_2}\right] \approx P[R_2 - R_1]$$

R_2 is the USD swap rate, but now we actually need to adjust it by the basis swap amount. Thus

$$\text{EUR hedge cost} \approx P[R_2 + R_{basis} - R_1] \tag{2}$$

Because (1) and (2) are approximately equal to each other, it can be calculated either way, depending on the data that is available. One would usually use equation (2), as the basis swap is explicitly incorporated, but if one wished to use the spot and forward FX rates, then it is possible to express the quantity $[R_2+R_{basis}-R_1]$ in terms of these FX rates as in equation (1), because the forward FX rate in the market does incorporate the basis.

It's not difficult to extend this to the multi-year case. We know that for n years,

$$FX = FR_n \frac{(1+R_1)^n}{(1+R_2)^n}$$

So the total EUR hedge cost over the whole deal is given by

$$\text{EUR hedge cost} = P\left[1 - \frac{(1+R_1)^n}{(1+R_2)^n}\right] \approx P\left[\frac{n(R_2 - R_1)}{1+nR_2}\right] \approx P \times n[R_2 - R_1]$$

$$\text{EUR annual hedge cost} \approx P[R_2 - R_1] \approx P\left(1 - \left[\frac{FX}{FR_n}\right]\right)/n$$

if we use a binomial expansion and take only the first order. Once more, of course, we actually need to include the basis swap, so the actual annual cost will be $P[R_2+R\_basis-R_1]$.

$$\text{EUR annual hedge cost} \approx P[R_2 + R_{basis} - R_1] \approx P\left(1 - \left[\frac{FX}{FR_n}\right]\right)/n \tag{3}$$

So we may now calculate a hedged yield pickup, which is actually accessible to the EUR-based investor. It is FX hedged and relatively risk-free. Note that equation (3), where the hedge cost is expressed in terms of the FX spot and forward rates, is a novel way of calculating hedge cost. It is useful in that it is an alternative way of arriving at the answer from other data series than those usually used.

Practical Calculation of Maturity-Matched Yield Pickup

From now on, we can omit the principal amount P in expressions, as it will always cancel on both sides of the equation and there is no loss of generality in expressing all quantities as percentages.

Once we have the hedge cost, we may derive the annualised yield pickup very simply, as the following:

$$\text{Yield pickup} = [B_2 - B_1] - \text{Hedge Cost}$$

As previously discussed, in a perfectly efficient market, this would be zero, but in the 'real world' it is often substantial.

In practice, we may derive this yield pickup three ways.

(1) Using bond yields, swap rates and cross-currency basis swaps

$$\text{Yield pickup} = [B_2 - B_1] - [R_2 + R_{basis} - R_1]$$

(2) Using asset swap spreads, 3s6s basis swaps and cross-currency basis swaps

$$\text{Yield pickup} = [A_1 - A_2] - C_1 + R_{basis}$$

(3) Using bond yields and spot and forward FX rates

$$\text{Yield pickup} = [B_2 - B_1] - \left(1 - \left[\frac{FX}{FR_n}\right]\right)/n \tag{4}$$

Where, for a EUR investor buying a USD government bond,

B_1 = EUR bond yield
B_2 = USD bond yield
R_1 = EUR swap rate
R_2 = USD swap rate
R_{basis} = XCCY basis swap
A_1 = EUR asset swap
A_2 = USD asset swap
C_1 = 3s6s basis
FX = spot foreign exchange rate
FR_n = forward foreign exchange rate for tenor n
n = tenor in years

Note that the 3s6s basis (i.e. the difference between swap rates referenced to 3m and 6m Libor) may sometimes be needed if the other interest rates differ in their coupon frequency, and that the asset swap spread is $A_1 - A_2$ rather than $A_2 - A_1$ because it is always quoted as a positive spread over the government bond. Additionally, one may need to be careful of the sign of the basis swap, which is usually quoted as a spread to the non-USD interest rate, so if the basis-adjusted EUR interest rate is lower than the actual rate, then the basis swap will be a negative number.

Having done all of this, we see in Figure 4.1 that the three ways of calculating the yield pickup match beautifully.

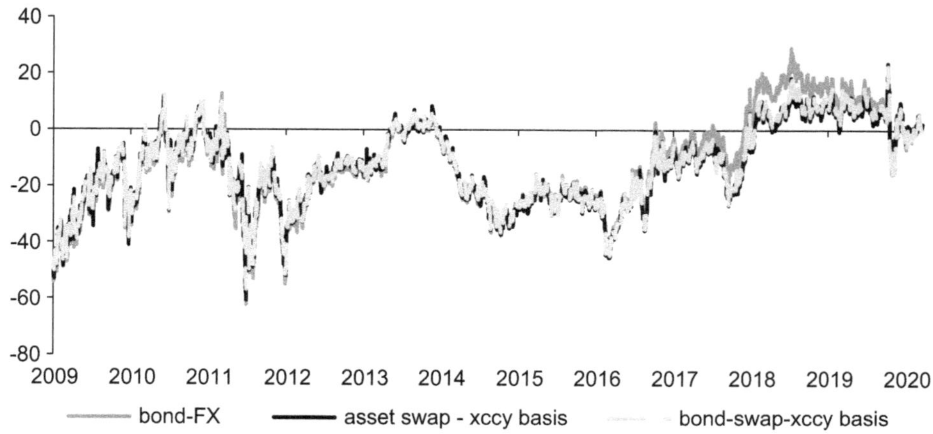

Figure 4.1: Maturity-matched FX hedged yield pickup for 2y USD bonds vs EUR vs German bonds, in bp.
Source: Commerzbank Research, Bloomberg

Historical Results for G10 Maturity-Matched Yield Pickup

It is interesting to see how the available yield pickup has varied over time, tenor and currency pair. In Figures 4.2 and 4.4, we show the generic bond yields, and in Figures 4.3 and 4.5, we show the pickup for 2y bonds since 2009 – it can be seen that recently, Japan has held the most promise.

It's obvious that the 'pickup' is not always positive – the point one can make is that a negative pickup from the perspective of one currency of a pair is a positive one from the other currency's perspective. Thus, the 2017 positive pickup in Japan was an opportunity for EUR investors; the negative pickup available in 2016 for USD vs EUR was attractive for USD investors.

The same effect is visible to a greater extent for longer tenors. In Figure 4.6 through Figure 4.9, we plot the same data for 10y bonds.

We see that the available yield pickup often comes close to 1%, which is a considerable amount in this era of close-to-zero rates.

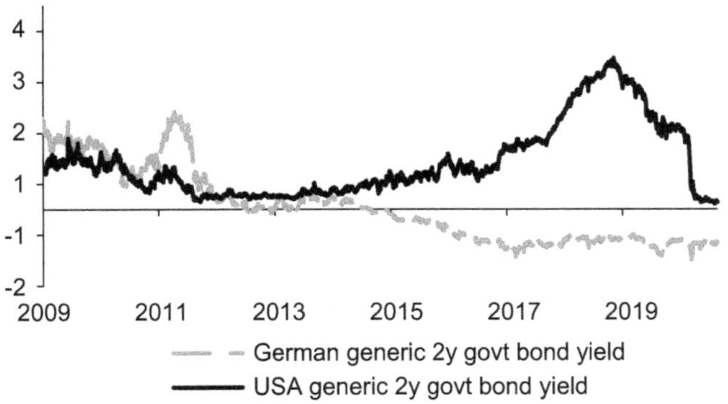

Figure 4.2: Generic bond yields for 2y USD and EUR bonds, in %.
Source: Bloomberg, Commerzbank Research

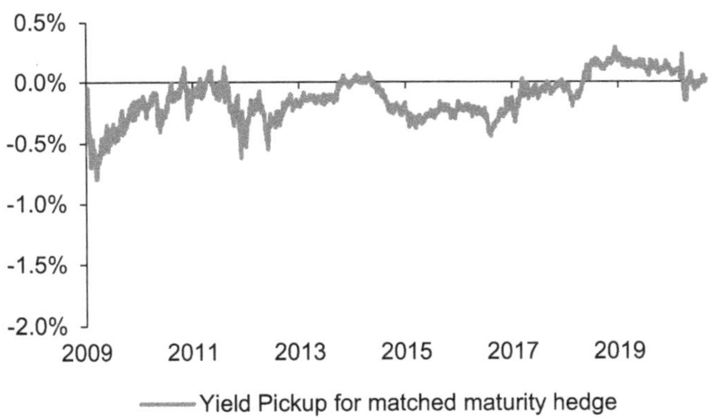

Figure 4.3: Maturity-matched FX hedged yield pickup vs EUR for 2y USD and EUR bonds, in %.
Source: Bloomberg, Commerzbank Research

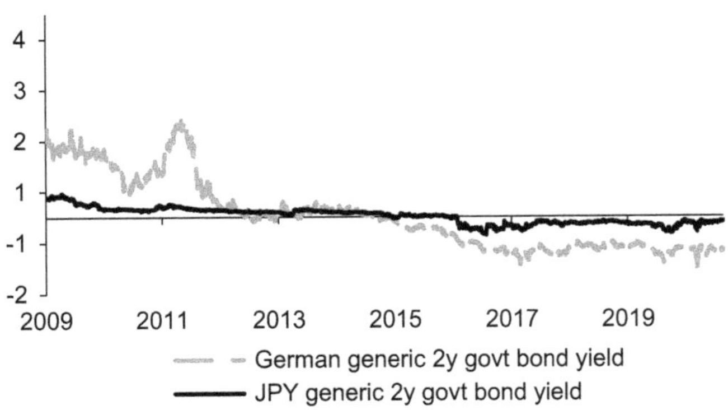

Figure 4.4: Generic bond yields for 2y JPY and EUR bonds, in %.
Source: Bloomberg, Commerzbank Research

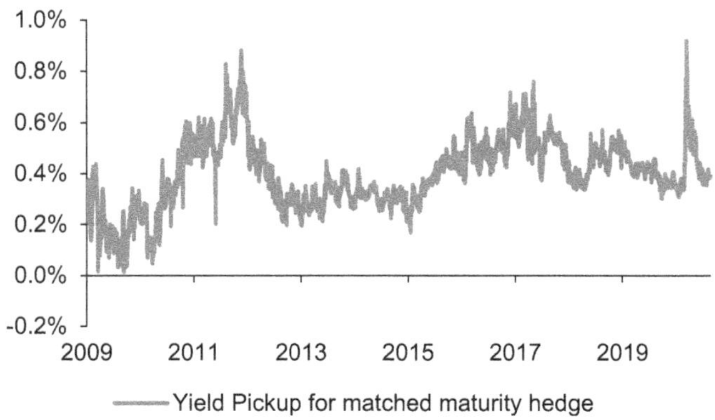

Figure 4.5: Maturity-matched FX hedged yield pickup vs EUR for 2y JPY and EUR bonds, in %. Source: Bloomberg, Commerzbank Research

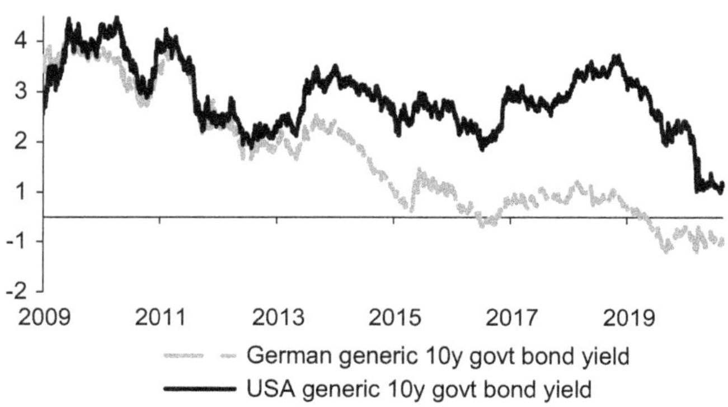

Figure 4.6: Generic bond yields for 10y USD and EUR bonds, in %. Source: Bloomberg, Commerzbank Research

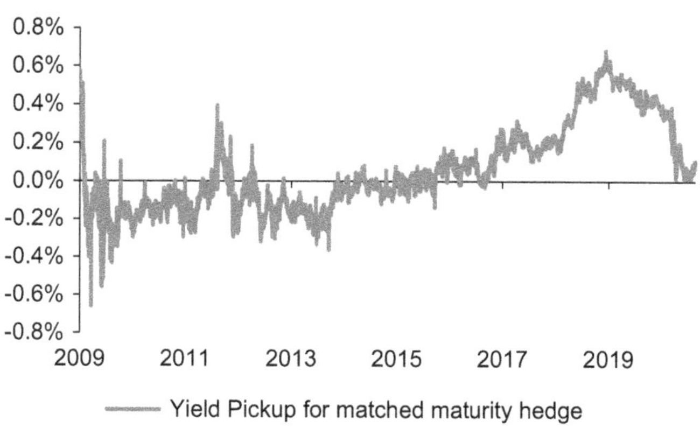

Figure 4.7: Maturity-matched FX hedged yield pickup vs EUR for 10y USD and EUR bonds, in %. Source: Bloomberg, Commerzbank Research

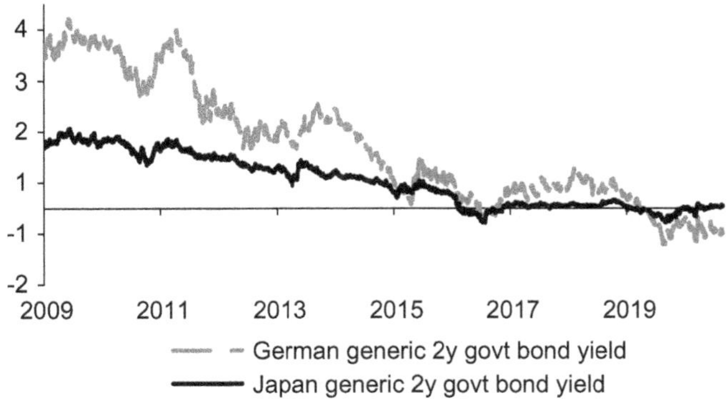

Figure 4.8: Generic bond yields for 10y JPY and EUR bond, in %.
Source: Bloomberg, Commerzbank Research

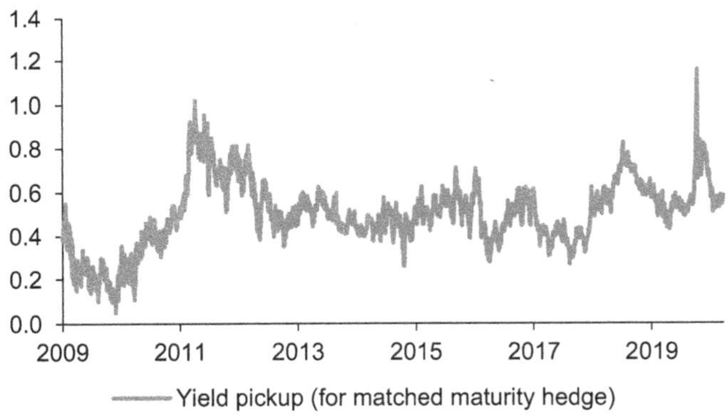

Figure 4.9: Maturity-matched FX hedged yield pickup vs EUR for 10y JPY bond, in %.
Source: Bloomberg, Commerzbank Research

Rolling Hedges

Taking a Short-Term View

An investor may want to gain some pickup but not lock in an FX hedge for the whole lifetime of the bond. In this case, it's straightforward to do a short-dated FX hedge – 3m is a popular tenor – and roll the hedge if desired, to continue with the deal at the end of this period. But it's important to realise that this is a very different deal than the maturity-matched hedge.

It's popular to compare the annualised yield pickup between both deal types – but it is essential to recall that for the maturity-matched case, that pickup is delivered for every year of the tenor of the bond, while for the 3m case, the pickup is only available for 3m, and will be a quarter of the annualised amount. Comparing the two annualised rates as if they were equivalent involves some absolutely heroic assumptions, as we do not know what the short-term rolling rate will be after the first roll date.

But if we assume that the short-term swap rates and cross-currency basis stay the same for the life of the deal (which they have never done since the markets started trading), then the two may be compared. Certainly, the comparison is valid for the first three months of the deal. If interest rates and bases were to develop exactly as predicted by forwards, then the return of the maturity-matched and rolling trade should be identical. As this is also a heroic assumption, the P&L of investors with rolling hedges is exposed to interest rate changes.

How do we calculate the rolling pickup? We have in fact done all the work earlier. There are no asset swaps available for quarterly periods, but we can still use methods (1) and (3), as described here.

(1) Using bond yields, swap rates and cross-currency basis swaps

$$\text{Yield pickup} = [B_2 - B_1] - [R_2 + R_{basis} - R_1]$$

(3) Using bond yields and spot and forward FX rates

$$\text{Yield pickup} = [B_2 - B_1] - \left(1 - \left[\frac{FX}{FR_n}\right]\right)/n$$

In these expressions, for the 3m rolling hedge of bonds of any longer tenor, the swap rates R are the 3m interest rates, the basis swap is the 3m tenor, the FX rate is 3m forward, and n is actually ¼ as the hedge is for ¼ of a year.

Possible Actions at 'Roll Point'

Let's now consider what the investor might do once the short hedge comes to an end. The FX rate and the yield curves will have changed during the course of the hedge. Thus, for a EUR-based investor who bought a USD bond at the start of the hedge, the value of the USD bond has changed in EUR terms.

But the FX hedge will deliver a payment that will make up this difference precisely. So if the investor wishes to maintain their exposure as the same amount of EUR, they can use the FX hedge maturity to buy or sell an additional amount of the USD bond which should result in a constant EUR exposure, and they can put in place another rolling hedge, this time for the new amount of USD per EUR. But the new pickup available for the new rolling hedge will not be the same as the old. It may be completely different – better or worse – leaving the investor to regret or rejoice in his or her original decision to roll rather than hedge for the full maturity of the deal.

Additionally, maintaining a rolling hedge program with a constant EUR exposure requires constant adjustment of the USD notional, although the FX hedges will cover this difference.

Historical Results for G10 Rolling Yield Pickup

We plot the rolling pickup throughout history for the same set of G10 currencies for the 2y case. It is easy to see that there are significant differences between the matched maturity and rolling hedges (Figures 4.10–4.13).

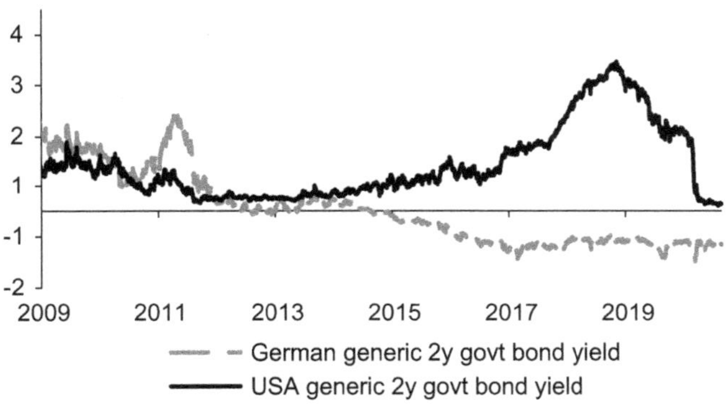

Figure 4.10: Generic bond yields for 2y USD and EUR bond, in %.
Source: Bloomberg, Commerzbank Research

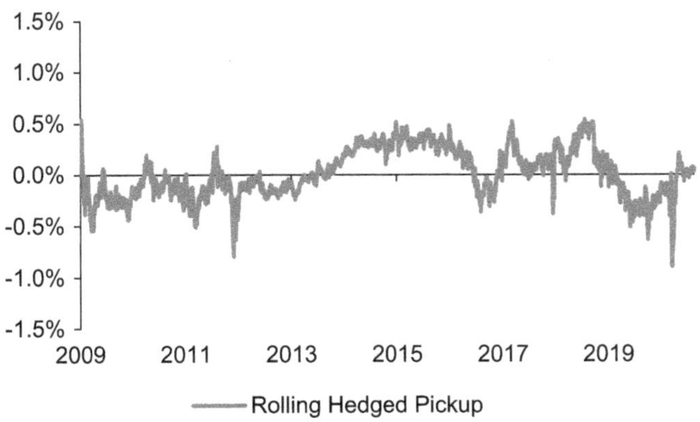

Figure 4.11: 3m FX hedged yield pickup vs EUR for 2y USD and EUR bond, in %.
Source: Bloomberg, Commerzbank Research

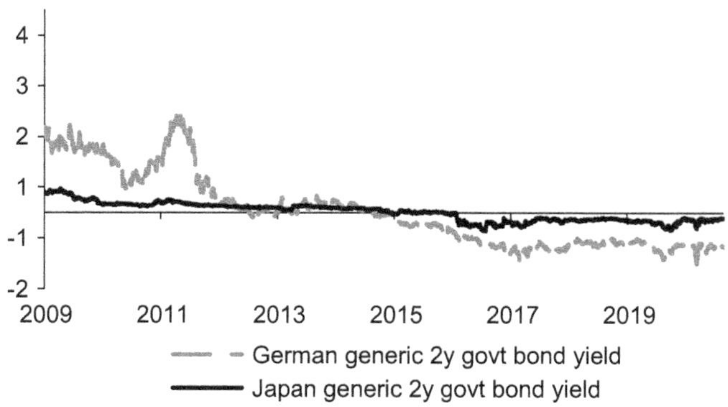

Figure 4.12: Generic bond yields for 2y JPY and EUR bond, in %.
Source: Bloomberg, Commerzbank Research

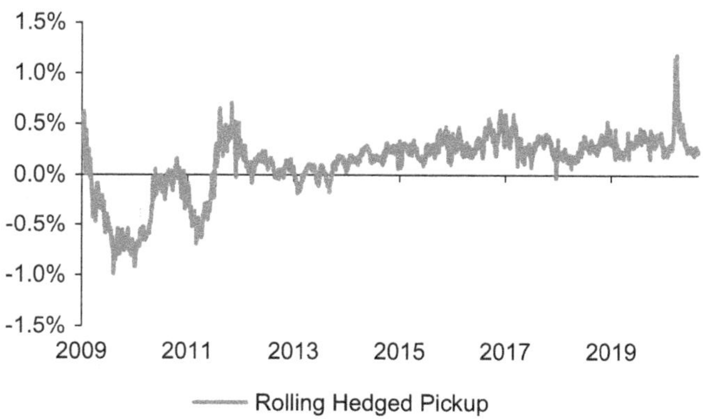

Figure 4.13: 3m FX hedged yield pickup vs EUR for 2y JPY and EUR bond, in %.
Source: Bloomberg, Commerzbank Research

In the following section, we repeat the calculation for 10y bonds. The pickup often looks substantial, but it is worth remembering that this is the annualised figure; in reality, for the 3m tenor it would be ¼ of that amount (Figures 4.14–4.17).

What underlying drivers are we seeing for these changes? It's interesting to look at what is causing the evolution in available pickup. For the 3m rolling hedge of the 10y EUR bond (top left), we see that the spread between the EUR and USD bonds was widest in 2018. And yet, the available rolling pickup, which initially increased along with the spread, has narrowed since 2015 and has even reversed direction. This reduction is driven by the short-dated differentials; since 2015, they have been steadily moving lower, eroding much of the gain from the longer tenors.

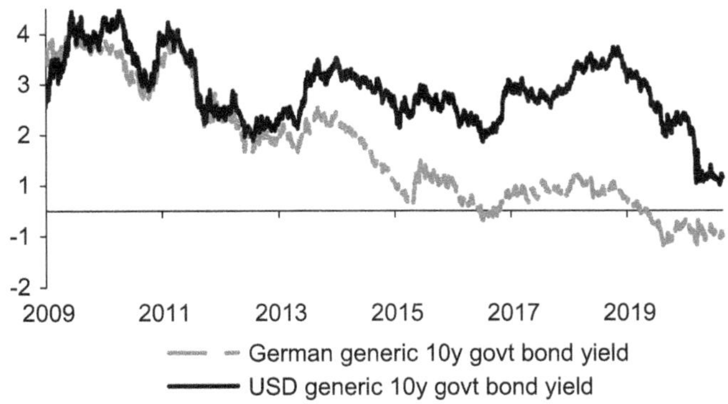

Figure 4.14: Generic bond yields for 10y USD and EUR bond, in %.
Source: Bloomberg, Commerzbank Research

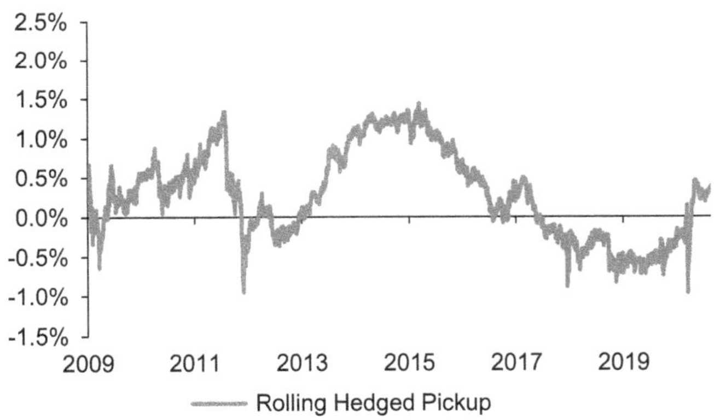

Figure 4.15: 3m FX hedged yield pickup vs EUR for 10y USD and EUR bond, in %.
Source: Bloomberg, Commerzbank Research

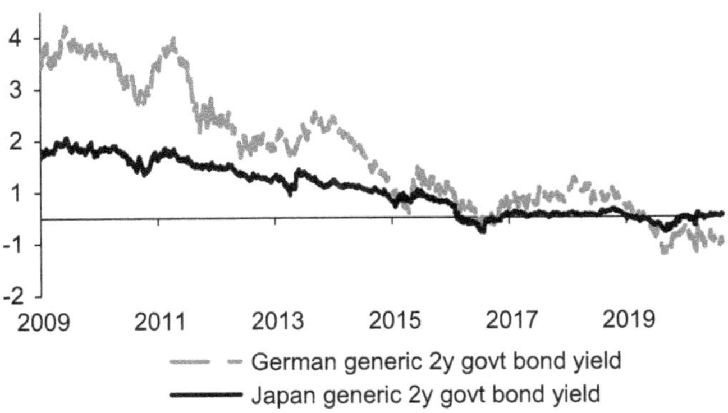

Figure 4.16: Generic bond yields for 10y JPY and EUR bond, in %.
Source: Bloomberg, Commerzbank Research

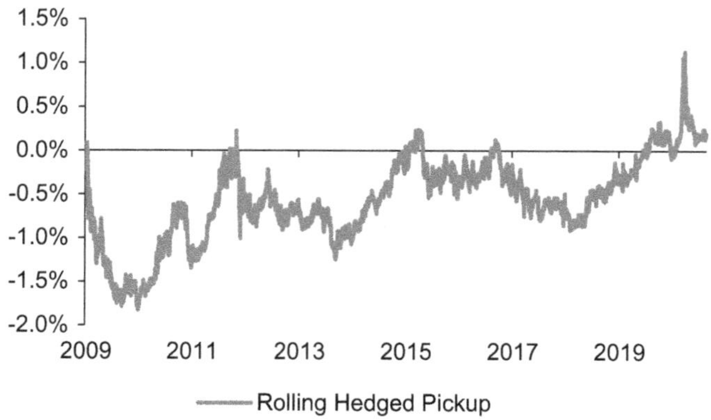

Figure 4.17: 3m FX hedged yield pickup vs EUR for 10y JPY and EUR bond, in %.
Source: Bloomberg, Commerzbank Research

Rolling Pickup 'One Period On' and for the Tenor of the Instrument

Now, let us look at what really happens in the case of rolling hedges. In the following figures, we plot the 3m rolling hedged pickup for the EURUSD case, for a 2y and 5y bond. This is the grey line. Then we plot the next quarter actual pickup (black line). This is of course the current one shifted by 3m. Finally, we plot the average 3m-hedged pickup for the tenor of the bond – for the 5y case, this ends early, as we need 5y of data to get the result (Figures 4.18 and 4.19).

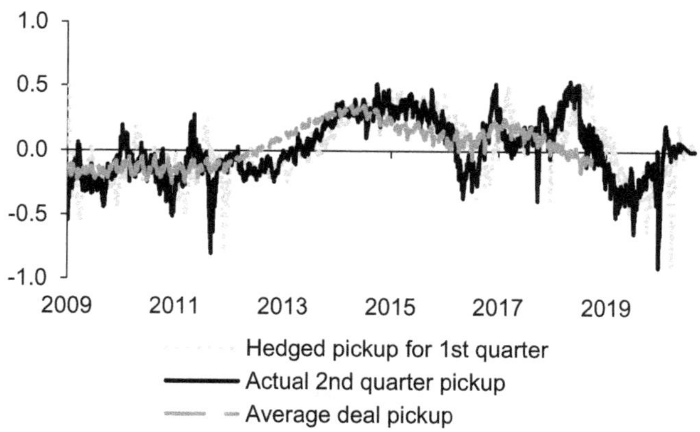

Figure 4.18: Rolling FX hedged yield pickup vs EUR for 2y USD bond, in %.
Source: Bloomberg, Commerzbank Research

It's crystal clear that the assumption that the yield pickup from one 3m period to the next could remain constant is ridiculous. Over the life of the deal, the average pickup of course becomes smoother for the longer deal tenors, and reflects more of

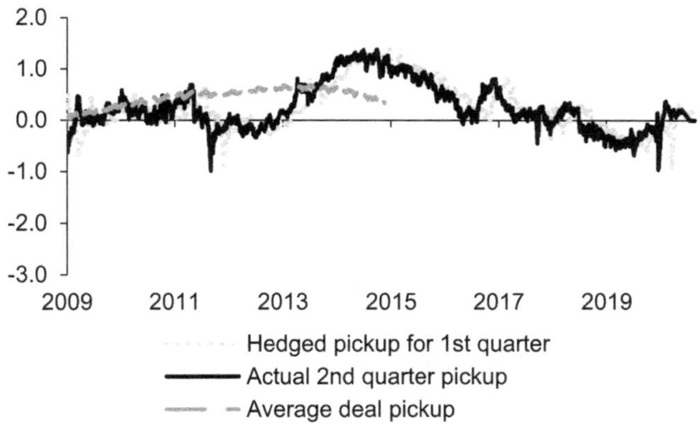

Figure 4.19: Rolling FX hedged yield pickup vs EUR for 5y USD bond, in %.
Source: Bloomberg, Commerzbank Research

a slow variation in interest rate differentials. But once more, the idea that it can be forecast by looking at the first rolling pickup is absolutely unrealistic.

Translation Effect

Finally, we can take a look at the case where the investor crosses their fingers and hopes that they can harvest the interest rate differential of the bonds without hedging. To do this, we can simply reuse equation (4), as follows:

$$\text{Yield pickup} = [B_2 - B_1] - \left(1 - \left[\frac{FX}{FR_n}\right]\right)/n$$

The beauty of our somewhat novel way of writing the yield pickup in terms of the FX rates is that if we want to understand the impact of the 'no hedge' case, we simply replace the forward rate FR_n with the spot rate at the end of the period – we can call it FX_n. It is only worth looking at the 2y case, as otherwise we have less data at the end of the period to view, but it makes the point very well indeed. We need different scales for the two returns to be visible on the same graph – the maximum range for the hedged pickup is just over 1%, but this is nearer 30% for the unhedged case.

This is not surprising, looking at the dynamics of the spot rate in that period. But it serves to underline that there are very good reasons for all the attention given to hedging the FX risk of fixed income instruments – not to do so exposes the investor to risk levels an order of magnitude larger (Figures 4.20 and 4.21).

Note that the last two years of the two-year return in these figures are of course unavailable.

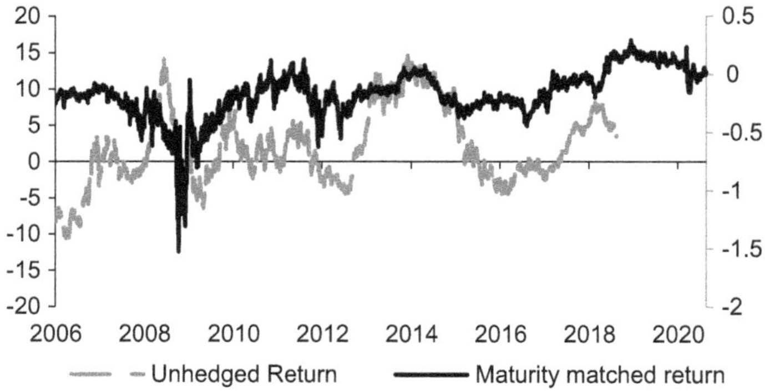

Figure 4.20: Maturity-matched FX hedged yield pickup vs EUR with unhedged return for 2y USD bond, in %.
Source: Bloomberg, Commerzbank Research

Figure 4.21: EURUSD spot exchange rate.
Source: Bloomberg, Commerzbank Research

Volatility Breakdown – What is Driving the Performance?

It is interesting to look at the contributions to the overall volatility of the various different returns. We can do this empirically by looking at the data, but also our equation (4) can be used quite elegantly to show theoretically where the dominant volatility sources originate.

We have

$$\text{Yield pickup} = [B_2 - B_1] - \left(1 - \left[\frac{FX}{FR_n}\right]\right)/n$$

Using normal propagation of error techniques, we know that if

$$f = aX - bY$$

where a and b are constants, and A and B are the sources of variation, then

$$\sigma_f = \sqrt{a^2\sigma_X^2 + b^2\sigma_Y^2 - 2ab\sigma_{XY}} \tag{5}$$

where

σ_f = standard deviation of function f
σ_X and σ_Y = standard deviation of function X and function Y
σ_{XY} = covariance of function X and function Y

So by expressing the yield pickup in the manner here where the yield differential and FX contributions are separated, we can set

$$X = [B_2 - B_1] \text{ (yield differential)}$$

$$a = 1$$

$$Y = \left(1 - \left[\frac{FX}{FR_n}\right]\right) / \text{n (FX term)}$$

$$b = 1 \text{ (but don't confuse } b \text{ with B1 and B2)}$$

We have set a and b equal to 1 so that the contributions are clear to see. Note that if the two variables X and Y are relatively uncorrelated then the covariance will be close to zero (i.e., the sum of the contributions from the differential and the FX term will be roughly equal to the covariance term). In Table 4.1, we tabulate the volatility contributions for different tenors of USD pickup for a EUR-based investor for the differently hedged cases.

We show both the standard deviation (s.d.), which is the traditional measure of volatility, and the variance, which is the square of the volatility. Although the standard deviation is more familiar, the contributions from the yield differential and the FX component are delivered via equation (4) where the s.d. is the root of the sum of the squares of the contributions and the covariance term, whereas the variances are additive so are perhaps easier to understand. Note that there is no 30y FX hedge data available.

What is interesting in Table 4.1 is the fact that the contributions to the volatility of the pickup from the yield differential and the FX term are very similar indeed, especially for the shorter-dated bonds. The FX term becomes more important for longer tenors, as might be expected. However, especially for the short-dated case, the covariance term is extremely important. If there was no covariance (i.e., no correlation), then the s.d. would be larger. The positive correlation of the yield differential and the FX term mean that overall, the yield pickup volatility is lower than it might be. This is hardly surprising, as the FX term is derived from the hedge, which in an arbitrage-free world would reduce the pickup to zero.

Table 4.1: Volatility contributions for matched maturity FX hedge, USD bonds, data since 2000, in %.

Standard Deviation (s.d.) and variance (var) of contributions to yield pickup				
	2Y	**5Y**	**10Y**	**30Y**
s.d. of pickup	0.18%	0.24%	0.48%	–
s.d. of yield differential	1.20%	1.03%	0.81%	–
s.d. of FX term	1.13%	0.87%	0.84%	–
Covar term	2.69%	1.75%	1.13%	–
var of pickup	0.03%	0.06%	0.23%	–
var of yield differential	1.44%	1.05%	0.65%	–
var of FX term	1.29%	0.76%	0.71%	–
Covar term	2.69%	1.75%	1.13%	–

Source: Bloomberg, Commerzbank Research

Table 4.2: Volatility contributions for rolling FX hedge, USD bonds, data since 2000, in %.

Standard Deviation (s.d.) and variance (var) of contributions to yield pickup				
	2Y	**5Y**	**10Y**	**30Y**
s.d. of pickup	0.44%	0.68%	0.82%	1.00%
s.d. of yield differential	1.20%	1.03%	0.81%	0.68%
s.d. of FX term	1.30%	1.30%	1.30%	1.30%
Covar term	2.94%	2.29%	1.67%	1.17%
var of pickup	0.19%	0.46%	0.68%	1.00%
var of yield differential	1.44%	1.05%	0.65%	0.46%
var of FX term	1.70%	1.70%	1.70%	1.70%
Covar term	2.94%	2.29%	1.67%	1.17%

Source: Bloomberg, Commerzbank Research

Next, in Table 4.2, we show the same table for the rolling hedge. Here, also, the covariance term is important. In this case, however, the FX term is relatively more important than the yield differential. Note that the FX term is the same in all cases, as they are all hedged with the rolling 3m strategy.

Finally, in Table 4.3, we show the unhedged case. Here, covariance is irrelevant, as everything is dominated by the FX volatility. This emphasises our point

Table 4.3: Volatility contributions for unhedged case, USD bonds, data since 2000, in %.

Standard Deviation (s.d.) and variance (var) of contributions to yield pickup				
	2Y	**5Y**	**10Y**	**30Y**
s.d. of pickup	6.43%	3.54%	1.97%	–
s.d. of yield differential	1.20%	1.03%	0.81%	–
s.d. of FX term	6.32%	3.45%	1.85%	–
Covar term	−0.05%	0.41%	0.21%	–
var of pickup	41.38%	12.54%	3.87%	–
var of yield differential	1.44%	1.05%	0.65%	–
var of FX term	39.89%	11.90%	3.43%	–
Covar term	−0.05%	0.41%	0.21%	–

Source: Bloomberg, Commerzbank Research

about the translation effect – the risks of not hedging dwarf any residual risks from an FX hedged strategy, no matter what it is.

Numerical Example

For those who would like to replicate some of these calculations, we give a detailed example in Table 4.4 (base data) and Table 4.5.

Table 4.4: Base data for calculation.

	Govt Bond		**Swap Rate**		**FX xccy basis to Euro**
	Germany	**USA**	**Germany**	**USA**	**USA**
Tenor					
3M			−0.318	0.953	−49.993
2Y	−0.731	1.1102	−0.268	1.326	−44.250
5Y	−0.396	1.8374	0.007	1.828	−44.500
10Y	0.382	2.4071	0.65	2.249	−43.125
30Y	1.125	3.1053	1.306	2.557	−24.250

Source: Bloomberg, Commerzbank Research

Note that the EUR swap rate in Table 4.4 is vs the 3m floating rate to match the US data. Using this data set, we construct a set of yield pickups in Table 4.5.

Table 4.5: Pickup results, 8th December 2016.

	Yield Pickup		
	USA		
FX Hedge	**None**	**Rolling**	**Maturity matched**
Tenor			
2Y	1.84	0.07	−0.195
5Y	2.23	0.46	−0.032
10Y	2.03	0.25	−0.005
30Y	1.98	0.21	0.487

Source: Bloomberg, Commerzbank Research

Let's go through the top line of the pickup in Table 4.5 in detail.

1.84 is simply the difference between the EUR and USD government bond rates for the 2y tenor, so

$$1.84 = 1.11 - (-0.73)$$

Then to this we can add the rolling hedge cost, which is the difference between the two swap rates, plus the cross-currency basis:

$$0.07 = 1.84 + (-0.318 - 0.953) + (-49.99/100)$$

Note that the cross-currency basis swap number needs to be divided by 100, as it is quoted differently in Bloomberg.

Or we can use the maturity-matched hedge, as follows:

$$-0.19 = 1.84 + (-0.268 - 1.326) + (-44.25/100)$$

Chapter 5
Introducing the Conversion Factor

Maybe you've never heard of the conversion factor.[1] You are in good company; many of my colleagues had not, and it was news to me when I first investigated it a few years ago. Though it isn't a new concept, it is a surprising and somewhat unexpected consequence of combining credit spreads with different yield curves, and has significant consequences for issuers and investors.

The Issuer's Choices

When choosing to issue, the modern treasurer has a bewildering set of choices. The following is a simplified list of the various decisions that the issuer needs to make before settling on a currency of issue.

Tenor

Internal needs will determine the tenor of the issue. But this choice may eliminate some currencies in which certain tenors are more readily available for historical reasons. In most cases, the currency of choice, however, is not independent from the companies' operating environment, with FX debt often met by operating income sources in the same currency, reducing the need to hedge cash flows.

Credit Spread

This is perhaps the critical question. The credit spread is typically defined as the difference between the interest rate on a corporate's bond, and the interest rate of the swap curve in the same currency. It can vary from one currency to another. Usually, credit spreads will be somewhat wider for currencies that are not the home currency of the corporate, but this may not be so for large multinationals, or sometimes specific industries. Central banks directly intervening in corporate bond markets can introduce another distorting factor. If a cheaper borrowing rate relative to the local market is available in a different currency, it is worth a look.

1 *This chapter was first published as Commerzbank's Rates Radar, combining 'Corporate Issuance and conversion factors', May 2017, and 'Conversion factor for investors', December 2018.*

https://doi.org/10.1515/9783110688733-005

Cross-Currency Basis

If there were no cross-currency basis, then this would have the effect of eliminating any difference in the local and foreign swap curves, leaving only the spread factor. However, the existence of the basis means that the rates at which FX hedges can be done are not exactly those which eliminate this difference; they can be as large as 1% different, and are often 0.5% different. So the basis may enhance the spread effect or reduce it.

Conversion Factor

This factor is often the one that no one has ever heard of! We discuss the conversion factor in more detail in the following section, as it is a factor which ranges from very close to zero to about 10%, and is applied to the spread. It is due to different yield curves in the different currencies.

Fees and Charges

Capital costs, regulatory issues and XVA charges mean that fees are complex to calculate and depend at least partly on the relative credit rating of the banks managing the issue and the corporation issuing the bond. In this chapter, we ignore these charges but it is worth noting that they can be significant.

What is the Conversion Factor?

The conversion factor comes from the relative cost of credit in different yield environments and the structure of interest rates for the two currencies in question. It is not connected with the FX rate between the two currencies, but is purely a function of the level of interest rates and the shapes of the yield curve.

(1) The conversion factor is the number of basis point per annum in one currency, which equals 1 basis point in the other currency.
(2) The conversion factor is the factor which equates the PV's of identical future cashflows in different currencies.

It arises because credit spreads in the post-crisis world are so much more significant than they were before. A highly rated corporate whose credit spread is close to zero (that is, it can borrow at a rate close to the prevailing local swap rate in the market) need not worry about conversion factors. As long as its bonds are highly rated in both its home currency and the currency it wants to issue debt in, then nothing more is needed, and the cross-currency basis swap level will be the only significant consideration.

However, this may not be the case! A credit spread of some hundred basis points is nothing unusual for some issuers, and this is where the conversion factor becomes important.

We can think about the issuance situation of a corporate with a large credit spread either as a completely different yield curve, or as the local swap curve with a factor added on. As the latter is the market convention, the conversion factor arises as an approximation to the perhaps more mathematically correct approach of using issuer-specific yield curves and forward rates for each currency under consideration.

Simplest Possible Example – 1-Year Bond, Zero Basis, USD Corporate

Let's take a look at an unrealistic but simple example for the sake of clarity.

- EUR issue – swap rate 1%, credit spread 2%, thus coupon = 3%
- USD issue – swap rate 5%, credit spread 2%, thus coupon = 7%
- The single coupon is paid at the end of the year.

If we assume that the basis is zero, then the corporate cannot gain an advantage by issuing in Europe where rates are lower, and then hedging the FX risk. The US corporate, if it hedges the FX risk it acquires by issuing at 1% in EUR, will come back to the home value of 5% via the FX hedge.

Now, as the credit spreads are the same, there should be no difference between issuing in either currency, right? Wrong!

We need to think about the Present Value (PV) of the credit spread. In EUR, we would discount the spread using the 1% swap rate – so ignoring any day count issues and assuming that all rates are in annual terms, we have

$$PV_{EUR} = \frac{2\%}{1+1\%} = 1.98\%$$

However, in USD, there is a different swap rate, so we have

$$PV_{USD} = \frac{2\%}{1+5\%} = 1.90\%$$

To equate the two PVs, we must increase the USD spread by a factor of 1.98%/1.90% = 1.039. This is the conversion factor. So now the total USD spread is 2.08%, from the point of view of the EUR corporate.

So this means that unless the corporate can find an advantage of more than 8bp from other factors, it's not worth issuing in USD. If, for example, the credit spread were lower in USD, at perhaps 1%, then indeed it could be worth doing, though the conversion factor would eat into that differential, transforming the effective EUR credit spread to 1.04% from the point of view of the EUR issuer.

More Realistic – Using the Yield Curve

If only life were as simple as this example. But bonds pay coupons at different frequencies, and swap rates vary with the tenor. What's important to realise is that you have to find the relevant conversion factor for the coupon stream of the bond. Not only does the conversion factor vary with the tenor, but it will also vary with the payment frequency (though to a lesser extent). So although it's popular to quote a '10y conversion factor', it should strictly be a '10y conversion factor for annual payments'. Let's have a look at these features.

The easiest way to calculate the conversion factor between two cashflow streams is to look at the PV of the sum of 1 basis point at each payment date in each currency. In practice, this is as simple as calculating a discount factor for each payment date, adding them up for each currency, and taking the ratio of the sum. An example is shown in Table 5.1.

As can be seen, the longer dated conversion factor can add another 9% of spread value to the total cost of the issuance at the current time.

It is easy to check the calculation – for the 5-year conversion factor for annual payments, add up the first 5 discount factors for each currency and divide the USD result by the EUR result. However, if we do the calculation for 6-month payments (out only to 5 years this time to fit the data in!), then the results are slightly different. See Table 5.2 which illustrates this point.

If we compare the 5y conversion factor in both tables, we see that it is 1.0524 for the annual payment case, and 1.0525 for the semi-annual payment case. Though very small for these low-interest rate environments, for longer tenors and higher differentials, it could become more significant.

Another Way to Think about It

Why does the conversion factor arise? One final way in which it might be useful to think of it is a consequence of the individual credit curve of a corporate vs the swap curve. Forward FX rates, and indeed all FX hedge valuations, are calculated using the swap curves in different currencies. But the credit curve of a corporate will (almost always) trade above the swap curve. So the FX hedge cost does not take into account this differential, which is the credit spread. If it did, we would have no need to calculate conversion factors. But then different companies would have different forward rates and liquidity for any single credit curve would be very low. It is

Table 5.1: Conversion factor calculation out to 10y as of 7 Apr 2017, for EUR and USD, for annual payment dates, rates in %, discount factors and conversion factors are numbers with no unit.

USD										
Date	**1Y**	**2Y**	**3Y**	**4Y**	**5Y**	**6Y**	**7Y**	**8Y**	**9Y**	**10Y**
Swap Rates	1.4042	1.6185	1.7875	1.9203	2.0266			2.2529	2.3087	2.3564
07-Apr-17 Friday	07/04/2018	07/04/2019	07/04/2020	07/04/2021	07/04/2022	07/04/2023	07/04/2024	07/04/2025	07/04/2026	07/04/2027
Discount Factor	0.9886	0.9739	0.9570	0.9338	0.9199	0.9005	0.8808	0.8611	0.8415	0.8220
EUR										
Date	1Y	2Y	3Y	4Y	5Y	6Y	7Y	8Y	9Y	10Y
Swap Rates	−0.2210	−0.1535	−0.0650	0.0320	0.1550			0.5160	0.6270	0.7360
07-Apr-17 Friday	07/04/2018	07/04/2019	07/04/2020	07/04/2021	07/04/2022	07/04/2023	07/04/2024	07/04/2025	07/04/2026	07/04/2027
Discount Factor	1.0035	1.0063	1.0076	1.0072	1.0043	0.9983	0.9896	0.9782	0.9647	0.9497
Conversion Factor	1.0151	1.0241	1.0335	1.0431	1.0524	1.0613	1.0697	1.0774	1.0844	1.0908

Source: Commerzbank, Bloomberg

Table 5.2: Conversion factor calculation out to 5 1/2 y as of 7 Apr 2017, for EUR and USD, for semi-annual payment dates, rates in %, discount factors and conversion factors are numbers with no unit.

USD										
Date	**1Y**	**18M**	**2Y**	**30M**	**3Y**	**42M**	**4Y**	**54M**	**5Y**	**66M**
Swap Rates	1.4042		1.6185		1.7875		1.9203		2.0266	
07-Apr-17 Friday	07/04/2018	07/10/2019	07/04/2020	07/04/2021	07/04/2022	07/04/2023	07/04/2024	07/04/2025	07/04/2026	07/04/2027
Discount Factor	0.9886	0.9816	0.9739	0.9656	0.9570	0.9480	0.9388	0.9294	0.9199	0.9103
EUR										
Date	1Y	18M	2Y	30M	3Y	42M	4Y	54M	5Y	66M
Swap Rates	−0.2210		−0.1535		−0.0650		0.0320		0.1550	
07-Apr-17 Friday	07/04/2018	07/10/2019	07/04/2020	07/04/2021	07/04/2022	07/04/2023	07/04/2024	07/04/2025	07/04/2026	07/04/2027
Discount Factor	1.0035	1.0050	1.0063	1.0071	1.0076	1.0077	1.0072	1.0061	1.0043	1.0017
Conversion Factor	1.0151	1.0194	1.0240	1.0287	1.0335	1.0383	1.0431	1.0478	1.0525	1.0571

Source: Commerzbank, Bloomberg

far better to calculate all hedges using the highly liquid swap curve and then separately account for credit spreads using conversion factors.

Still, we need to keep in mind that conversion factors calculated from swap rates remain only an approximation, as the shape of the credit curves can vary as well in the currencies under consideration. So theoretically, even if the swap rates were the same in both currencies – that is, the calculated conversion factors were equal to 1 – the PVs of future cashflows in different currencies can vary.

Examples of Conversion Factors

In the following Figures 5.1–5.4, we have plotted conversion factors for different currencies over time. DF denotes Discount Factor, so the reader can recalculate if desired.

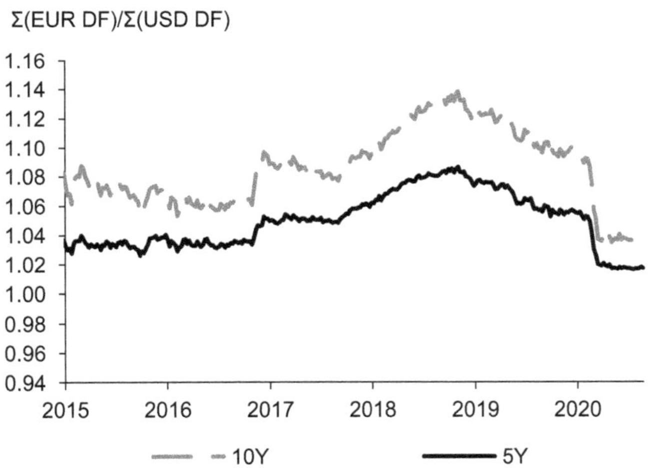

Figure 5.1: EURUSD conversion factor.
Source: Commerzbank, Bloomberg

It's clear that the conversion factor is affected by most events that impact perceptions of the future yield environment. The EURCHF peg break is clear in early January 2015, while the late 2016 election in the USA had a strong influence on the EURUSD factor given the sharp re-pricing of the US curve.

Forecasting Conversion Factors

It could be useful for corporates to have some forecasts of conversion factor levels. Fortunately, if we have forecasts available of market interest rates, we can use these to create discount factors (if the forecast rates curves are smooth enough), and from these,

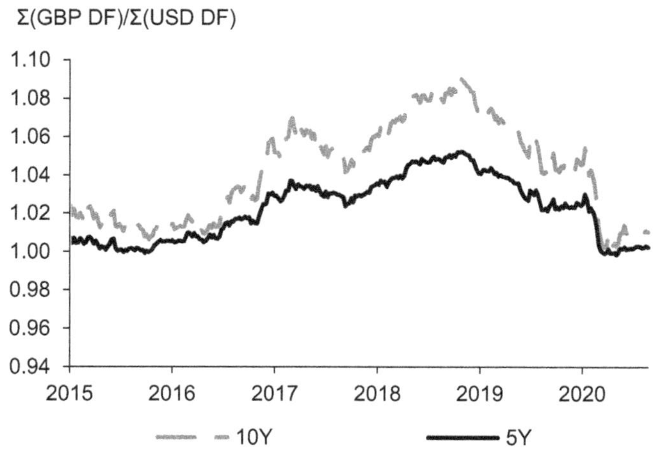

Figure 5.2: GBPUSD conversion factor.
Source: Commerzbank, Bloomberg

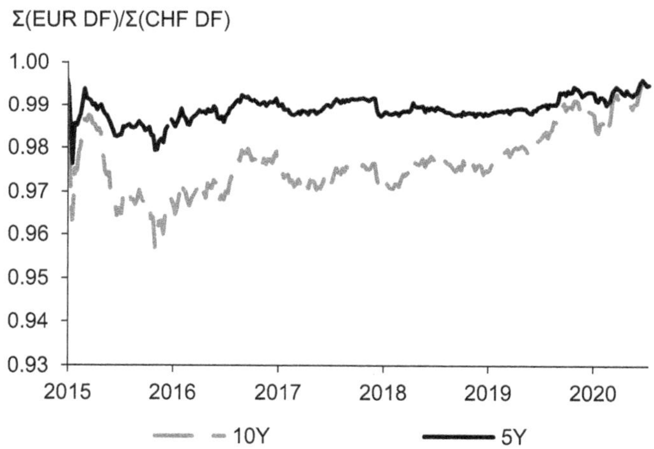

Figure 5.3: EURCHF conversion factor.
Source: Commerzbank, Bloomberg

we can quickly derive the conversion factors. Ideally we would have rates forecast at every annual tenor to create the discount factors, but in reality, forecasts often miss out interim tenors like 7y and 8y. When this is the case, we linearly interpolate the rates to use in the discount factor calculation.

While this is not a method that would be used in an accurate valuation scenario (which would also use Libor rates, spreads, FRAs and so on), in this case it is probably accurate enough. In Figures 5.5 and 5.6 we show the accurate discount curve from a test data set (created using Commerzbank's in-house valuation software DIVA) and the

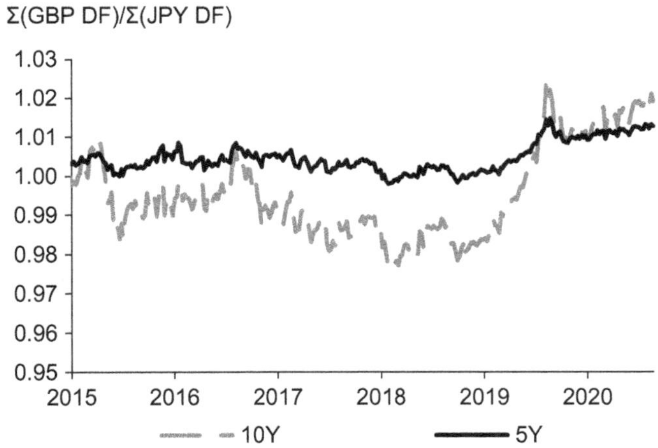

Figure 5.4: GBPJPY conversion factor.
Source: Commerzbank, Bloomberg

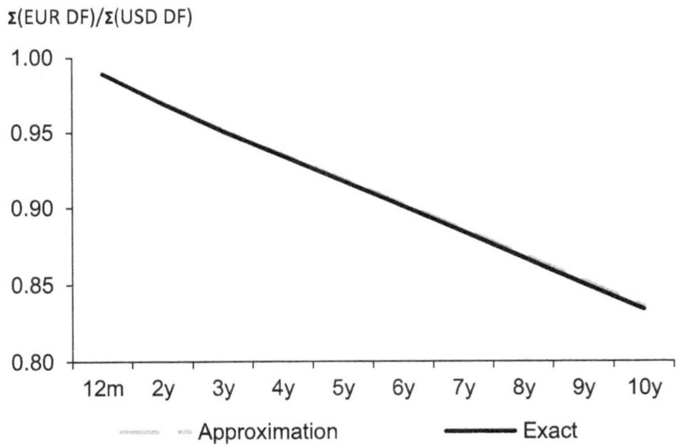

Figure 5.5: Discount factor comparison.
Source: Commerzbank, Bloomberg

Σ(GBP DF)/Σ(EUR DF)

12m	2y	5y	10y
1.11%	1.58%	1.70%	1.80%

Figure 5.6: Underlying data (sparse set to mimic).
Source: Commerzbank, Bloomberg

approximate one, using the method which we also use for the forecasts. As can be seen, they are very close. The approximation formula for the discount factor (DF) for an n-year point which we use can be seen here, where r_n is the n-year interest rate.[2]

$$DF_n = \frac{1 - r_n \sum_{i=1}^{i=n-1} DF_i}{1 + r_n}$$

Because a set of forecast data is rarely complete, we used the 4 rates here as our test forecast rates and interpolated linearly as needed to create the discount factors. It is very close to the accurate method using the same data set.

Now we can proceed to use our Commerzbank forecast data to create a set of discount factors and conversion factors (Table 5.4). At the time of writing in 2017, we did not know how accurate the forecasts would be. Now, however, in 2020, we have the opportunity to see how well they worked!

Table 5.3 shows the forecasts as of April 2017 for EUR OIS and IRS levels, for end 2017 and end 2018.

Table 5.3: OIS and IRS Commerzbank forecasts, as of April 2017, rates in %.

	12m	2y	3y	4y	5y	6y	7y	8y	9y	10y
EUR end 2017	**−0.35%**	**0.00%**	**0.10%**	**0.20%**	**0.30%**	**0.43%**	**0.56%**	**0.69%**	**0.82%**	**0.95%**
EUR end 2017	**−0.20%**	**0.15%**	**0.25%**	**0.35%**	**0.45%**	**0.64%**	**0.83%**	**1.02%**	**1.21%**	**1.40%**
USD end 2018	**1.65%**	**2.05%**	2.23%	2.42%	**2.60%**	2.61%	2.62%	2.63%	2.64%	**2.65%**
USD end 2018	**2.35%**	**2.70%**	2.78%	2.87%	**2.95%**	2.95%	2.95%	2.95%	2.95%	**2.95%**

Source: Commerzbank, Bloomberg

These forecast factors are substantial; the longer tenors are introducing an additional 10% to spread costs, which is at the highs of previous historical results. For corporates with substantial credit spreads, this is very much worth considering.

The graphs in Figures 5.7 and 5.8 show the forecast conversion factors by tenor, for end 2017 and end 2018 (in Figure 5.7), and we also combine this data with the previous historical data for the 10y conversion factor in Figure 5.8. We see that in April 2017, the conversion factor was forecast to rise to much higher levels. What actually happened, though? Well, at the current time of writing, we are able to see how well the forecast did – and the answer is: quite well! The black line on the same graph reveals that for once, the future was fairly well-predicted.

Obviously, we can't generalise from this single instance, but clearly this method of forecasting conversion factors works at least some of the time . . .

2 Day count fractions would be used in a valuation context.

Table 5.4: Calculated discount factors and forecast conversion factors, EUR and USD discount factors (top 4 rows) and forecast conversion factors.

	3m	6m	9m	12m	2y	3y	4y	5y	6y	7y	8y	9y	10y
EUR 1y ahead	100.09%	100.18%	100.26%	100.35%	100.00%	99.70%	99.20%	98.51%	97.44%	96.13%	94.58%	92.79%	90.79%
EUR 2y ahead	100.09%	100.18%	100.19%	100.20%	99.70%	99.25%	98.61%	97.77%	96.21%	94.31%	92.06%	89.50%	86.64%
USD 1y ahead	99.65%	99.28%	98.89%	98.38%	96.01%	93.57%	90.85%	97.87%	85.59%	83.35%	81.15%	78.99%	76.88%
USD 2y ahead	99.45%	98.91%	98.38%	97.70%	94.80%	92.08%	89.28%	86.42%	83.95%	81.54%	79.20%	76.93%	74.73%
CF 1y ahead	100.44%	100.90%	101.39%	102.01%	103.07%	104.20%	105.40%	106.66%	107.78%	108.77%	109.65%	110.42%	111.10%
CF 1y ahead	100.64%	101.28%	101.84%	102.56%	103.84%	105.12%	106.39%	107.66%	108.73%	109.63%	110.37%	110.96%	111.40%

Source: Commerzbank, Bloomberg

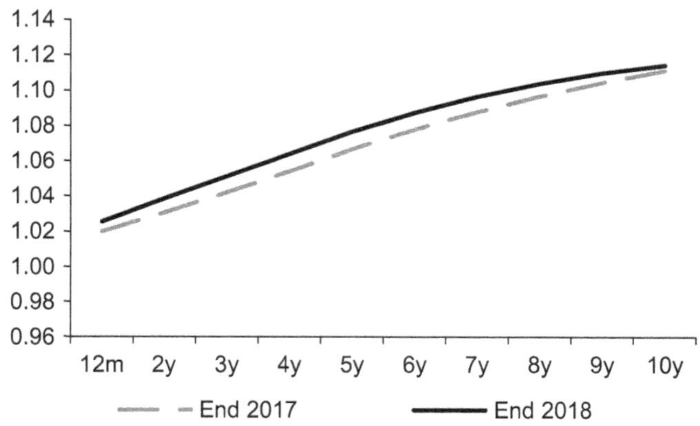

Figure 5.7: Forecast conversion factors, by tenor.
Source: Commerzbank, Bloomberg

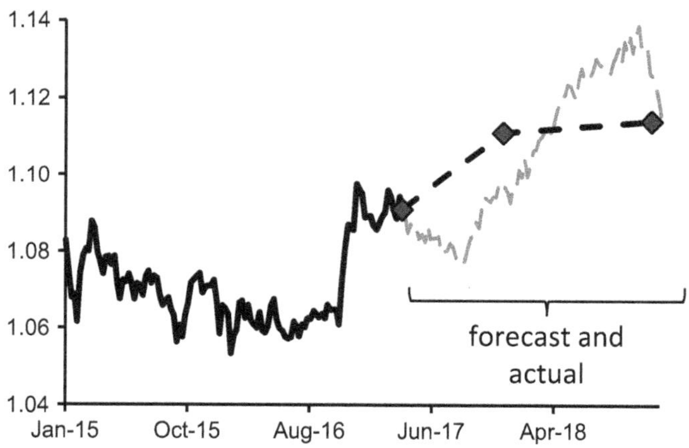

Figure 5.8: 10y EURUSD conversion factor, history and forecast.
Source: Commerzbank, Bloomberg

Translating Spreads across Currencies

We have said that the conversion factor affects the credit spread available to issuers who issue in non-domestic currencies, but how exactly does this work? Let us consider the case of a EUR issuer who would like to know how their credit spread would translate if they issued in USD. To calculate what an additional spread for the USD asset on the USD curve would look like when translated back to EUR, we must add the USD spread, modified by the 10y conversion factor, to the basis.

$$\text{Spread}_{\text{USD investment}}\,(\text{EUR}) = \text{Spread}_{\text{USD investment}}\,(\text{USD})/\text{Conversion Factor} + \text{basis}$$

Clearly, as the spread increases, the conversion factor term becomes more important, but when spreads are close to zero, the basis is the only thing that matters. We illustrate this graphically in Figure 5.9.

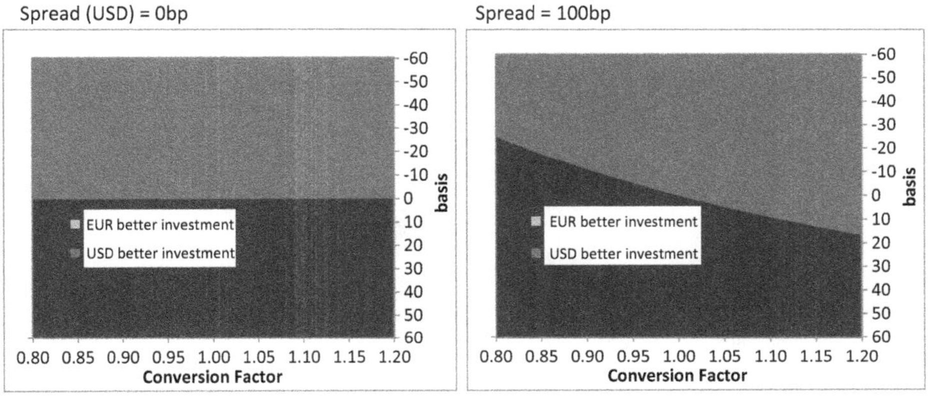

Figure 5.9: Xccy basis and conversion factor currency decision for 2 spreads.
Source: Commerzbank, Bloomberg

When $\text{Spread}_{\text{USD investment}}$ (EUR) is less than $\text{Spread}_{\text{USD investment}}$ (USD), the EUR will be the preferred investment on a currency-adjusted basis. Given that the basis is generally negative, looking at the left-hand graph, we see that for the case of low spreads, the EUR asset will be preferred.

From the right-hand graph, we can see the effect of introducing a credit spread on the USD asset. The conversion factor now enters and its importance increases with the credit spread; in Figure 5.10, we repeat the analysis for multiple values of Spread (USD) – suddenly, with this graph, the investor can make an informed choice about currency, taking into account credit spread, conversion factor and the value of the xccy basis. The different lines on the chart are the borderlines between the USD or EUR asset being more favourable.

Today, we are in the top-right quadrant in the area of EUR preference. The numbers correspond to time periods indicated in Figure 5.11. Not only can these charts guide the investment decision in the current moment, but they can also help include views on the future. How does the investor expect spreads, the basis, and the curves to evolve? They can study the chart and decide which currency is preferred. We see for example that the current situation is well within the EUR preference zone, and there would have to be a substantial change in multiple parameters to mean that the EUR choice was not the right one. For example, the conversion factor could become smaller than 1 – but that would entail the EUR yield curve being higher than the USD one, which is absolutely unlikely in the medium-term. Or the

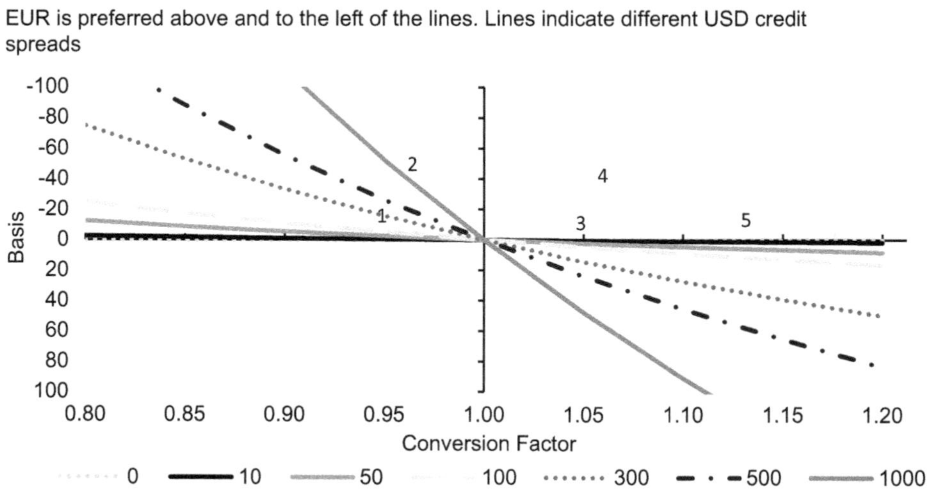

Figure 5.10: Xccy basis and conversion factor currency decision for multiple spreads.
Source: Commerzbank, Bloomberg

xccy basis could change sign, but that has never been the case except very briefly and to a tiny degree in 2014.

We should note that some of the areas of the graph are unlikely ever to be 'occupied' – would we ever see a strongly positive basis, for example, with a conversion factor less than 1? But if the market ever gets there, this chart can still be used to judge which currency to select.

We can compare the graph in Figure 5.10 to the time series in Figure 5.11. The numbers which match those in Figure 5.10 indicate which conditions prevailed at different times.

A degree of offset, not always apparent but worth remarking upon, is observable between the conversion factor and the basis, and is particularly apparent at the current time; the drivers of this behaviour would be interesting to explore.

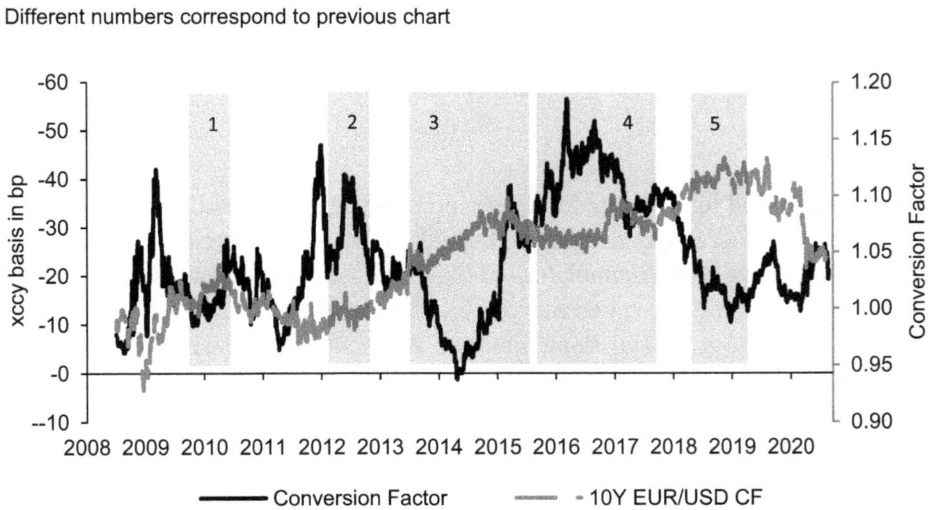

Figure 5.11: Xccy basis and conversion factor currency decision time series.
Source: Commerzbank, Bloomberg

Chapter 6
An Empirical Method of Calculating the Term Premium

Interest rates tend to be higher for longer term instruments, reflecting the additional risk to the lender of longer term loans. Essentially, over a long period, unpredictable and unforeseeable risks accumulate, and the lender (usually) demands an additional return to their capital to compensate for this. This is one explanation for the tendency of yield curves to in general slope upwards. While simple in theory, this term premium is not directly observable and more difficult to measure than one might expect. We present a straightforward empirical calculation method using forward rate errors which works for all liquid currencies and has excellent correlation with more complex methods.

Introduction

The term premium is important for investors, issuers and policy makers.[1] Negative rates emphasise the question of whether global fixed income benchmarks expose investors to rate-free risk rather than risk-free returns. Capturing the term premium allows investors to compare risk/reward across asset markets, and issuers to understand their funding cost and manage their primary market activities. For central banks, variations in the term premium can complicate the transmission of monetary policy, thus rendering the impact of actions like rate cuts and non-standard measures difficult to predict. This is particularly relevant as reducing long term interest rates and pushing investors into higher yielding assets via a lower term premium is typically cited as a central argument for quantitative easing, most recently by ECB Chief Economist Praet [16].

And, the term premium adds significant uncertainly to the various forecasts which derive from interest rate term spreads. So it is more difficult to influence interest rates, and more difficult to predict the effect of the adjusted rates!

The term premium also relates to economic activity. Various studies connect term premium to GDP and to the probability of recession; however, difficulties in separating term premium from market expectations mean that there is disagreement over its exact effects [11].

1 This chapter was previously published in *Quantitative Finance*, October 2017, DOI: 10.1080/14697688.2017.1355588, reproduced with permission. Please note, for this reason, references are included at the end of this chapter as well as in the Bibliography.

https://doi.org/10.1515/9783110688733-006

Our method has various advantages. The term premium is notoriously difficult to measure given the interaction with other unobservable yield components, model uncertainty and data issues. We have derived a method of calculating the term premium by using the 'forward errors' from the swap curve i.e., understanding how moves predicted by forward rates differ from actual realised moves, as an average over time. This allows us to easily discover the term premium for any currency and tenor.

Why is the Term Premium Important?

It has been observed for many years that interest rates are higher for longer term instruments. Besides expectations regarding future short term rates, this reflects the additional risk to the lender compared to rolling over short term instruments and, in liquid markets, the higher price sensitivity of longer-dated bonds or swaps. The difference between genuine short rate expectations and the observable yield is called the term premium. On the surface it seems to be a simple concept and makes intuitive sense; the normal upwards sloping shape of yield curves is due to expectations of future moves, overlaid onto a term premium curve. Some definitions then further separate the term premium component into a part due to inflation expectations and a pure term risk part.

The term premium turns out to be both more important, and less easy to calculate, than might initially be supposed. In the next sections we will focus on calculation methods; in this section, we discuss why it would be very useful to have a robust term premium estimate, not only for investors but also for policy makers at Central Banks and other governmental institutions.

- Time variation in term premium complicates the transmission mechanism of monetary policy. Central banks would like to be able to influence the longer term interest rates most relevant for the decisions of households and businesses [10]. A historical example would be the tightening of monetary policy in the USA from 2004 to 2006; this was offset in the long end by a fall in rates which was largely attributed to a fall in term premiums. In 2005 Fed Chairman Greenspan suggested that "a significant portion of the sharp decline in the 10y rate 1y forward over the past year appears to have resulted from a fall in term premiums". His successor in 2006, Ben Bernanke, appeared to agree, stating "When the term premium declines, a higher short term rate is required to obtain the long term rate and overall mix of financial conditions consistent with maximum sustainable employment and stable prices." [1].
- The term premium has become highly relevant in the current era of unconventional policy measures amid very low or negative rates and flat curves. Policy makers would like to know the likely impact upon longer term yields of the volume and maturity of government debt they remove from the market via quantitative easing. The results would also have implications for the exit from such measures, as well as the links between monetary and fiscal policy and debt

management. Various studies (see [15] for an excellent overview) show that increases in central bank holdings of debt can significantly reduce the term premium, and forcing investors into higher yielding assets via a lower term premium is typically a key argument for quantitative easing. The ratio of privately held to total outstanding debt is also significant.

- Term premium adds significant uncertainly to the various forecasts which derive from interest rate term spreads. Many models, some used by policy makers, use term spreads for recession and economic activity forecasting [11]. An inverted yield curve has from the 1970s been a leading indicator of a slowdown. However, a yield curve inversion, especially when overall levels of rates are low, could well be driven more by term premium effects than by 'true' inversion; a forecasting model which separates the components would be very valuable. In an Economic Letter from the San Francisco Fed, [4], it is stated that "understanding long term interest rate fluctuation requires on to understand what the term premium is and how it may change over time." The BIS agrees; in one Quarterly Review, we read that "The term structure of interest rates can be an invaluable source of information to Central Banks . . . . However, this requires separating expectations of future interest rates from the term premium." [12]
- Term premium may relate to economic activity. Some studies suggest that the term premium may help to forecast GDP [13], though uncertainties as to how to measure it mean that different methods disagree about whether it is procyclical or countercyclical! More recently [14] Ben Bernanke stated "Researchers have found that term premiums tend to rise in recessions; they also rise in periods in which there is greater disagreement among economic forecasters."
- An understanding of the term premium could be very useful for positioning. Carry strategies and yield curve trades become possible once term premium and market expectations can be reliably separated (it is essentially the term premium that makes carry strategies profitable in the long-run). A good term premium model would hence be of significant interest to investors and hedgers. The same holds for issuers as it allows a decomposition of the respective funding costs and hence better management of primary market activities (e.g. by taking advantage of low/falling term premiums).

The Term Premium and Forward Rates

While the concept of a term premium is simple in theory, its consequences in a world of liquidly traded instruments of varying tenors are interesting (as it were . . .). Moreover, it is not directly observable and thus has to be estimated. The yield curve, available in all liquid currencies, describes interest rates as a function of tenor, and a natural product of this is the construction of forward interest rates; the arbitrage-free contracts for borrowing or lending in the future.

The calculations for forward rates are trivial, complicated only by coupon frequency and day count conventions. As a simple example, a 1 year investment must be equivalent to two consecutive 6 month investments, where the proceeds of the first are invested into the second. This defines the forward rate available for the second 6 month investment.

But, these forward rates can be interpreted as the market 'prediction' of what will occur. If there were no term premium, then it is feasible that these predictions could be the market's best guess for the future. As it is, the yield curve embodies at least two drivers; a view on the future, and the term premium. It is also driven by credit and liquidity variations as well as inflation expectations, but at this stage we would like to consider these as included in the 'view on the future' part and not the term premium.

We would like to be able to assign values for the term premium. Part of the difficulty of doing this is that it is unlikely to stay constant; at least a slow variation through time is to be expected, possibly with faster changes during market crises. But overall we would expect it to change only slightly from one period to the next. If we had values for the term premium, then we might expect a degree of predictive power from the forward rates, as they are likely to embody all available information about future interest rate regimes.

This paper suggests a relatively simple way of extracting an empirical term premium from forward rates, which agrees well with more complex methods.

An Empirical Method for Determining the Term Premium

Calculation Method

The problem with calculating the term premium is that, although it is a simple concept, it is difficult to calculate. Consider a yield curve today. It forecasts its own evolution. Which is the timescale to consider? A month ahead, a year, five? We have market rates going out to 30 years, and forward rates going out beyond that. The entire spot and forward curve structure on any one day are mathematically related by arbitrage constraints. In addition, the term premium interacts with other unobservable components of nominal yields like liquidity and inflation (risk) premia, and separating these is not straightforward.

To account for these issues while fitting across time series is not simple, and various models of the term structure must be assumed. An empirical method which works mostly in the data space would be useful and much easier to use, if available.

We would like to find the adjustment which makes the curve today an unbiased predictor of the curve in the future. Let us say that we start on average with the black central curve on the following illustration in Figure 6.1, which predicts the yellow forward curve at a time in the future. In fact, at that future time, the actual rates are more like the grey curve. We have added some scatter to show that there is considerable variation in both. To be strict we ought to have added scatter on the starting curve as well but refrained in the interests of clarity.

Consider taking the median of the quantity (forecast move – actual move). This is of course not one quantity but many; over what period do we calculate the median, and for which time forward of moves? And once we choose the period and the move time forward, we don't have one number, but a curve for which we need to separately calculate the median for each rate tenor. But for each time forward, for a given calculation period, if we take this median curve away from the 'forecast' curve, we will have the future curve about which 50% of actual rates lie above, and 50% below.

Does this help us approximate a term premium? It may get us some of the way there; it certainly allows us to generate a 'neutral' forward curve which lies in the centre of the actual rate evolution. If we use this median forward curve to derive a starting spot curve, we have something which fits many of the criteria for a term premium, in that without it, the forward curve is a forecast of the actual future rates.

However, we have a slight problem, as mentioned above; the calculation will be different for every time forward. We don't have just one median curve, we have a family going out through future time. What can we do with this family of curves? Initially, it is worth taking a look at them and seeing what they imply. It certainly gets us a little closer to the idea of a term premium from empirical data. Moreover, there is a potential further use from constructing this move matrix. Potentially a fitting method could be used to derive from them the 'most likely' starting curve, which could indeed have a claim on being a true term premium.

The implied moves in yellow differ from the actual moves in grey

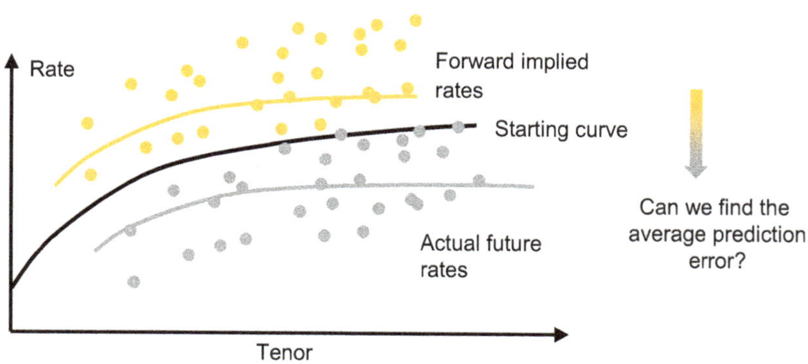

Figure 6.1: Illustration of forward rate error model.
Source: Commerzbank Research

Quick Review of Previous Term Premium Calculation Methods

How does this relate to other models of the term premium? We list some of the more important approaches below.

(1) A vector-autoregression (VAR) approach has been used to forecast interest rates. The idea in this case is that the variation which is not captured by the forecast, on average, is the term premium
(2) One could also use a macroeconomic model to do the forecast. An example of this is the Rudebusch and Wu 2003 model [1].
(3) Cochrane and Piazzesi derive a purely empirical forecast model to forecast long term US treasury excess return, with the unexplained part once more being assigned to the term premium [2].
(4) Kim and Wright [8] fit a 3-factor affine term structure model to US treasury yields since 1990. A variation of the model also incorporates inflation data. The term premium is defined as the difference between the yield and the expected short term interest rate.
(5) Adrian, Crump and Moench use a linear regression approach to fit the evolution of the yield curve, using multiple tenors simultaneously, and their term premium is that portion of the curve shifts unexplained by the forward rates. This is an elegant but complex paper [3], which is somewhat similar to [8].
(6) Hordahl and Tristani derive a very different model using inflation forecasts and bond yields, maintaining an affine form for curves, but without utilising forward rates as forecasts [5].
(7) Survey-based measures. One could in theory survey market participants about their interest rate forecasts and calculate the term premium as difference between the consensus forecast and the market forwards. Yet such surveys are infrequent and may still differ from the market's genuine rate expectations.

It would be good to be able to compare the range of results which these various different methods give, but to duplicate them all would be a large task! Fortunately, we may get part of the way there with the help of some useful review papers from the St Louis and the San Francisco Federal Reserve Banks, published in 2007 [1, 4]. In Figures 6.2 and 6.3 we reproduce their graphs, and overlay onto the second a schematic of the results of Adrian, Crump and Moench.

We include both graphs as this allows us to view some additional models. Although there is significant disagreement about term premium levels among the methods, most of them exhibit a similar form and overall variation, and are clearly correlated. The Adrian, Crump and Moench data is not perfectly to scale, having been overlaid onto the graph image for illustration purposes, but it is clearly related to other models. It goes out to later dates, but we do not show these for clarity.

The discerning reader may note that those series which may be directly compared between the two graphs, which ought to be quite identical, exhibit very small differences. This is one more problem to add to the pile of understanding and

This data includes the Kim-Wright method

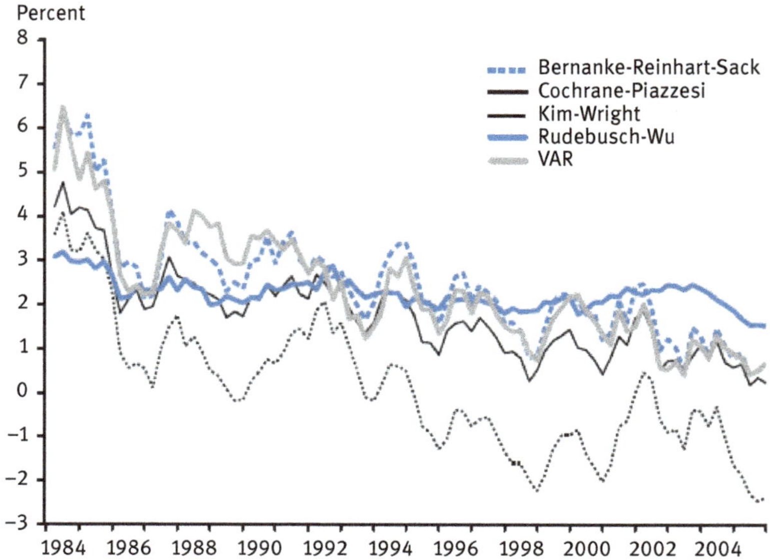

Figure 6.2: 10y USD term premium using different methods, up to 2006.
Source: Rudebusch et al. [1]

The Adrian-Crump-Moench data is manually overlaid from [3]

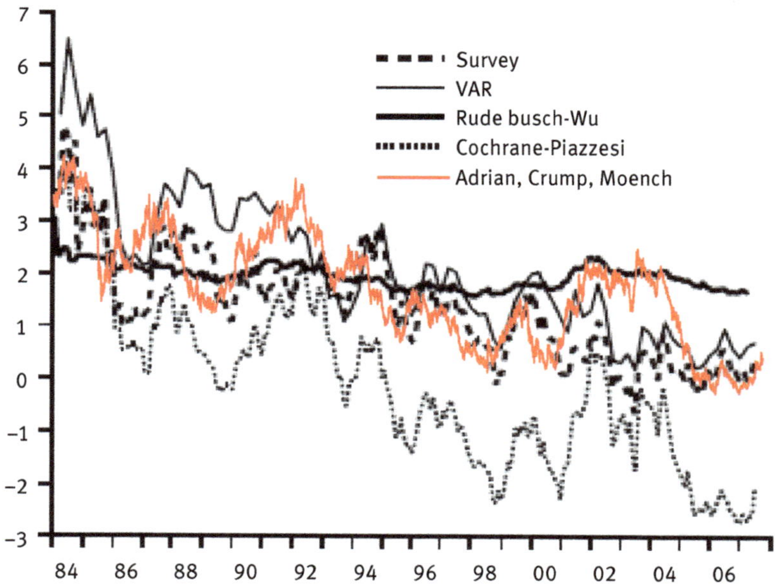

Figure 6.3: 10y USD term premium using different methods, up to 2007.
Source: Crump et al. [3]

estimating term premium – many papers are published in several updated forms, and the calibration of the various models can differ among the versions, leading to small differences.

We have not shown any data from the Hordahl and Tristani method, mainly because their paper does not have any graphs of term premium data! However, the BIS use a variant of their model for their regular term premium updates, which we assess later. See the Appendix 6.A for a discussion of this data issue.

Results

Median (Predicted – Actual) Moves for USD

Having established that the quantity median (predicted – actual) moves may be of interest in term premium calculations, we present some results. In Figure 6.4 we graph the neutral forward curves families up to ten years forward for the USD swap curve. What are we actually looking at? Each point is given by

Median over all data of (predicted move – actual move)
Predicted move = forward rate – spot rate (for the various tenors)
Actual move = spot rate at maturity – spot rate at inception (for the various tenors)

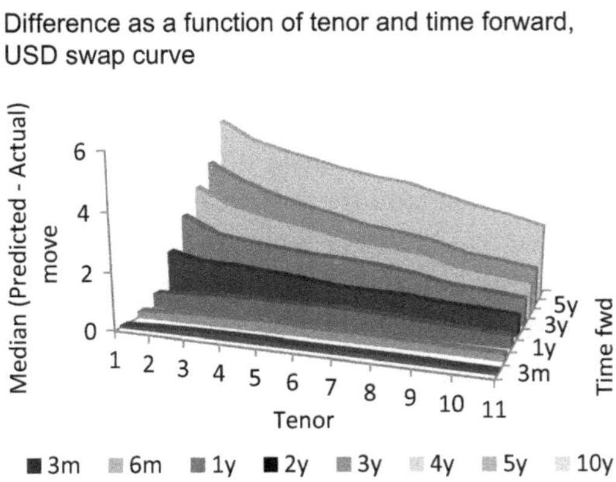

Figure 6.4: Predicted – actual move.
Source: Bloomberg, Commerzbank Research

Each curve is in some sense a 'forecast' of a curve in the future, the time horizon being given by the 'Time fwd' on the axis. The general pattern is that the curves begin fairly flat, and at the 2 year time forward, are at a level of 1% or similar. After this they become strongly downward sloping, with at the 10 year forward point, the short tenors at a level of something like 4% and the longer tenors at perhaps 3%. What are we seeing?

In all tenors and short times forward (<2y), the predicted move is a little more than the actual move overall. This is very consistent with a term premium effect. But for longer times forward, we see a very large effect for short tenors (predicted move much larger than actual move) which is not as great for longer tenors.

The effect for longer times forward could well be a simple consequence of yield curve shape. Curves tend to be steeper at the short tenor end and flatter for longer tenors. Thus, after 10 years, the predicted move for a short term rate is quite large, but the predicted move for a long term rate will be smaller. Additionally, short term rates have historically been more volatile, reflecting Central Bank rate expectations (at least before the negative interest rate policy regime). More volatile rates attract higher risk premiums.

Finally, we can say that as in general rates have come down rather then moved up (by more than the amount that the consensus had predicted during most years under observation), overall, the value of (Predicted – Actual) moves is positive.

Choice of Forward Curve

What part of this picture would be useful to determine the term premium? We need to choose how to proceed. One thing which is important to recall is this; one starting yield curve predicts all forward curves. So if the set of 'predicted – actual' moves was perfectly consistent with a single starting curve, then we would only need one forward curve to derive all others, including the starting curve.

But this is absolutely unlikely. We would not expect these empirical curves to conform to this set of constraints. In practice, we could try to fit a starting curve to a number of different forward curves, or we could select a single forward curve and 'back out' the starting curve from it. This latter approach is certainly easier from a mechanical and computational point of view. The 1-year forward curve is a good place to start, as it would be needed in any case to derive the shorter rates for the starting curve; curves from longer times forward could only contribute to longer tenors on the starting curve. Moreover, longer times forward might be generally less relevant to deriving the underlying starting term premium curve. There is much more information available for a shorter term 'forecast' over a year or so than a longer term one over 5 or 10 years, and data is better quality. Thus our initial method for deriving the starting curve (term premium) will be to take the implied 'neutral' curve 1 year forward, as given by the 'predicted – actual' data, for each currency.

The other desirable thing about selecting the 1 year forward curve is that it simplifies the algebra!

Lookback Period

In order to derive a starting curve, we need to decide how much data to incorporate into it. By definition, we will be using a certain amount of time averaging, as we are taking the median of a set of differences through time. If the term premium and other parameters were stationary or close to stationary, then we would take as long a period as possible to get the best statistics. As we are pretty sure that they are not stationary, but believe that they are time varying, we face the usual trade-off between statistics and varying parameters.

We can probably assume that the term premium can change considerably within the course of a year, and so initially we tested 1m, 6m and 1y as our averaging periods, finally settling on 1m which was most consistent with other models.

What might cause fluctuations over short time periods? Anything which affects market participants' long term view. It is well known that long term views change over the short term! An extreme example might be the autumn of 2008 when the Lehman crisis caused global risk levels to soar, and term premiums to spike. Closer to today, the end of 2015/start of 2016 when rapid oil depreciation caused global growth and deflation fears saw a quickly declining term premium given rising odds for more policy easing / less policy tightening from the major central banks. Though one might argue that risk premia should increase during stress periods, the term premium has the potential go lower when interest rates are anticipated to fall, as borrowers face less difficulty in paying off debts.

Discount Factor Calculation

How to get from this set of median(Predicted-Actual) curves to a term premium? First we need to derive a set of discount factors. The median(Predicted-Actual) curves represents a set of forward rates, and we have selected the 1y forward data. Linear interpolation is used to create rates like the 6 year tenor which are not quoted.

Let DF_n be the discount factor for tenor from 0 to n years.

Let r_{mn} be the interest rate from time m to time n.

We know that

$$DF_1 = \frac{1}{1 + r_{01}}$$

$$DF_2 = \frac{1}{(1 + r_{02})^2}$$

And also, from the definition of the forward rate,

$$(1 + r_{02})^2 = (1 + r_{01})(1 + r_{12})$$

So

$$1 + r_{12} = \frac{DF_1}{DF_2}$$

It is easy to see, that if we have a whole set of r_{mn}, that we can easily derive all the discount factors, and thus all of the r_{0n} which are our 'term premium' starting curve – but there is a catch. We need the first rate to start off with, otherwise there is no unique solution. And that is just what we don't have. An alternative method would be to have the last rate on the far end of the tenor curve, which could be obtained by saying that the curve is flat for very long tenors. While appealing, this leads to very unstable fits at the short end and had to be abandoned. Another method which we attempted was to match the sub-1-year discount factors derived from FRA rates to the short end of the curve, but similarly, these were unstable. A simple assumption is that $r_{01} = r_{12}$, which is unlikely to be accurate but will give an approximate value and enables us to build a discount curve. Once the discount curve is built we can use it to derive the term premium curve, using

$$r_{0n} = \left[\frac{1}{DF_n}\right]^{1/n} - 1$$

The final calculation for the term premium therefore consists of the following steps:

(1) **Create time series of Median(predicted moves – actual moves) for each swap tenor.** This uses a scrolling window approach with a predefined lookback period, so each item in the series will incorporate an exogenously defined number of data points, like 1 month or 1 quarter. The move window is 1 year. This forward error series is taken to be a set of 1 year forward rates. We want to use it to derive a starting curve.

(2) **Use linear interpolation to create fill in the gaps.** This created forward curve will have missing tenors (like 6 years or 11 years). We use simple linear interpolation to fill them in

(3) **Back out the discount factors from this set of 1 year forward rates.** Unfortunately we need to make an assumption at either the long end or the short end of the curve to do this, as we have one fewer rate than we need to get a unique solution. We assume that the 1 year rate = the 1 year forward rate, which gives an approximate value

(4) **Use the discount factors to derive the term premium curve.**

10y Term Premium Results

A popular tenor for term premium in the literature is 10y. Using this method, for the 10y US term premium through time, and a 1m lookback period, we obtain a time series for this tenor of term premium. How might we check that this result is reasonable? Some data, namely Kim and Wright, Adrian, Crump and Moench, and the BIS variant of the Hordahl and Tristani method, may be downloaded and are regularly updated. We graph them together, in Figure 6.5, for the period where all series are available.

Our own empirical method is James-Leister-Rieger

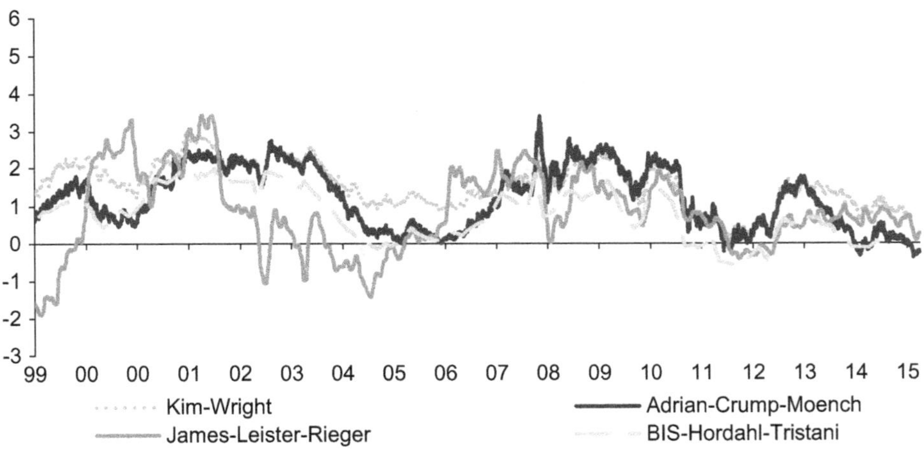

Figure 6.5: 10y USD term premium using different methods (%).
Source: Commerzbank Research, [3, 5, 6] *and* [8], *US treasury data*

We can see that the overall form and magnitude of the 10 year term premium are very similar for all the models graphed. Our James-Leister-Rieger method gives overall slightly lower values with a greater tendency to dip into negative territory but the patterns of return are almost identical. This is encouraging, as the Adrian-Crump-Moench for example uses a sophisticated state variable method to derive the term premium from forward rate errors. Our method is more empirical but derives from similar underlying assumptions. The USD swap spread dynamics vs. the treasury curve could explain at least part of this effect; the 10y spread fell 80 bp from Q1 2000 to Q1 2003, but this fall was not seen in the treasury market. Post 2008 swap spreads to treasuries are much more stable, and our method agrees more closely with the others in this period as well.

More recently, we see rising a term premium towards the end of the year as the rate hike cycle was thought to be starting, followed by a drop off, reflecting deflationary fears.

2y Term Premium Results

When we try to extract the 2 year term premium rate using this same method, however, we run into problems. The rate is unstable and varies from 5% to −2%. This is probably due to the approximations made at the shortest end of the curve, but as previously discussed, it is not easy to find a better data set for the shortest rates. Part of the problem is that we are requiring the term premium to have a proper affine form and to be directly derived from a consistent set of discount factors. The form that this forces upon the curve 'flips' very easily at the short end.

However, do we really require that the term premium curve have this form? There are no practical arbitrage constraints which would force it to conform. It is more reasonable to simply require that it be fairly smooth. Moreover, it seems possible to make one more simplifying assumption; we can say that the term premium is zero for zero time. Thus the 'short rate' of the term premium curve can be set to zero, and we can retain some of the better fitted long term rates to allow us to create a smooth curve which passes through all the selected points.

We use a Lagrange interpolation so that

$$y = \frac{(x-x_2)(x-x_3)}{(x_1-x_2)(x_1-x_3)}y_1 + \frac{(x-x_1)(x-x_3)}{(x_2-x_1)(x_2-x_3)}y_2 + \frac{(x-x_1)(x-x_2)}{(x_3-x_1)(x_3-x_2)}y_3$$

Additionally, y_1 = term premium for zero time = 0. y_2 and y_3 can be set to be something like the 10y and 20y rates, and x are the tenors. This method (with a 1m lookback) yields the following result for the US 2 year rate.

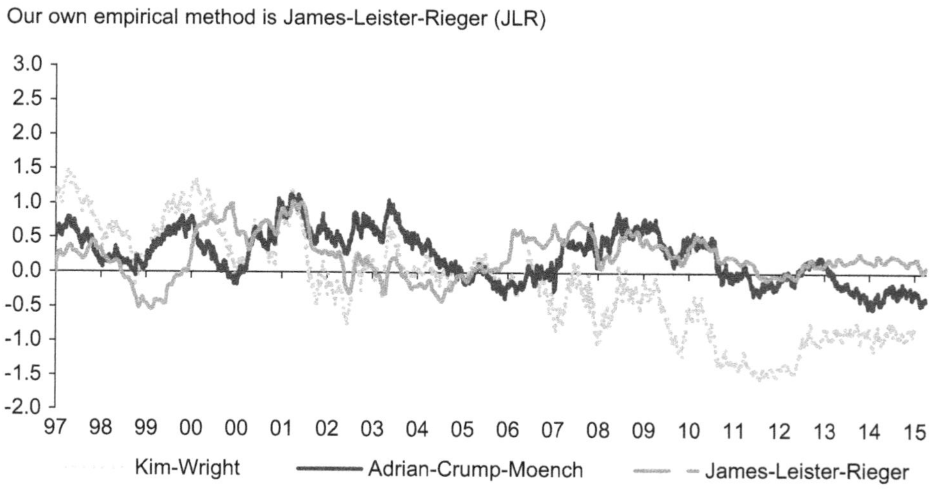

Figure 6.6: 2y USD term premium using different methods (%).
Source: Commerzbank Research [3] and [8], US treasury data

Once more we see that the results are close both in magnitude and form, though we have a longer data series. Unfortunately there is no 2y data available for the BIS Hordahl and Tristani model, but the James-Leister-Rieger 2y results (Figure 6.6) are pleasingly close to both the Adrian, Crump and Moench model and the Kim and Wright model, showing strong similarities to each at different times.

Comparison with BSI EUR Data from Quarterly Report

The BSI produce a quarterly report [6, 7], which frequently contains some term premium estimates. The data for the Hordahl and Tristani model are in fact taken from the data download facility for this report. Fortunately, they also include EUR data which we can use to compare our term premium estimates with as well (Figures 6.7 and 6.8).

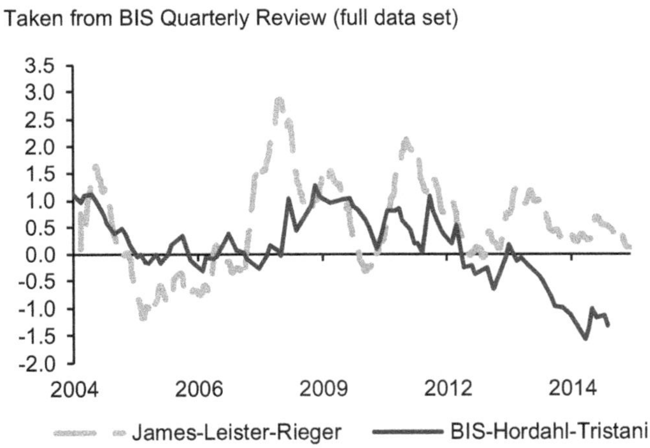

Figure 6.7: 10y EUR Comparison with BIS term premium data (%).
Source: Commerzbank Research, [7]

There is certainly a similarity in level and form once more. The BIS variant of the Hordahl and Tristani model has some divergences, including a greater recent decline. It is hard to understand how the early 2015 BIS result of −2% for a term premium can be justified. With a TP of −2% and observed forward rates of ~1.5% the corresponding 'short rate expectation' would be 3.5%, which seems quite high. See Appendix 6.A for a discussion on the derivation of this model.

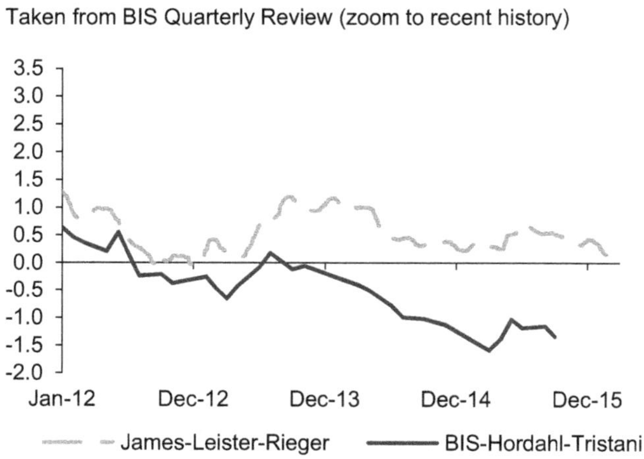

Figure 6.8: 10y EUR Comparison with BIS term premium data (%) (focus on recent history).
Source: Commerzbank Research, [7]

Recent Results: A General Pitfall with Term Premium Methods

As our results emerged, naturally we sought to connect changes in term premium with observed changes in market conditions. We focussed on events in 2015, when the Euro term premium was perceived to fall early in the year before rising sharply in the yield spike of May and June. But, we did not see what we expected. There was no sharp rise and no indication that the term premium had reacted to the abrupt increase in yields. Carefully scrutinising the data to understand this result, we came to an interesting realisation. We had assigned the 'date' of a term premium number to the point in time when it was fully known; i.e., at the point where the actual move was completed and could be compared with its forecast of a year earlier. But – though this is the earliest point that the term premium could be known, it is not the point at which it occurred. That point, in fact, should be the point at which the forecast was known, i.e., a year previous to the date we had assigned it.

This is a problem! Most of the term premium methods we have examined rely on evolution vs expectation/predictability. Basically, if one is looking at a 1-year timeframe, one cannot properly compare predicted and actual rates until the predicted rates are realised. So one does not have a 'true' measure of the term premium until the goodness of prediction is known, i.e., until a year has passed.

However, all is not lost. At all points in time, we have the implied move derived from the forward curve, and this gives us the information about market expectations. As we move forward in time, we may collect data about the actual move – for example, after 6 months, we can see whether markets have moved towards or away from the forecast, and after 11 months we will be nearly there. Thus, we may construct a term premium 'estimate' for the final year which initially relies more on the forecast than the realised result, but which contains market expectations about term premium. Below left we show some 2015 results; we can see that the yield spike in May/June 2015 looks precisely as we would expect. This method has a downside, however. The last year of data will slowly evolve so the curve above will not be 'fixed' until a year has passed. If a sudden sharp move occurred then the curve might change noticeably month-on-month. As an example, if we had looked at this data in December of 2015, we would see the slightly lower black line. It is encouraging that the overall form of the data does not change; the sharp rise in May/June is faithfully portrayed (Figure 6.9).

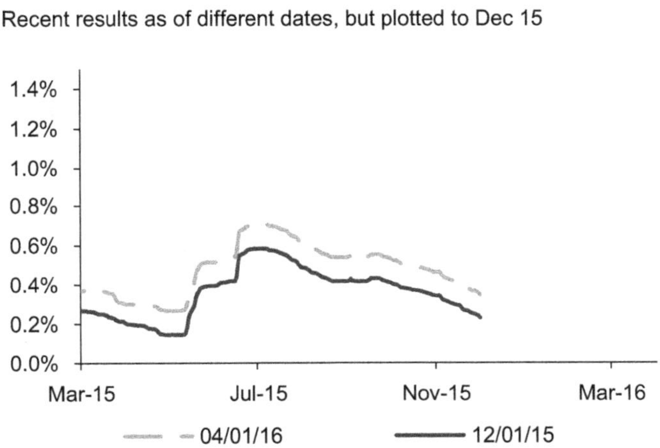

Figure 6.9: EUR 10y term premium as of different points.
Source: Bloomberg, Commerzbank Research

Is this 'term premium estimate' a good enough measure to use day-on-day? It uses all available data at any point in time and embodies market expectations, though not market evolution. As long as its conceptual pitfalls are fully understood, it certainly offers an insight into the market view of the price of risk, and moreover it could be interesting to look back a year to see how the curve has evolved as the data series extend.

We may summarise this by saying that today our method calculates the term premium estimate; after a year has passed, we can know the 'true' term premium.

Discussion of Results

We have certainly derived an empirical data based method of finding the term premium which is consistent with several far more complex models, and is pleasingly intuitive. The levels of the term premium seem broadly consistent with other results; the patterns of return are very similar though levels can be a little different, but this is not unexpected given the broad range of results among other term premium models.

Have we done this in too complicated a way? Given that our final stage involved an assumption of zero rates for zero tenor, could we have short cut the process by assuming this earlier?

This was one of the (several) ways we attempted to model the short end of the curve, and the problem that arose was that it increased (again) instability at the short end, introducing a steep gradient which led to a noisy fit. Introducing the zero rates right at the last stage meant that all data could be incorporated up to that point, so contributions to the level of the term premium from both long and short rates are preserved.

The effects of varying some of our fitting choices and parameters have been investigated. The lookback period seems to work well at up to 62 days. Additionally, we investigated the effect on the 2 USD year term premium of varying the selection of long term rates. As long as the tenors are greater than 10 years there is little effect other than a slight overall level change.

What further investigations would be useful? It would be valuable to understand exactly the effect of the input data set. Our input data is from the swap markets and it would be interesting to substitute sovereign bond data for the swap rates – this is what is used in the BIS study and the one by Adrian et al. [3]. One could argue, however, that perhaps swap data gives the term premium relevant to general market participants whereas bond data incorporates different credit effects. On the other hand, swap spreads themselves represent a risk premium which has been significant since 2008. So the difference between the swap term premium and the government bond term premium could reveal interesting effects.

Appendix 6.A: BIS Report Graphs

One method of discovering term premium is laid out in [5] by Hordahl et al. This is apparently used by the BIS in their quarterly report, which we compare our results to as well. Hordahl et al. do a multi-factor panel estimation of their model, which, although it maintains an affine form to the bond yield curve, does not use forward rates as an input. Thus, one would anticipate that this effect where the slope of the curve is important would be less picked up by their method. They also incorporate data from inflation surveys – it is a very different approach to the term premium problem.

Their results are, as might be expected, not similar to other methods – indeed, with the incorporation of inflation data, it could be said that they are not really measuring the same thing. Below right is the graph of the 10 year term premium for USD and Eurozone from their paper in [5]. By comparing it with the data taken from the BIS paper, which apparently uses the same method to calculate the term premium for USD on the left, we see that there is very little resemblance, either with the dynamics, or the range. The results from the paper are confined to a tight range around zero, whereas the BIS data have in general been higher.

A careful reading of the paper reveals the likely answer, however. The Hordahl paper is actually focussed more on the inflation risk premium, and it is these that appear in the graph (Figure 6.11). Quoting from the paper, we then find in footnote 8, that 'Our model can also be used to compute nominal and real term premium for any maturity. We do not report these variables, because our focus is on the inflation risk premium.' Additionally, a further BIS paper by Mohanty and Rishabh [9], which graphs the same data as in Figure 6.10, has in a footnote to the graph that the data is the "sum of inflation and real risk premium, the latter calculated using the BIS term structure model". Thus the BIS term premium data seems to be derived both from the Hordahl paper and an internal model. It is fairly closely correlated with other results for the USD, though as stated the use of French government bond data for the EUR results could cause differences.

A final comment is that the BIS data appears to evolve slightly through time. The 10 term premium data taken from the September review [6] differs somewhat from the apparently identical data in the December review [7]. As the overall form of the graph is very similar, it seems likely that some kind of market calibration is to blame.

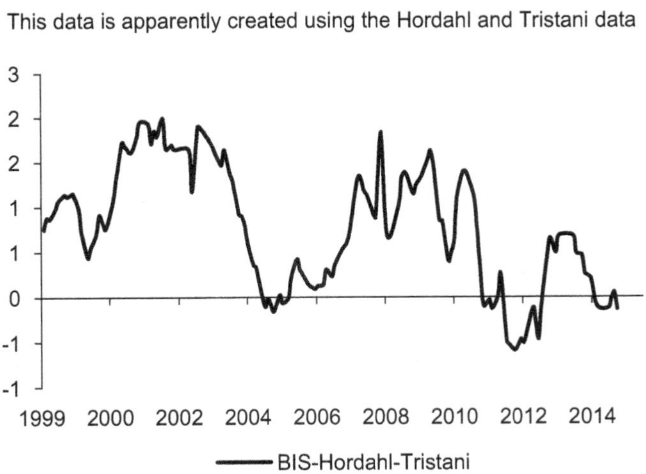

Figure 6.10: 10y USD treasury term premium from BIS data.
Source: Bloomberg, BIS [6]

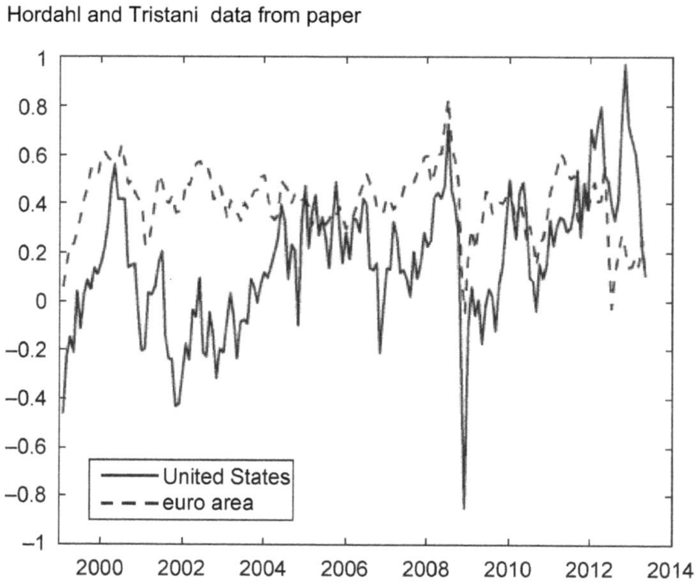

Figure 6.11: 10y USD treasury inflation based term premium.
Source: Bloomberg, Hordahl et al. [5]

References

[1] Glenn Rudebusch, Brian Sack, and Eric Swanson. 2007. "Macroeconomic Implications of Changes in the Term Premium." FRB St. Louis Review 89 (4) (July/August) pp. 241–269. http://research.stlouisfed.org/publications/review/07/07/Rudebusch.pdf

[2] John Cochrane and Monika Piazzesi. 2005. "Bond Risk Premia." American Economic Review 95 (1) (March) pp. 138–160. http://www.nber.org/papers/w9178

[3] Tobias Adrian, Richard K. Crump and Emanuel Moench, 2008, updated 2013. "Pricing the Term Structure with Linear Regressions", FRB New York Staff Report #340, https://www.newyorkfed.org/research/data_indicators/term_premia.html

[4] Eric Swanson, 2007 FRBSF Economic Letter. "What We Do and Don't Know about the Term Premium" http://www.frbsf.org/economic-research/publications/economic-letter/2007/july/term-premium/

[5] Peter Hordahl and Oreste Tristani, International Journal of Central Banking, Sep 2014, "Inflation Risk Premia in the Euro Area and the United States" http://www.ijcb.org/journal/ijcb14q3a1.htm

[6] Bank of International Settlements Quarterly Review, Sep 2015, http://www.bis.org/publ/qtrpdf/r_qt1509.htm

[7] Bank of International Settlements Quarterly Review, Dec 2015, http://www.bis.org/publ/qtrpdf/r_qt1512.htm

[8] Kim and Wright, 2005 Federal Reserve Board, Washington, "An Arbitrage-Free Three-Factor Term Structure Model and the Recent Behavior of Long-Term Yields and Distant-Horizon Forward Rates" http://www.federalreserve.gov/pubs/feds/2005/200533/200533abs.html

[9] Mohanty and Rishabh, BIS working papers no 546, March 2016, "Financial intermediation and monetary policy transmission in EMEs: What has changed post-2008 crisis?" http://www.bis.org/publ/work546.pdf

[10] Jonathan H. Wright, Finance and Economics Discussion Series, Federal Reserve Board, Washington DC, 2008 "Term Premiums and Inflation Uncertainty: Empirical Evidence from an International Panel Dataset" http://www.federalreserve.gov/pubs/feds/2008/200825/200825pap.pdf

[11] Joshua V. Rosenberg and Samuel Maurer, Federal Reserve Bank of New Hor, Economic Policy Review July 2008 "Signal or noise? Implications of the term premium for recession forecasting" https://www.newyorkfed.org/medialibrary/media/research/epr/08v14n1/0807rose.pdf

[12] Don H. Kim and Athanasios Orphanides, Bank of International Settlements Quarterly Review, Jun 2007, "The bond market term premium: what is it, and how do we measure it?" http://www.bis.org/publ/qtrpdf/r_qt0706e.pdf

[13] James Hamilton, Econbrowser November 2006, "The Yield Curve and the term premium" http://econbrowserlcom/archives/2006/the-yield-curve_2

[14] Ben Bernanke, April 2015, Brookings "Bernanke's Blog", http://www.brookings.edu/blogs/ben-bernanke/posts/2015/04/13-interest-rate-term-premiums

[15] Jagjit Chadha, Centre for Economic Policy Review, Vox Policy Portal, November 2014, "The impact of the maturity of US government debt on forward rates and the term premium: New results from old data" http://www.voxeu.org/article/government-debt-and-term-premium-new-results-old-data

[16] Speech by Peter Praet, Member of the Executive Board of the ECB, at ECB and Its Watchers XVII conference organised by Center for Financial Studies, Frankfurt, 7 April 2016 http://www.ecb.europa.eu/press/key/date/2016/htmfal/sp160407.en.html

Chapter 7
An Update of the Term Premium Calculation

Introduction

Chapter 6 is simply a reproduction of the 2017 paper which introduced our model for the Term Premium. In 2019, we updated the results as yields fell to lower levels than ever before, and this chapter contains a further update where possible.[1] We were able to source data from a selection of different models to form a useful comparison.

Evolution of Yield Curves

As explained in Chapter 6, the term premium is difficult to measure and extract from the other factors that determine the level and shape of the interest rate yield curve. With interest rates in many major economies dipping in and out of negative territory, even at longer-dated maturities, the term premium can now be the dominant factor that determines whether the yield curve slope is positive or negative. Inverted yield curves have historically been a harbinger of recessions and economic problems, as they signal that monetary policy is restrictive (short-term rates set by the central bank are higher than the market's equilibrium rate), and thus embody a market view of an economic slowdown ahead. Thus, it becomes a matter of critical interest to be able to extract the 'true' yield curve, the actual market view on future interest rate, separate from the term premium.

Figures 7.1 and 7.2 show the evolution of the USD and EUR yield curves, at quarterly frequency, as a surface.

It is argued in Cohen et al. (2018), Li et al. (2017) and Swanson (2007) that the general lowering and flattening or even inversion of the yield curve as seen in Figures 7.1 and 7.2 is largely due to falling-term premia over the same period. Accordingly, studies (e.g. Haltom et al. [2018]) argue that curve inversions are no longer as valid a proxy for recessions as in the past, as the falling-term premium (and thus the curve flattening) relates to factors other than recessions fears.

The term premium is a critical element in monetary policy. For one, dissecting significant rate moves into changes in genuine rate expectations and varying risk premia is crucial for determining the policy response. While monetary policy can directly address short-rate expectations via rate cuts (and hikes), adjusting the term premium is primarily done via QE.

1 This chapter was first published as Commerzbank's Rates Radar, 'The term premium and curve signals', November 2019.

https://doi.org/10.1515/9783110688733-007

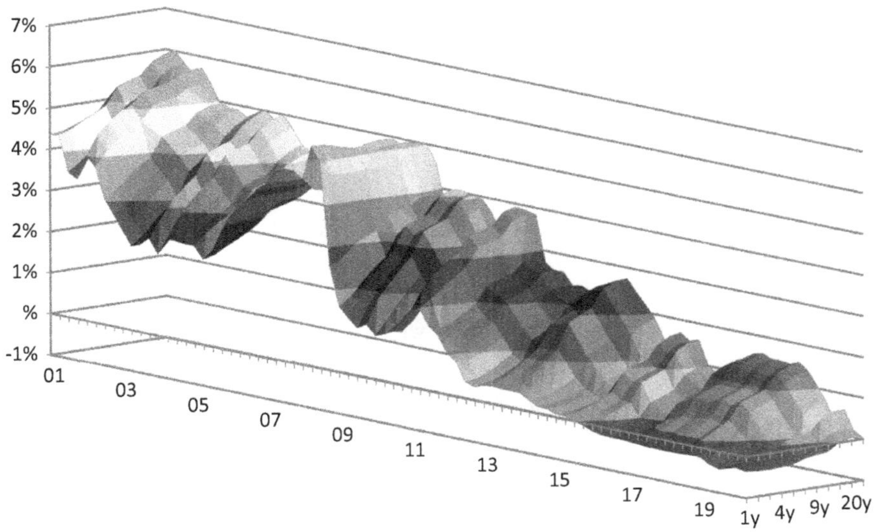

Figure 7.1: Evolution of EUR yield curve, various tenors, in %.
Source: Bloomberg

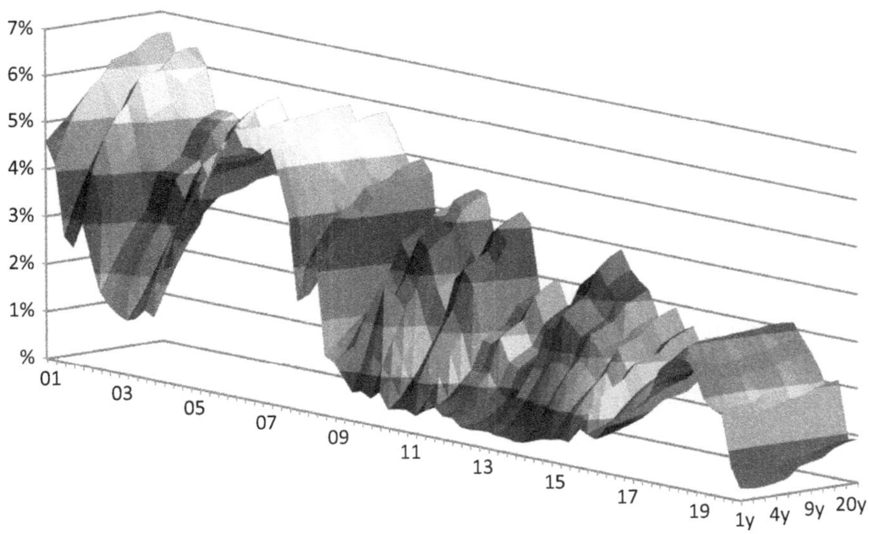

Figure 7.2: Evolution of USD yield curve, various tenors, in %.
Source: Bloomberg

Various papers conclude that monetary policy can only impact long-term yields by modifying term premia (Bernanke et al. [2005], Crump et al. [2016], and Kopp and Williams [2018]). Policymakers would like to know the likely impact upon longer-term yields of the volume and maturity of government debt they remove from the market via quantitative easing.

Policymakers could also refrain from countering a change in yields driven by changes in the term premium if it were deemed to be driven by factors outside its control, like the so-called savings glut (more savings chasing fewer investments in an ageing society), a general flight-to-safety or hedging demand from ALM investors. The same holds true for a shift in the market's risk assessment, which does not equate to unwarranted policy easing or tightening (note for example that regarding declining EUR inflation break-evens, the ECB frequently attributes these to a declining inflation risk premium, which does not warrant a policy response).

Investors would like to be able to capture the term premium and compare risk/reward across currencies and asset classes, while a robust risk-free rate is a key input into equity (and other DCF) valuation models. Likewise, issuers could understand which parts of their funding costs reflect their unique credit profile and which are simply due to fluctuations in the term premium (i.e. the fundamental market price of risk demanded by investors).

Accordingly, the lack of clarity about variations in the term premium arising from various approaches to measuring it (i.e. model risk) makes the impact of rate cuts and non-standard measures even harder to predict than they would be otherwise.

Crucially, varying signals from different term premium models imply different policy responses as well as relative value and valuation assessments. A good understanding of term premia values and their variation has seldom been more important than it is today.

Term Premium Values Over Time

There have been a number of different attempts to calculate current and historical values of the term premium. A literature review might discover perhaps 15 separate methods, some of these subdivided into several variants. The data that they are based on is varied; yield curves through time are of course popular sources of term premium information, but so are inflation, economic inputs, and surveys of market participants. What is surprising is not so much that they all give different results, but that they all do tend to agree on overall shape and direction, to an extent. It is difficult to source live or even historical data for all of them, as many are not published in data form or updated, but for those which we could discover, we have graphed the results in Figure 7.3. Although most models in theory would give a term premium value as a function of tenor, in practice the 10y term premium is the most often calculated and published. Although it should be possible to generalise any model to any currency, in practice the US dollar tends to get most of the attention.

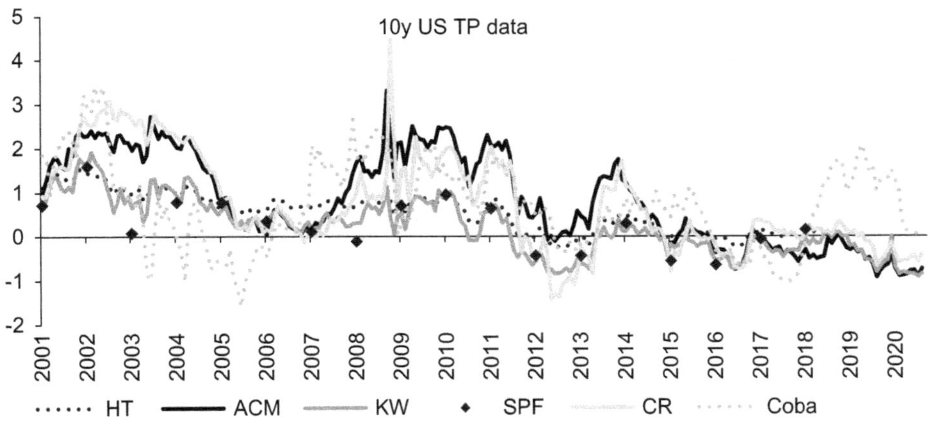

Figure 7.3: Term premium results, 10y term premium, in %.
Source: Bloomberg, Commerzbank Research, San Francisco Federal Reserve, St. Louis Federal Reserve, BIS Quarterly Report Sep 2018

Overall, it is certainly true to say that there has been a decline in term premium values over time. All show a peak and then decline at the start of the millennium, and all show a spike and decline after the 2008 crisis. After that period, there is a brief recovery in 2014, followed by an overall downtrend until the present day.

Term Premium Models; Similarities and Differences

As can be seen in Figure 7.3, we have six separate models that give term premium results for a period since 2001. We can categorise them by the data that they use as inputs, as well as the pricing model and estimation technique to compute the pricing factors they use to create the final term premium number. Note however that not all of the models are quite up to date, as not all data were available for the most recent time.

Overall, those that include only yield curve data (like ACM and Coba) tend to be the most volatile and perhaps the most responsive, though anomalous curve behaviour can translate into noisy results. Those models that access broader data sources, like Hordahl-Tristani, tend to be less volatile and give smoother returns.

1. HT: Hordahl-Tristani (Hordahl and Tristani [2014]) – Input data is nominal and real (index-linked) yields, inflation, survey data on future short-term interest rates and future inflation rates, and a measure of economic slack (the output gap). The method uses a forward-looking Phillips curve model.
2. ACM: Adrian, Crump and Moench (Adrian et al. [2013]) – Uses only yield curve data as inputs. Uses an affine term structure model with principal components of bond yields as pricing factors that are assumed to follow an vector autoregressive (VAR) process.

3. KW: Kim-Wright (Kim and Wright [2005]) – Similar to ACM, but KW incorporates Blue Chip surveys of professional forecasters' short-rate expectations in the data set used to estimate the model.
4. SPF: Survey of Professional Forecasters – This is a model-free estimate, calculated as the 10y yield minus the corresponding 10y average short rate expectation, as reported once a year by the Survey of Professional Forecasters (SPF).
5. CR: Christensen and Rudebusch (Christensen and Rudebusch [2019]) – This model uses inflation-indexed US Treasuries (TIPS) and a dynamic term structure model.
6. Coba: Commerzbank Research (see James et al. [2016] and Chapter 6) – This model takes swap rates as inputs but uniquely includes historical yields as well as current yields. The method assumes that forward rates, in the absence of a term premium, would be on average a good predictor of the future, and takes this 'forward error' to be a forward curve of the term premium spot curve.

It is useful to look at the volatilities of the different models to see how their construction and methodology affect their output. In Table 7.1, we see that the models that incorporate econometric data like HT have lower volatility, whereas those with only yield curve data like ACM and Coba are higher. Note that the SPF data is annual, so this figure is only from linear interpolation and is thus bound to be lower.

Table 7.1: Volatilities of term premium models, standard deviation of monthly changes in %.

Model	HT	ACM	KW	SPF	CR	Coba
St. Dev.	0.47%	1.05%	0.64%	0.53%	1.08%	1.00%

Source: Commerzbank Research

Aggregating Model Results

Is there any utility in attempting to pin down the sources of the differences in levels that these models give? Can we approach a 'true' term premium any more closely? There are some useful discussion papers on this topic (for a good summary, see Cohen et al. [2018]), but it seems that there is no consensus as to the 'best' one out there. All term premium estimates are model-dependent and are subject to parameter uncertainty. Some are not 'up to date' until a while after their initial publication, and values will change due to macro data revisions and delays. For example, in the case of the Coba model, it is not 'accurate' until there is a year of back-data included (i.e. the initial forwards are realised and can be 'evaluated'), though before that time, the model gives approximate results.

Recent problems with econometric models have arisen where they need adjustment to cope with the relatively new phenomenon of rates being bounded at zero or slightly below it. Thus, we do not attempt to pick and choose, but it is interesting to look at an aggregation of available data and the degree of model variation as a function of time.

In Figure 7.4, we graph a simple average of the available models (the black line). For each month, we then calculate a standard deviation of the cross section of the model results (so, seven data points for each standard deviation calculation). Then we use this to put 1 standard deviation band around the monthly results. The bands provide an indication of the spread of model values at each point in time; wider bands indicate a greater degree of model 'disagreement'. Finally, the shaded grey area is the actual value of this standard deviation.

Unsurprisingly, there is significant noise around the 2008 financial crisis. After this, the models tend to agree more and more closely up to around 2016, with more divergence thereafter as yield curves entered often uncharted territory. What is notable, however, is the correlation between the level of standard deviation and rises in the term premium. The models seem to diverge more on the way up and achieve a degree of consensus on the way down.

It is clear that we are on a downward slope. Current values of the aggregated term premium are headed for a record low, with models lining up to agree. Is the current decline to record lows in long-term yields due to (1) caution about the future and insurance-buying behaviour, or (2) is it just that the market has decided that policy normalisation is a long way off? If (1), then the term premium would be the dominant driver, but (2) would indicate that rate expectations are responsible.

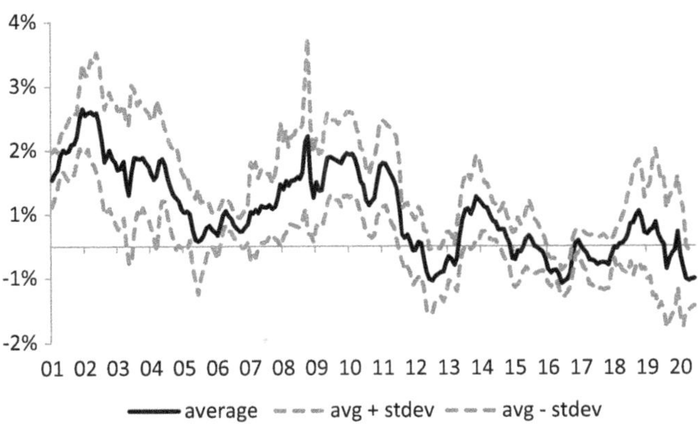

Figure 7.4: Average 10y USD term premium, term premium averaged over models, with standard deviation bands.
Source: Bloomberg, Commerzbank Research, San Francisco Federal Reserve, St. Louis Federal Reserve, BIS Quarterly Report Sep 2018

Chapter 8
Forward Curves, Duration and Convexity

The shape of the yield curve has implications that are not always well understood.[1] A curve whose slope 'rolls off' can imply a future curve inversion, even when such an inversion is very unlikely to take place. Since the 2008 crisis, curves have become lower and flatter, and their implied 'forecasts' start to look improbable. In this chapter, we report and update a study where we analysed the actual evolution of curves long-term relative to their implied forecasts, and we show that in particular, forecasts of curve slope are likely to be biased. We investigate whether yield curve convexity is a driver of this effect.

Are the Forwards a Useful Forecast?

Investors frequently take curve slope positions in liquid fixed income products. For example, if they have a view that the EUR yield curve is likely to steepen in the near future, they might do a 2's–10's trade. If the curve does steepen beyond the slope implied by the forward curve, the trade will deliver a profit. Investors can trade all parts of the curve from a few months tenor to 50 years, and more complex views where the anticipated yield curve evolution could involve a change in curvature can also be expressed, often with 3 or 4 rather than 2 positions on the curve.

Forecasting these changes is both a science and an art, but one factor that is frequently taken into consideration is the implied forward evolution of the yield curve. Each rate has a forward curve, and thus a combination of forward curves (or forward surface) will allow us to create a forward evolution path for the curve slope. Are forward curve slopes a useful indicator for the development of the curve?

Why are Forward Curves so 'Abnormal'?

Any prudent investor should always be circumspect about market anomalies and ask whether or not there is a justification, which could point to hidden risks when trying to exploit this.

When it comes to forward yield curves, combined technical and fundamental factors explain the unusually flat curves, giving us confidence about a systematic flattening bias in forwards that should not be realised on average.

1 This chapter was first published as Commerzbank's Rates Radar 'Can you trust forward curves?', June 2018.

https://doi.org/10.1515/9783110688733-008

Arithmetically, a forward curve is always flatter than the spot curve if the spot curve exhibits a concave shape – that is, if the shorter part of the curve is steeper than the longer part of the curve. All major yield curves persistently show this pattern because central bank key rate expectations dominate the shorter part of the curve out to 5y, the term premium effect dominates intermediate maturities out to 10/15y maturities while convexity and supply/demand effects dominate the ultralong part of the curve.

Recall that convexity describes the change in duration for a given change in the underlying yield. When yields fall, the duration of a bond with positive convexity increases, and vice versa. For a long bond investor, convexity is therefore a positive attribute. Your duration increases when the market rallies, which means your bond price increases become larger, and the converse is true in a bear market. This also explains why the larger the convexity value, the higher the expected yield volatility. Finally, the convexity of a non-callable bond rises significantly with time to maturity, so that ultralong bonds have much higher convexity. For any given level of expected volatility, the convexity value of a longer-dated bond will therefore be higher, and the yield of this bond will hence be lower.

Besides these technical aspects, supply/demand imbalances are also more relevant for longer maturities. Given the long liabilities of pension funds and life insurers and the persistent duration gap of most of these ALM accounts, there is strong structural demand for ultralong duration. At the same time, although prudent issuers should try to increase their duration in order to reduce refinancing risk, most issuers have the bulk of their funding in shorter/intermediate maturities, because this generates interest rate savings in the longer run (given the 'normal' curve slope).

Everything considered, a 'normal' curve slope tends to be not only upward-sloping, but also concave – that is, the shorter part out to 10/15y is steeper than the ultralong part. In turn, this means that the forward curve is usually flatter than the spot curve.

Simple Spot and Forward Curve Evolution

It is possible to look at the simplest cases of curve evolution using the derivation for the forward rates from discount factors.

Let DF_n be the discount factor for tenor from 0 to n years.

Let r_{mn} be the interest rate from time m to time n.

We know that

$$DF_1 = \frac{1}{1 + r_{01}}$$

$$DF_2 = \frac{1}{(1 + r_{02})^2}$$

And also, from the definition of the forward rate,

$$(1+r_{02})^2 = (1+r_{01})(1+r_{12})$$

So

$$1+r_{12} = \frac{DF_1}{DF_2}$$

Using this expression, we derive a set of 1y forward rates from simple spot curves, and plot them in Figures 8.1 and 8.2.

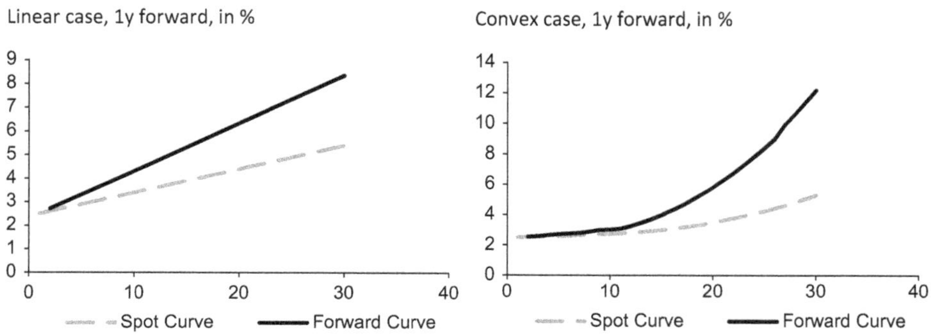

Figure 8.1: Linear and convex spot interest curve shapes.

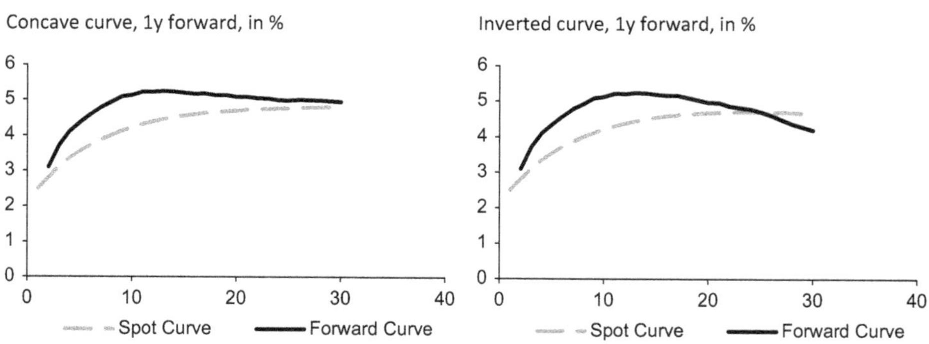

Figure 8.2: Concave and inverted curves.
Source: Commerzbank

The first chart in Figure 8.2 is perhaps most similar to developed market curves on average. A remarkable feature of this is that even though the spot curve increases throughout the tenor range, the roll-off in slope means that the forward curve is actually inverted. These examples clearly show that a curve that remains static is almost certainly not forecasting its own evolution. So most persistent curve shapes may well be generating opportunities. Note that the spot curves in the concave and inverted cases are not the same, though they look similar; the slight additional roll-off for the inverted case is much more exaggerated in the forward.

Forward Implied Slopes vs Realised Data

To investigate whether forward implied slopes are useful forecasting indicators for future curve evolution, initially we examine the history of the EUR and USD 2–10y curve slope. We plot the spot differential of 12y and 10y swap rates together with the same difference 1y forward in Figure 8.3. We use swap rates because of good availability, simplicity (no time decay or benchmark roll) and because they are highly correlated with other fixed income products; the conclusions we draw from this study are likely to be highly transferable to other rates.

Note that in the charts in Figure 8.3 we plot the forward curve slope and the actual curve slope at the same date, so that the forecast and its result are simultaneous. This means that the end of the chart lacks data for the period that has been forecast but has not yet arrived.

What can we say about these charts? Initially, we see a correlation with current values and forecast values. That is hardly news; forward rates are famously prone to predicting the future to continue trends seen in the immediate past. The range of values attained by the actual slope is very much greater than those forecast. The implied slopes are forever predicting convergence which is not, on average, taking place. We can perhaps interpret this as indicating that the size of moves of longer-term rates is more overestimated relative to shorter-term rates, which could mean that degrees of flattening and steepening are usually forecast to be smaller than they should be, and that as the forecast tenor increases, the size of forecast moves grows, though not enough.

As can be seen in the Appendices, this situation is not confined to EUR; it is present in all of the G10 currencies we examined, though we only give the USD for comparison purposes. As the forward tenor increases, the ratio of the standard deviation of the implied forward distribution to the actual distribution at the future time referenced by the forward comes closer to 1, and as the slope tenor increases, the ratio decreases.

However, recall that the forward 'forecast' is only ever purporting to forecast the mean of a distribution – there is always a range of values allowed around this, which would be indicated by the swaption volatility. While we do not examine this effect here, it could well be that a more complete treatment that includes the implied volatilities would resolve the difference between the implied and actual range of moves. More relevant, however, is the question of whether there is any systematic bias in the forecast.

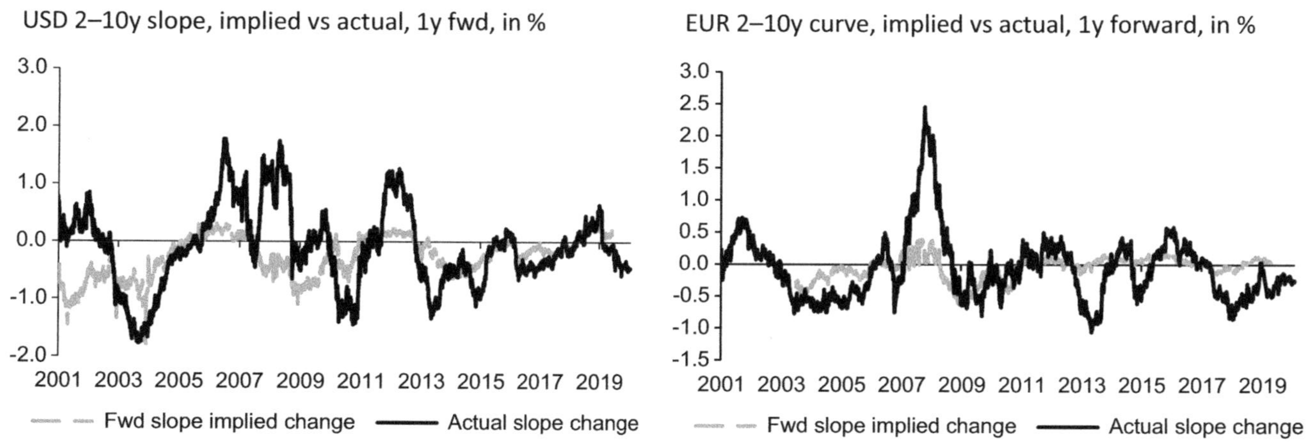

Figure 8.3: Implied forward curves are too flat and too stale.
Source: Commerzbank, Bloomberg

Analysis of Mean Forecast Slope vs Mean Actual Slope

To understand if there is any systematic effect initially unseen due to volatility, we analyse the mean value of curve shifts, implied vs actual. We show the 1y case in Figure 8.4; other forward times are in the Appendices. Most of the numbers are well below 1, indicating that the average forecast move is larger than the average actual move.

EUR IRS slopes, 1y forward, mean(actual)/mean(forward), all data since 2001

	Tenor 2					
Tenor 1	1y	2y	5y	10y	15y	20y
2y	-0.112					
3y	-0.194	-0.461				
4y	-0.275	-0.709				
5y	-0.371	-1.234				
8y	-3.425	2.679	0.433			
9y	-1.271	1.460	0.354			
10y	-2.036	1.024	0.303			
15y	1.059	0.403	0.167	0.061		
20y	0.594	0.309	0.142	0.063	0.066	
30y	0.462	0.272	0.136	0.075	0.091	0.123

Figure 8.4: Ratio of means of actual moves/forward moves.
Source: Commerzbank, Bloomberg

Somehow, though the range of values of moves is underestimated by the forward slope, the average magnitude of the predicted slope is larger than actually occurs (see charts in Figure 8.4). Additionally, the results in the tables are often negative, indicating that the direction of the mean forecast was incorrect.

Resolving the Apparent Contradiction

These two empirical observations do not in fact contradict each other. What we are seeing is a consequence of bias. On average, the forward curve in EUR has been biased. Yield curves normally slope up due to the term premium, with the shorter part of the curve being steeper. The slope forecast that this slope of the spot curve delivers will inevitably be a flattening one. While some exceptions exist, this will tend to be the rule. However, curves have not inevitably flattened – on average, there has been a degree of steepening, as the very low rates available for short tenors have limited ability to drag down 10y+ rates to their levels.

While there has been a persistent bias to the slope forecast values, this has not been the case for the actual slope evolution, which has been on average close to zero. In most cases, forwards predict too much flattening, but if there is a major flattening move, they miss that one as well (and also any big steepening moves). We can thus resolve the contradiction; forwards can indeed forecast too small a range of future values, while their average forecast value is larger in magnitude but more negative than the average actual slope change value.

Forward Implied Slopes and Direction

The previous analysis, indicating the presence of bias, points the way to the next investigation. To analyse volatility effects, we looked at the 2–10y slope, but we anticipate finding more evidence of consistent bias in the longer tenors, due to effects like term premium becoming more important. Due to term premium and other risk premia, in all liquid currencies, yield curves tend to slope upwards and level off. The short-dated end of the curve is more active and variable, primarily due to the different policy outlooks for the respective central banks, but in the post-10y tenors, curves tend to look far more similar across currencies and time periods. Thus, to gain a picture of bias overall, we should investigate the whole curve and not neglect longer rates. Additionally, any effects present in aggregate over the whole period may be due to dominant sub-samples, so it is essential to analyse different data periods as well.

Analysis of Whole Data Period

For different liquid currencies, we first look at the full data period from 2001–2020 in Figures 8.5 to 8.10. We examine three different curve slope sections; the 1–2y, 2–10y and 10–30y. We look at the average forecast slope change from 1 to 5 years forward, and compare it with the actual change over the same period. The slope is defined to be the yield of the longer tenor minus the yield of the shorter tenor – hence a negative number, in either forwards or actual changes, indicates a curve flattening in that set of tenors, while a positive number indicates a steepening.

There is a very clear picture here. Overall, but most clearly in the longer tenors, the predicted change is a flattening which in general fails to materialise. The move predicted is consistently negative, but actual moves over the same period have been close to neutral for all curve sections. The effect is roughly linear with time forward. Especially over longer tenors and times forward, it can be substantial.

Analysis of Sub-periods

We examined three sub-periods; the pre-crisis time of 2001 to 2007, the post-crisis from 2007 to 2014, and the modern-day low interest regime in 2014 to 2020. These

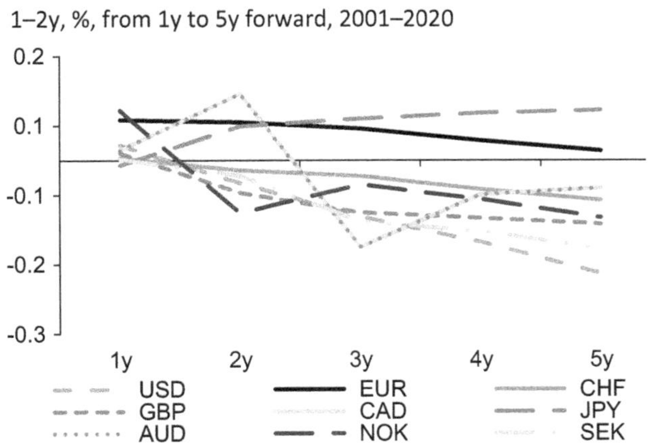

Figure 8.5: Implied slope change (1–2y).
Source: Commerzbank, Bloomberg

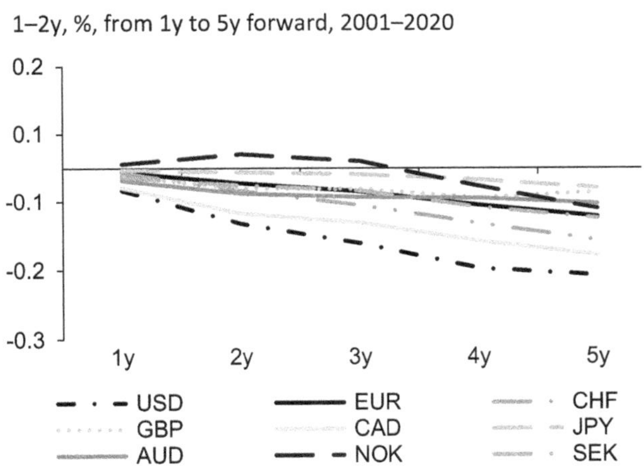

Figure 8.6: Actual slope change (1–2y).
Source: Commerzbank, Bloomberg

results are statistically less good especially for longer times forward, as in a 7y data set, the 5y forward data will have only 2y of useful information, so they need to be taken with a grain of salt. The graphs for these different periods can be found in the Appendices, but we summarise the results as follows:

(1) 2001–2007: All sections of the curve imply a flattening on average. Actual results, however, vary greatly by currency pair, with no consistent pattern. The range of actual moves is larger than the implied forward moves.
(2) 2007–2014: This period in general had steepening realised curves, with flattening implied.

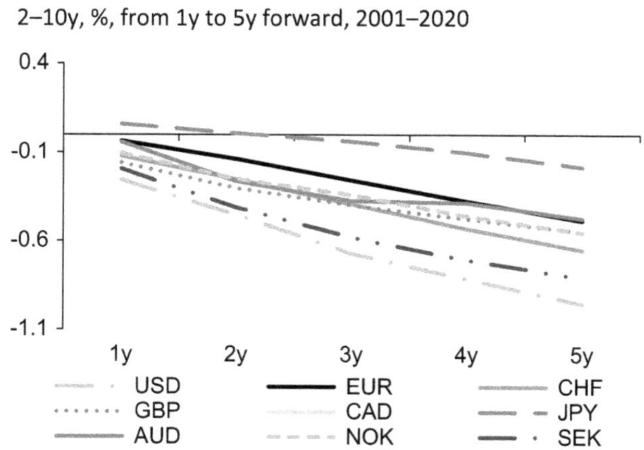

Figure 8.7: Implied slope change (2–10y).
Source: Commerzbank, Bloomberg

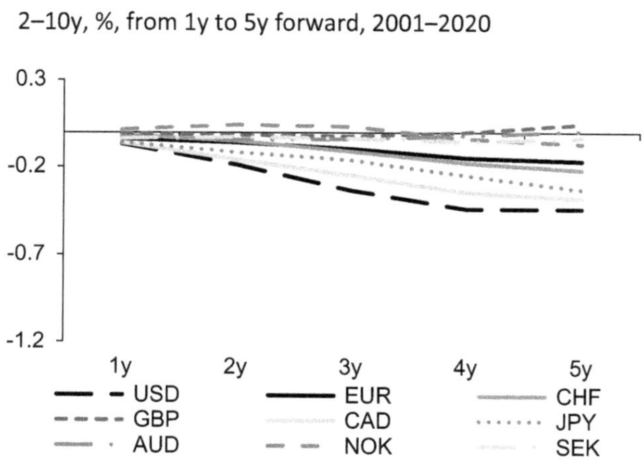

Figure 8.8: Actual slope change (2–10y).
Source: Commerzbank, Bloomberg

(3) 2014–2020: The most recent period shows noise in the shorter tenors but the longest end of the curve preserves the behaviour where the implied flattening is consistent, and on average, the realised flattening is less.

What does this mean? Perhaps in the longer tenors, the persistence over various periods of the implied flattening exceeding the realised might be useful.

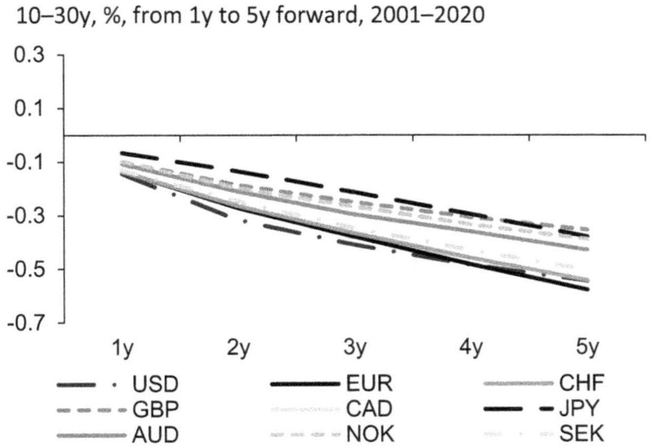

Figure 8.9: Implied slope change (10–30y).
Source: Commerzbank, Bloomberg

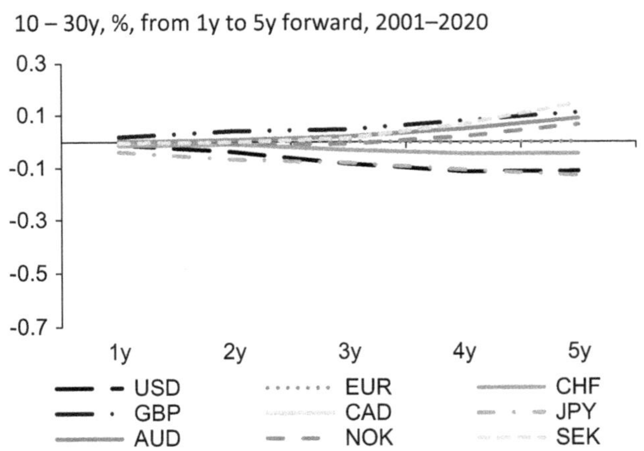

Figure 8.10: Actual slope change (10–30y).
Source: Commerzbank, Bloomberg

Can We Monetise This?

Initially, to analyse a tradable feature, we look only one year ahead. The obvious trade to do is a forward steepener trade, whose return is determined by the difference between the implied steepening and the actual. In Figure 8.11, we tabulate the average annual return of such a steepener trade, over the full data period, for EUR, for different sections of the curve.

1y forward steepener, for various tenors, full data period 2001–2020, in bp

Tenor 1 \ Tenor 2	1y	2y	5y	10y	15y	20y
2y	-8.05					
3y	-11.55	-3.50				
4y	-13.33	-5.27				
5y	-13.93	-5.87				
8y	-4.67	-4.73	1.09			
9y	-11.86	-3.88	1.95			
10y	-10.94	-2.95	2.87			
15y	-4.83	3.14	8.97	6.07		
20y	-1.42	6.57	12.38	9.48	3.42	
30y	0.95	8.93	14.73	11.79	5.70	2.29

Figure 8.11: Average deviation of steepener trade vs forwards.
Source: Commerzbank, Bloomberg

The sweet spot is very clear at the longer end of the curve. Let us focus on the 10–30y trade and look at different data periods. In Figure 8.12, we graph the return of this trade for our different data periods – it is fairly consistent and rarely makes a loss.

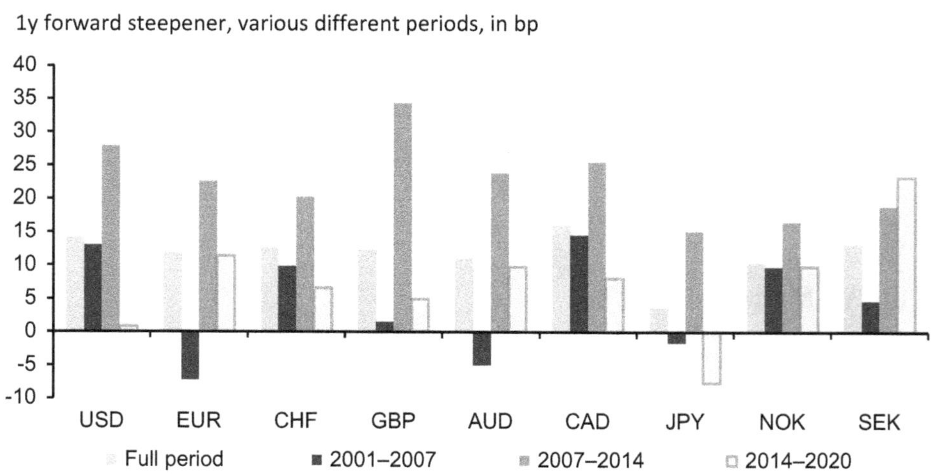

Figure 8.12: Average deviation of 10–30y steepener vs forwards (different periods).
Source: Commerzbank, Bloomberg

It is important to realise that this is only an indication of profitability; we have neglected bid-offer costs and have also neglected the fact that when we unwind the trade, we will use 9-year and 29-year rates, not 10-year or 30-year rates. Additionally, this result is valid for a trade held on the books for a year, which is not always desirable. However, it does indicate that the persistent curve behaviour holds potential and should be kept in mind when making investment decisions.

We can also create the chart in Figure 8.12 for the 5y forward case, as in Figure 8.13. In this case, we only look at the full period case and compare it with the 1y forward, as the data quality is less good for the sub-periods. Though not all investors will wish to wait 5 years to see their returns, for those who do, they are substantial. However, recall that these returns are over a 5y period and are approximately linear with time, so it might be better to simply repeat the 1y strategy every year for five years to generate similar results.

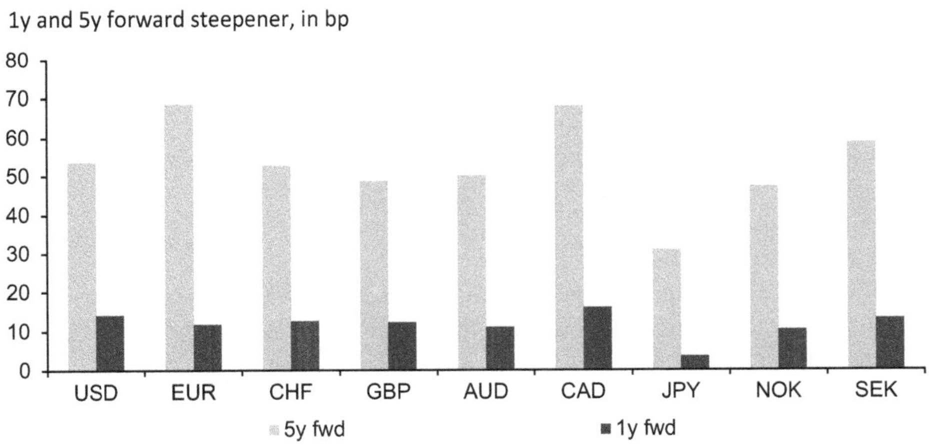

Figure 8.13: Average deviation of 10–30y steepener vs forwards.
Source: Commerzbank, Bloomberg

The Value of Convexity

It's natural to ask, 'Where on earth is this fairly consistent return coming from?' The natural first answer is 'probably something to do with convexity'. To understand how this might be so, first we define convexity for a coupon bond, and then show how it can take on a value along the yield curve. To do this, first we need to talk about the duration of a bond as well.

Defining Duration

The duration of a bond is a quantity with a story. Initially, as one might deduce from the name, it was connected with the tenor of the bond. Specifically, it is the weighted average of the times until the cashflows of the bond are received, as shown in Figure 8.14. This is usually known as the Macaulay Duration. There are two good ways to look at MacD – visually and algebraically. The first can lead to the second.

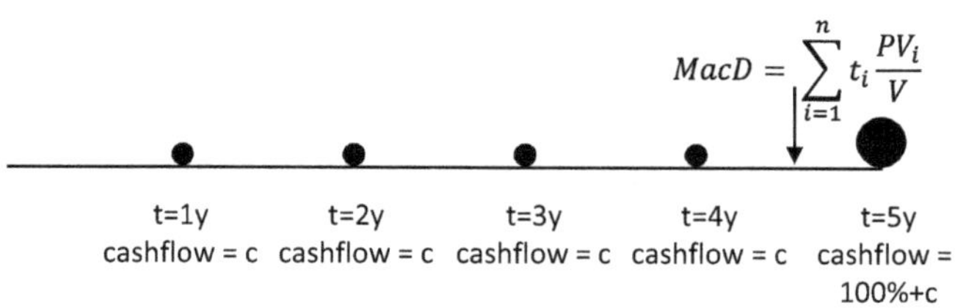

Figure 8.14: Macaulay Duration.

The weights of each maturity (t_i) of the cashflows are given by the PV of the cashflow divided by the total value of the bond, which gives the factor of PV_i/V. This ensures that the weights add to 100%.

In the diagram in Figure 8.14,
MacD = Macaulay Duration
t_i = maturity of cashflow (time from now until cashflow)
n = number of cashflows = number of years for annual coupon bond = 5
PV_i = PV of ith cashflow
V = value of bond
c = coupon of bond
and we will also need
y = yield of bond

One can see from the definition that the MacD is the 'balance point' of the bond, and it is useful when thinking about a kind of average lifetime of the bond.

We can put some numbers into this expression. First, we need the present value *P* of the bond; the following is the sum of the discounted cashflows.

$$P = \sum_{i=1}^{n-1} \frac{c}{(1+y)^i} + \frac{c+100\%}{(1+y)^n}$$

For a 5y bond, coupon 3%, yield 2%, this is:

$$P = \frac{0.03}{(1+0.02)^1} + \frac{0.03}{(1+0.02)^2} \frac{0.03}{(1+0.02)^3} \frac{0.03}{(1+0.02)^4} + \frac{1.03}{(1+0.02)^5}$$

$$P = 0.0294 + 0.0288 + 0.0283 + \ + 0.0277 \ + 0.9329$$

$$P = 1.0471 = 104.71\%$$

Now, let's use this to find the duration MacD:

$$MacD = \sum_{i=1}^{n} t_i \frac{PV_i}{V} \tag{1}$$

$$MacD = \frac{0.0294}{1.0471} + \frac{0.0288 \times 2}{1.0471} + \frac{0.0283 \times 3}{1.0471} + \frac{0.0277 \times 4}{1.0471} + \frac{0.9329 \times 5}{1.0471}$$

MacD = 4.725

Those reading this note who have a science background will note a similarity to this calculation and that for the centre of gravity of a rod.

However, these days, MacD is not used as often as its successor, the modified duration. Though similar in calculation method, the modified duration has a different and specific purpose. It is a price sensitivity, specifically the percentage derivative of price with respect to yield (or we could say the first order derivative of bond price with respect to yield). Perhaps it was realised that MacD possessed this quality to an extent, and thus, modified duration was a better realisation of sensitivity.

Modified duration is defined as follows:

$$ModD = \frac{MacD}{1+y} \tag{2}$$

In this example, ModD = 4.632

How do we use duration? (Please note that for the rest of this paper, duration will refer to ModD.) Let's take a look at the graph in Figure 8.15.

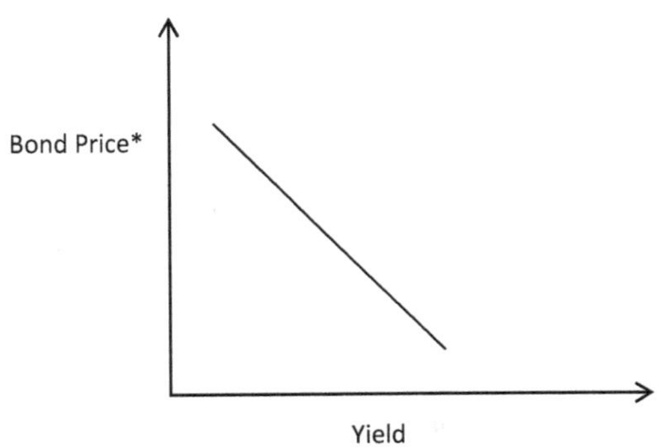

Figure 8.15: Linear price-yield relationship.
*Note that although this graph is always drawn with bond price on the y-axis, it is strictly bond return, as duration and later convexity are defined with respect to return Br rather than price. The graph would look just the same in form, but this distinction is important for later on.

If we can assume that the bond price and the bond yield have a linear relationship, then the duration is the ratio between them, or the slope of the line on the graph. Strictly, there needs to be a minus sign in the definition (2) as well, as the slope of the line is negative, though it is usually quoted as a positive number.

Though taking (1) and (2) together, the calculation of the duration will be a sum over the number of years in the tenor, by some algebraic wizardry, we can express it in closed form. To see the full derivation of this formula, see Chua (1984).

$$ModD = \frac{1}{1+y}\left[\frac{1+y}{y} - \frac{1+y+n(c-y)}{c[(1+y)^n - 1] + y}\right] \tag{3}$$

Note that if the bond is semi-annual or quarterly, this gets more complex, and there is also a correction for stub periods that can be added if desired.

A note on the yield term: This is the yield-to-maturity of the bond, which is the equivalent flat interest rate which would duplicate the value of the bond in the current yield-curve environment. Thus it changes as the interest rate environment changes and is a useful 'flat' rate to use for the bond lifetime.

Defining Convexity

If only life were this simple. But the price of the bond is not actually linear with respect to the yield – it is more like the graph in Figure 8.16.

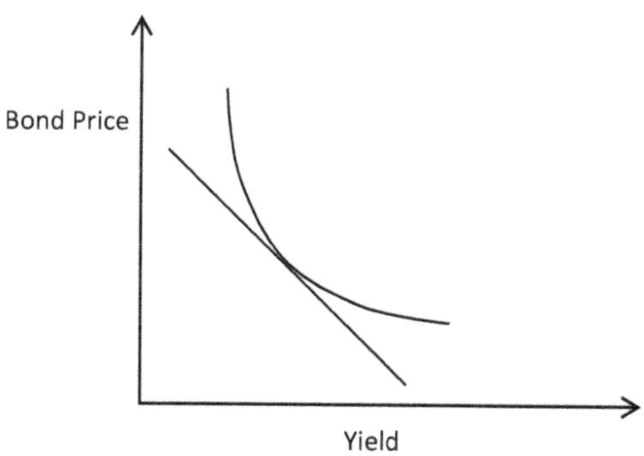

Figure 8.16: Non-linear price-yield relationship.

In fact, the relationship of price to yield is only modelled well by a linear approximation over a short range; for anything else, the curvature of the price-yield relationship is critical, and it is this curvature which is represented by convexity. We can see that this curvature is very beneficial to the owner of the bond. Why? Because the price is always better than the linear approximation would indicate. Thus, the convexity measures the change in duration (or slope of the graph) with respect to yield, or we can say it is the second derivative of bond price with respect to yield.

How are we going to calculate this? There are a few ways. First, let's look at good old finite differences. We can derive a value for duration this way as well. We set Δr to be 0.01%.

Table 8.1: Duration and convexity.

Finite Difference Duration and Convexity Calculation						Price
Price at discount rate r – Delta r	0.029415	0.028841	0.028278	0.027726	0.93336017	1.04762
Price at discount rate r	0.029412	0.028835	0.02827	0.027715	0.93290273	1.047135
Price at discount rate r + Delta r	0.029409	0.028829	0.028261	0.027704	0.93244556	1.04665

In Table 8.1, the central line is the same as the previous calculation for the duration; we are finding the present value of each cashflow of the bond and summing the values to get the price. But given that we know that the duration is the first derivative of the bond with respect to price, and the convexity is the second derivative, we can use simple finite difference methods to see that

$$ModD = \frac{P_{r-\Delta r} - P_{r+\Delta r}}{2 \times P_r \Delta r} = 4.632$$

$$Convexity = \frac{P_{r-\Delta r} + P_{r+\Delta r} - 2 \times P_r}{2 \times P_r \Delta r^2} = 13.361$$

In fact, it is usually quoted without the factor of ½, so

$$Convexity = \frac{P_{r-\Delta r} + P_{r+\Delta r} - 2 \times P_r}{P_r \Delta r^2} = 27.982$$

Another way of estimating the convexity of a bond is to say it is approximately equal to the square of the duration; this is only strictly true for zero-coupon bonds, but is a somewhat useful estimate for other cases.

If we wanted to express convexity as a sum over the tenor of the bond, similar to (1), then by taking the next derivative of price with respect to yield, we arrive at

$$Convexity = \frac{1}{P(1+y)^2} \sum_{i=1}^{n} PV_i \left(t_i^2 + t_i\right) = 27.982$$

Now, while the expression for duration as a closed form formula (3) is relatively well known, a similar expression for convexity is not generally found in the literature. There is an attempt to derive it in Miron and Swannell (1991), but it turns out to be incorrect. Therefore, we took the time to produce a correct closed-form formula for convexity, which makes it far easier to code into a spreadsheet and to look at dependencies. But it's a little longer than the formula for duration.

First, we define

$$V = \frac{1}{1+y}$$

Then

$$\begin{aligned} Convexity = & \frac{cV^4}{(1-V)^3}\left[n(1-n)(1-V)^2V^{n-2} - 2nV^{n-1}(1-V) + 2(1-V^n)\right] \\ & + \frac{2cV^3}{(1-V)^2}\left[-nV^{n-1}(1-V) + (1-V^n)\right] + (1+c)(n+1)nV^{n+2} = 27.982 \end{aligned} \quad (4)$$

It is very pleasing to be able to write convexity in this way, as it can be seen that it depends only on coupon, yield and tenor. Once more, several terms can be added to account for semi-annual or quarterly coupons or stub periods (see Chua [1984], though there are errors in this reference).

Numerical Calculation of Convexity

Obviously, this tendency for the price-yield curvature to benefit the bondholder is valuable. Also pretty obvious is that its value will be larger for larger bond volatilities. In other words, the more the price moves, the greater the convexity effect will be. Let's see if we can put numbers onto the effect.

We define bond return B_r as $\Delta P/P$, where P is the price of the bond. We know that bond return at time t is a function of yield at time t, y_t, so $B_r = B_r(y_t)$

Simply by using a Taylor expansion, we can say that

$$B_r(y_t) = B_r(y_0) + (y_t - y_0)B_r'(y_0) + \tfrac{1}{2}(y_t - y_0)^2 B_r''(y_0)$$

where y_0 is the forward bond yield for a forward contract maturing at time t, and B_r' and B_r'' are the first and second derivatives of bond return with respect to yield.

Of course, we know that B_r' =duration (ModD), and B_r''= convexity (C)!

Now, we take expectations of both sides of the equation.

$$E_t[B_r(y_t)] = B_r(y_0) + E_t(y_t - y_0)B_r'(y_0) + \tfrac{1}{2}E_t(y_t - y_0)^2 B_r''(y_0) \quad (5)$$

From this point, we can go two ways, and we find both in the literature. First of all,

$$E_t(y_t - y_0)^2 \approx \sigma_y^2 y_0^2 t \quad (6)$$

where σ_y is the relative yield volatility of the yield, i.e. the swaption volatility for the relevant time forward and tenor. For simplicity, we have used t=1 year ahead for the following calculations.

This is gives us the first result. The value of the convexity for a bond is defined as follows:

$$Convexity\ value = {}^{1}\!/_{2}\,\sigma_y{}^2 y_0{}^2 t \times C$$

This is the way you will see convexity value quoted in many texts, especially older ones. However, we need to be careful! These days, volatility in the fixed income world is quoted as 'basis point volatility', not 'relative yield volatility', as it used to be. Basis point volatility is the volatility of yield changes Δy, and today is something of the order of 1% for most developed markets. If you see an implied swaption volatility of '40', it will mean 40 basis points, or 0.4%. Some years ago, it was more usual to quote relative yield volatility – in which case, it might be something like 30%, and it was the volatility of yield changes relative to yield, i.e. $\Delta y/y$. Thus, if we are using basis point volatilities, we have

$$Convexity\ value = {}^{1}\!/_{2}\,\sigma_y{}^2 t \times C \tag{7}$$

Now, we can just use this as a formula to calculate the value of convexity at a future time t. Note that t is the time forward, not the tenor of the bond. The tenor of the bond will enter via the formula for C. But what yield should we put into the convexity C? That should be the yield that we assume will hold in the future. This is where forecasts and views can enter and affect the value of convexity that we believe will pertain to the future time. Similarly, we can put the volatility into the formula that we assume will exist at that time.

We can, if we wish, now make a further assumption. This is that the future return of the bond at maturity T is the forward return priced into the market. If this is the case, then

$$E_T[B_r(y_T)] = B_r(y_0)$$

and putting this into (5), we get

$$E_T(y_T - y_0)B_r{}'^{(y_0)} = {}^{1}\!/_{2}\,E_T(y_T - y_0)^2 B_r{}''(y_0)$$

And inserting Duration ModD and Convexity C, and using $E_t(y_0)=y_0$, we have

$$E_T(y_T) = y_0 - {}^{1}\!/_{2}\,E_T(y_t - y_0)^2 \frac{C}{ModD}$$

Which tells us that if we assume that the future bond return is the forward bond return at maturity T, then the forward yield should be adjusted, using equation (6), by

$$yield\ adjustment = -\tfrac{1}{2}\sigma_y^2 y_0^2 T \frac{C}{ModD}$$

or, with basis point volatilities,

$$yield\ adjustment = -\tfrac{1}{2}\sigma_y^2 T \frac{C}{ModD} \tag{8}$$

Though the forward yield assumption is certainly one assumption that may be made, it is not the only one, and convexity values may be calculated using wider assumptions than this by using (8) for a wide range of future scenarios. A popular assumption is that current bond returns (represented by current bond yields) will pertain in the future.

We can see that (7) and (8) are similar because a very rough approximation for the convexity calculation (only accurate for zero-coupon bonds) is that $C = ModD^2$. If we also say that ModD = T (modified duration is somewhat similar to tenor, once more only accurate for a zero-coupon bond), then they come out to be the same if time ahead = tenor.

Let's put some numbers into these calculations.

We can use the EUR German government bond yields and the current swaption volatilities to create Figures 8.17 and 8.18, taken from 26 June 2018. We need to input a value for the bond coupons, and also ideally have this value available back through time. There is not much smooth time series data available for long bond tenors – the available Bloomberg series are only given as averages for >10y tenors,

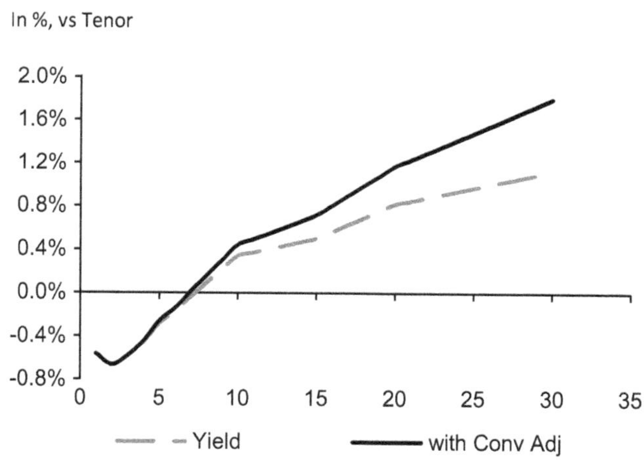

Figure 8.17: Convexity adjustment – bond returns constant.
Source: Commerzbank, Bloomberg

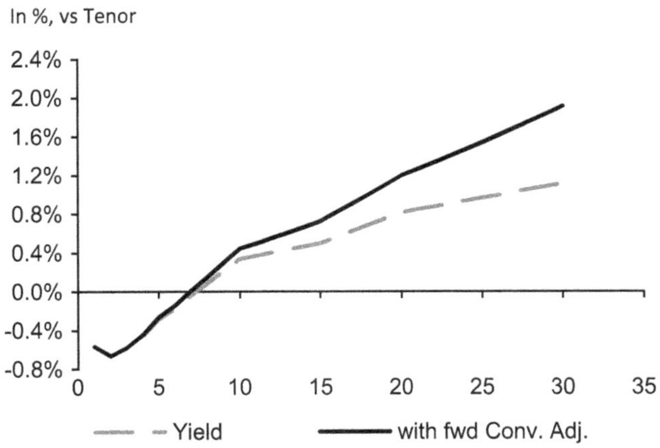

Figure 8.18: Convexity adjustment – bond prices follow forwards.
Source: Commerzbank, Bloomberg

for example. Thus we have taken the bond yield as equal to the coupon, which is a reasonable approximation over the long term.

How have we created the convexity adjustment? We have used (7) to calculate convexity value for Figure 8.17, and (8) for Figure 8.18, and then we added this amount to the bond yield. Figure 8.17 assumes that current bond returns (represented by yields) persist into the future, not that the bond prices will follow the forward price curve.

It is important to note that though the calculation for the value of convexity is fairly well known, there are different ideas about how to integrate it into the current yield curve. If we assume that the entire market knows the value of convexity and that this is priced into the curves, then the 'true' curve would be lower than the market values. This is assumed in Ilmanen (1995), but it is by no means universal, and would indicate that the 'true' long-dated returns are close to zero. If, rather, we believe that convexity value adds to the current returns, we would add the convexity value to the yield curve, as in Figures 8.17 and 8.19. It would certainly be possible to make a case that 'some part' of the convexity value is priced in, but that then involves another set of calculations and assumptions, all increasingly made with little data to rely upon. We have therefore used the simplest method and have added convexity value to the current curve, resulting in Figures 8.17 and 8.18.

Many previous papers have shown that generally, prices in FX and interest rates don't necessarily follow the forward curve. Thus if we use the current curve to calculate convexity value (as for Figure 8.17), how much value is there in the curve at the long end? Right at the long end, at the 30y tenor, we see nearly 70 bp of value, whereas at the 10y point, we see about 10 bp of value. Thus, is there perhaps 40 bp (average of 10 and 70) to capture at the current time? Or is some already priced in?

If we say that our 10y–30y steepener trade was at least partly driven by convexity, it regularly captured 15–20 bp of value. From our quick initial calculation, there is certainly enough convexity value in the curve to supply this, even if some is already priced in.

It is worth a quick note on bond returns vs bond yields. Strictly speaking, they are not the same, but for example in Figure 8.18, following Ilmanen (1995), we have conflated them, which is a frequent assumption. Ilmanen (1995) also assumes that the convexity-adjusted black curve in Figure 8.17 is analogous to a 1y forward curve and backs out a spot curve from it. However, to our mind, it is not clear what this spot curve would represent, as it is not necessarily a forecast or an adjustment.

The Long End of the Curve

There is increasing interest in very long-dated instruments from investors, not least because they have desirable high convexity. Though there is little useful timeseries data for bonds with tenors greater than 30 years, the swap market is another matter. Spot and forward swap data are available for the 50y tenor for some years. Though swaption volatility is not available, volatility curves tend to flatten at the long end so the 30y vol may be used as a proxy for the 50y. In Figures 8.19 and 8.20, we show the swap yield with and without convexity adjustment, and then in Figure 8.20, we show the 1y forward swap rate with the same adjustment, which is another way of looking at the expected return in a year's time. In fact, in the current environment, forward and spot curves are almost identical.

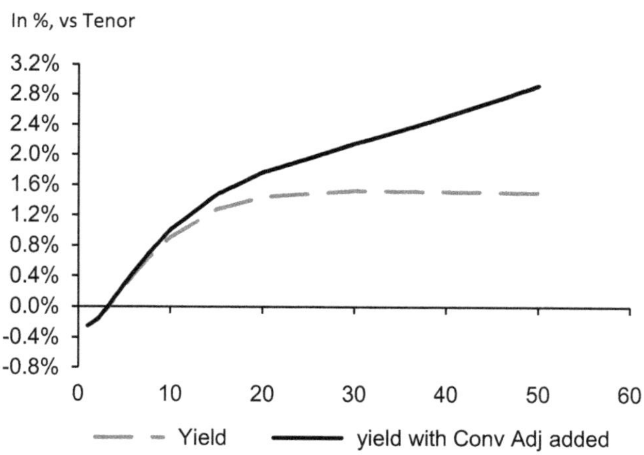

Figure 8.19: Convexity adjustment – swap yield.
Source: Commerzbank, Bloomberg

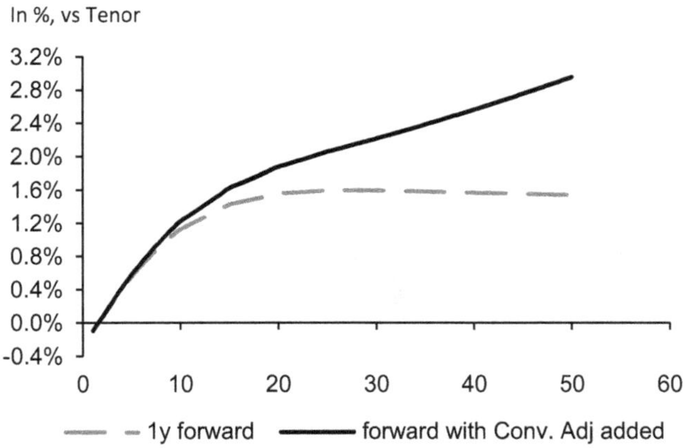

Figure 8.20: Convexity adjustment – 1y forward swap.
Source: Commerzbank, Bloomberg

As can be seen, the convexity adjustment means that longer-term instruments become much more desirable – which may go some way to explain investors' appetite for long-dated instruments.

Value of Convexity through Time

To see how this convexity adjustment has varied in the past, we take historical 1y forward swaption volatilities and German government bond rates, and look at the convexity value of the 30-year point by using the coupon timeseries scaled as previously described. In Figure 8.21, it is about 60–70 bp at the current time. We see that this is

Figure 8.21: Convexity adjustment – 30y German bonds.
Source: Commerzbank, Bloomberg

Figure 8.22: Convexity adjustment – 50y EUR swaps.
Source: Commerzbank, Bloomberg

in fact fairly modest and that convexity has had significant value in previous years. We then perform the same operation for the 50y swap rates to obtain Figure 8.22. As may be expected, they show similar patterns, but the adjustment is much larger for the longer tenor.

The swaption data was patchy and had to be interpolated and extrapolated at times, and we have also used an annual approximation for the calculation of convexity – however, this seems to make little difference.

Conclusion

Having identified a 10s–30s steepener trade in the long end of the yield curve which seems to deliver consistent returns over many currencies, delivering 15–20 bp of value annually, we find that the convexity value extant at those tenors is certainly enough to deliver that level of return, perhaps more. At the 30 year point, the current values of yield and convexity indicate that the convexity value is about 60–70 basis points, which is very significant in these low-yield times. However, in addition to delivering insight to the origin of the returns delivered by the trade, this substantial convexity value goes a long way to justifying the current flat curve and inverted forward curve. We can say that the longer tenor investments are still offering value despite the flat curve environment, once convexity effects are taken into consideration.

It is clear from this analysis that the market systematically undervalues convexity. Current values would indicate that the long-dated bonds are cheap, but today's convexity values are moderate compared to some in the past, so clearly this misvaluation has been in place for some time. This agrees with the persistence of the 10s–30s steepener trade.

As an example of how long-dated instruments can have unexpectedly good value, consider the UK government's decision in 2014 to repay part of the First World War debt. These bonds were issued as paying 5% and 3.5%, which at the time was low. In 2014, investors holding the 'consols' were doing very well! After one hundred years, the UK government paid off the bonds, along with some others, some of which were issued by William Gladstone in 1853 to consolidate the capital stock of the South Sea Company. It's safe to say that the holders of those bonds had done extremely well, on average, over the years.

Looking for other opportunities, it would seem that in general, 'non-inversion' curve plays, that the 10s–30s steepener belongs to, would be profitable. However, there are probably features of the shorter end of the curve that also fall into this category and would reward investors, which may repay further investigation.

Appendix 8.A: EUR Ratios

EUR Swap Slopes, 1y forward, s.d.(forward)/s.d.(actual)

	Tenor 2					
Tenor 1	1y	2y	5y	10y	15y	20y
2y	0.572					
3y	0.503	0.463				
4y	0.466	0.420				
5y	0.441	0.392				
8y	0.431	0.364	0.351			
9y	0.400	0.359	0.341			
10y	0.394	0.353	0.331			
15y	0.370	0.332	0.318	0.332		
20y	0.364	0.332	0.325	0.332	0.442	
30y	0.367	0.337	0.318	0.281	0.242	0.229

Figure 8.23: Ratio of standard deviations of forecast moves/actual moves (EUR 1y forward). Source: Commerzbank, Bloomberg

EUR Swap Slopes, 2y forward, s.d.(forward)/s.d.(actual)

	Tenor 2					
Tenor 1	1y	2y	5y	10y	15y	20y
2y	0.576					
3y	0.540	0.508				
4y	0.502	0.465				
5y	0.475	0.440				
8y	0.435	0.413	0.419			
9y	0.426	0.404	0.406			
10y	0.418	0.395	0.394			
15y	0.395	0.382	0.398	0.473		
20y	0.395	0.387	0.411	0.464	0.533	
30y	0.412	0.406	0.425	0.435	0.402	0.434

Figure 8.24: Ratio of standard deviations of forecast moves/actual moves (EUR 2y forward). Source: Commerzbank, Bloomberg

EUR Swap Slopes, 5y forward, s.d.(forward)/s.d.(actual)

	Tenor 2					
Tenor 1	1y	2y	5y	10y	15y	20y
2y	0.676					
3y	0.678	0.703				
4y	0.665	0.672				
5y	0.648	0.645				
8y	0.608	0.603	0.577			
9y	0.604	0.598	0.575			
10y	0.595	0.590	0.567			
15y	0.597	0.605	0.621	0.817		
20y	0.619	0.635	0.665	0.843	0.775	
30y	0.637	0.653	0.654	0.642	0.430	0.305

Figure 8.25: Ratio of standard deviation of forecast moves/actual moves (EUR 5y forward).
Source: Commerzbank, Bloomberg

EUR Swap Slopes, 1y forward, mean(actual)/mean(forward)

	Tenor 2					
Tenor 1	1y	2y	5y	10y	15y	20y
2y	-0.109					
3y	-0.189	-0.454				
4y	-0.270	-0.698				
5y	-0.366	-1.212				
8y	-3.275	2.746	0.438			
9y	-1.251	1.483	0.359			
10y	-1.994	1.036	0.308			
15y	1.071	0.407	0.171	0.064		
20y	0.600	0.313	0.146	0.067	0.071	
30y	0.469	0.277	0.141	0.080	0.099	0.134

Figure 8.26: Ratio of means of actual moves/forward moves (EUR 1y forward).
Source: Commerzbank, Bloomberg

EUR Swap Slopes, 1y forward, mean(actual)/mean(forward)

	Tenor 2					
Tenor 1	1y	2y	5y	10y	15y	20y
2y	-0.421					
3y	-0.634	-1.685				
4y	-0.977	-9.262				
5y	-1.623	3.319				
8y	2.695	0.715	0.245			
9y	1.491	0.566	0.193			
10y	1.055	0.463	0.157			
15y	0.400	0.231	0.068	-0.016		
20y	0.291	0.177	0.049	-0.014	-0.011	
30y	0.239	0.150	0.042	-0.009	-0.001	0.008

Figure 8.27: Ratio of means of actual moves/forward moves (EUR 2y forward). Source: Commerzbank, Bloomberg

EUR Swap Slopes, 1y forward, mean(actual)/mean(forward)

	Tenor 2					
Tenor 1	1y	2y	5y	10y	15y	20y
2y	-5.228					
3y	5.775	1.618				
4y	2.202	1.099				
5y	1.400	0.825				
8y	0.686	0.466	0.193			
9y	0.583	0.397	0.153			
10y	0.506	0.347	0.120			
15y	0.302	0.206	0.048	-0.036		
20y	0.249	0.171	0.041	-0.017	0.014	
30y	0.230	0.160	0.046	0.003	0.040	0.076

Figure 8.28: Ratio of means of actual moves/forward moves (EUR 5y forward). Source: Commerzbank, Bloomberg

Appendix 8.B: USD Ratios

USD Swap Slopes, 1y forward, s.d.(forward)/s.d.(actual)

	Tenor 2					
Tenor 1	1y	2y	5y	10y	15y	20y
2y	0.602					
3y	0.576	0.612				
4y	0.558	0.571				
5y	0.544	0.549				
8y	0.508	0.497	0.433			
9y	0.501	0.487	0.422			
10y	0.496	0.479	0.412			
15y	0.479	0.459	0.397	0.381		
20y	0.478	0.457	0.393	0.358	0.357	
30y	0.483	0.463	0.404	0.377	0.393	0.508

Figure 8.29: Ratio of standard deviations of forecast moves/actual moves (USD 1y forward).
Source: Commerzbank, Bloomberg

USD Swap Slopes, 2y forward, s.d.(forward)/s.d.(actual)

	Tenor 2					
Tenor 1	1y	2y	5y	10y	15y	20y
2y	0.694					
3y	0.652	0.615				
4y	0.616	0.578				
5y	0.594	0.556				
8y	0.546	0.512	0.546			
9y	0.537	0.503	0.514			
10y	0.544	0.518	0.504			
15y	0.511	0.481	0.465	0.844		
20y	0.508	0.481	0.467	0.671	0.548	
30y	0.515	0.491	0.482	0.631	0.559	0.659

Figure 8.30: Ratio of standard deviations of forecast moves/actual moves (USD 2y forward).
Source: Commerzbank, Bloomberg

USD Swap Slopes, 5y forward, s.d.(forward)/s.d.(actual)

Tenor 1 \ Tenor 2	1y	2y	5y	10y	15y	20y
2y	0.742					
3y	0.739	0.736				
4y	0.718	0.698				
5y	0.692	0.664				
8y	0.627	0.595	0.504			
9y	0.615	0.583	0.500			
10y	0.609	0.581	0.519			
15y	0.592	0.567	0.508	0.597		
20y	0.594	0.571	0.520	0.598	0.659	
30y	0.602	0.581	0.540	0.622	0.700	0.884

Figure 8.31: Ratio of standard deviations of forecast moves/actual moves (USD 5y forward).
Source: Commerzbank, Bloomberg

USD Swap Slopes, 1y forward, mean(actual)/mean(forward)[2]

Tenor 1 \ Tenor 2	1y	2y	5y	10y	15y	20y
2y	-1.422					
3y	-219.014	1.073				
4y	2.311	0.733				
5y	0.812	0.409				
8y	0.474	0.289	0.138			
9y	0.432	0.270	0.129			
10y	0.391	0.248	0.117			
15y	0.320	0.212	0.106	0.085		
20y	0.290	0.198	0.100	0.079	0.064	
30y	0.260	0.180	0.088	0.061	0.036	0.008

Figure 8.32: Ratio of means of actual moves/forward moves (USD 1y forward).
Source: Commerzbank, Bloomberg

2 The large value of the 1y–3y point is just due to a close-to-zero value for the denominator.

USD Swap Slopes, 1y forward, mean(actual)/mean(forward)

	Tenor 2					
Tenor 1	1y	2y	5y	10y	15y	20y
2y	2.647					
3y	1.423	0.873				
4y	1.029	0.688				
5y	0.840	0.585				
8y	0.563	0.414	0.225			
9y	0.532	0.395	0.220			
10y	0.546	0.409	0.246			
15y	0.435	0.329	0.196	0.129		
20y	0.402	0.309	0.187	0.130	0.129	
30y	0.372	0.285	0.168	0.111	0.086	0.043

Figure 8.33: Ratio of means of actual moves/forward moves (USD 2y forward).
Source: Commerzbank, Bloomberg

USD Swap Slopes, 1y forward, mean(actual)/mean(forward)

	Tenor 2					
Tenor 1	1y	2y	5y	10y	15y	20y
2y	0.993					
3y	0.800	0.648				
4y	0.709	0.589				
5y	0.654	0.553				
8y	0.560	0.483	0.370			
9y	0.540	0.468	0.358			
10y	0.533	0.462	0.358			
15y	0.475	0.411	0.313	0.249		
20y	0.452	0.392	0.300	0.241	0.221	
30y	0.425	0.367	0.273	0.205	0.156	0.087

Figure 8.34: Ratio of means of actual moves/forward moves (USD 5y forward).
Source: Commerzbank, Bloomberg

Appendix 8.C: Implied vs Actual Slope Changes, 2001–2007

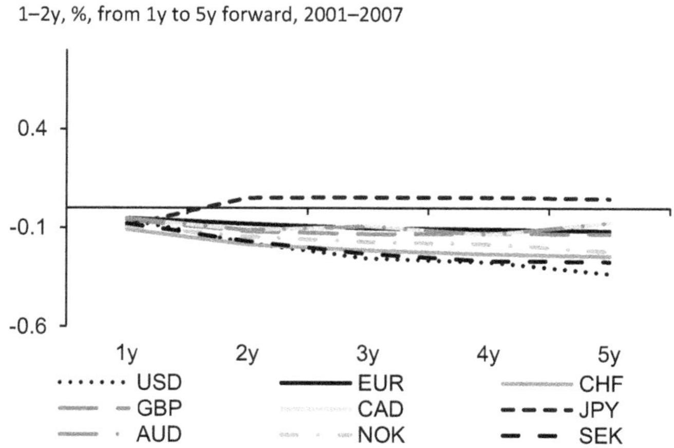

Figure 8.35: Implied slope change (2001–7, 1–2y).
Source: Commerzbank, Bloomberg

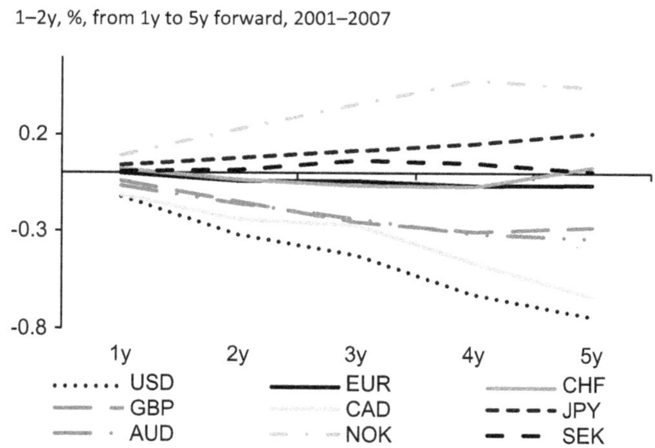

Figure 8.36: Actual slope change (2001–7, 1–2y).
Source: Commerzbank, Bloomberg

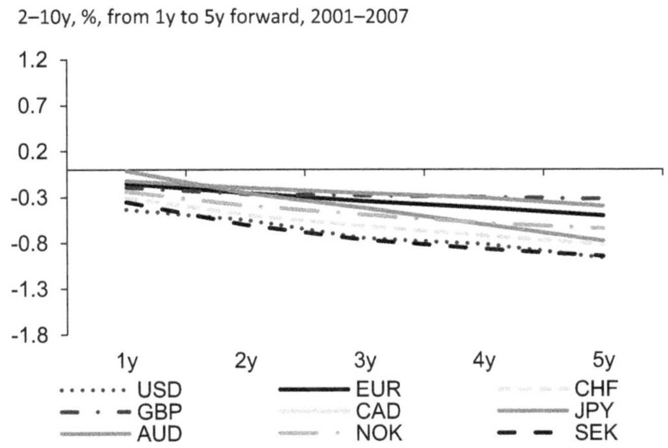

Figure 8.37: Implied slope change (2001–7, 2–10y).
Source: Commerzbank, Bloomberg

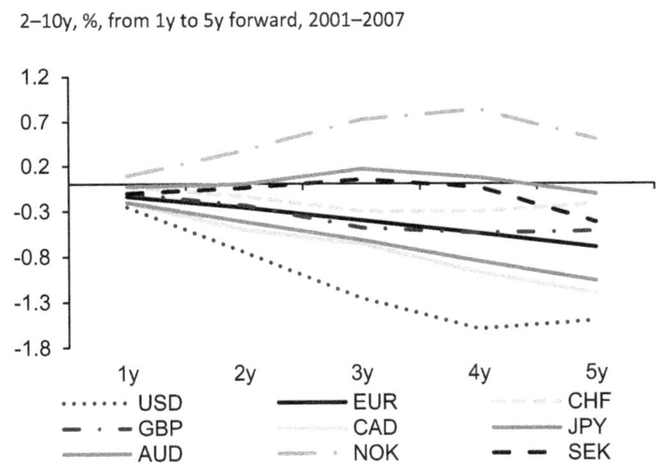

Figure 8.38: Actual slope change (2001–7, 2–10y).
Source: Commerzbank, Bloomberg

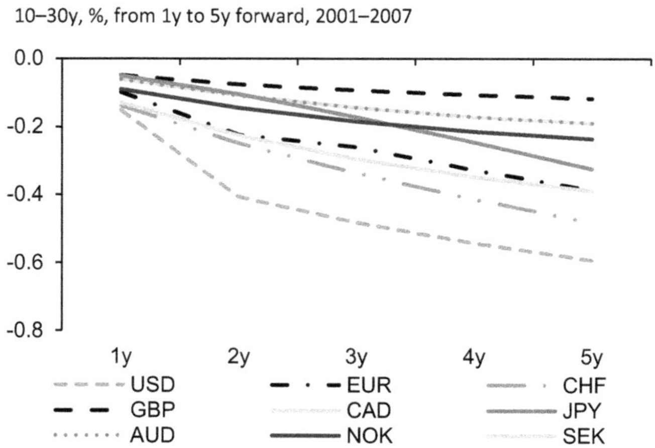

Figure 8.39: Implied slope change (2001–7, 10–30y).
Source: Commerzbank, Bloomberg

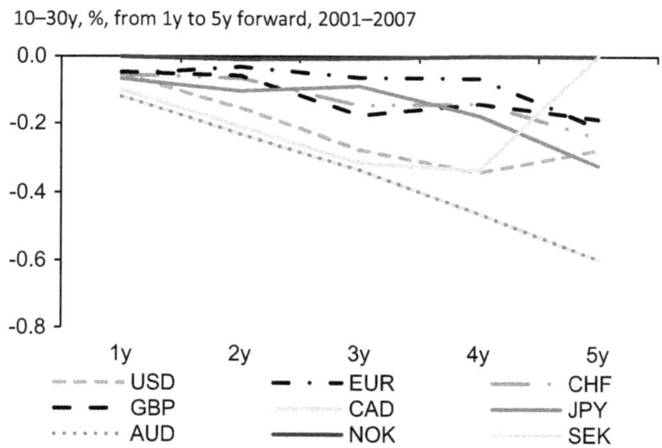

Figure 8.40: Actual slope change (2001–7, 10–30y).
Source: Commerzbank, Bloomberg

Appendix 8.D: Implied vs Actual Slope Changes, 2007–2014

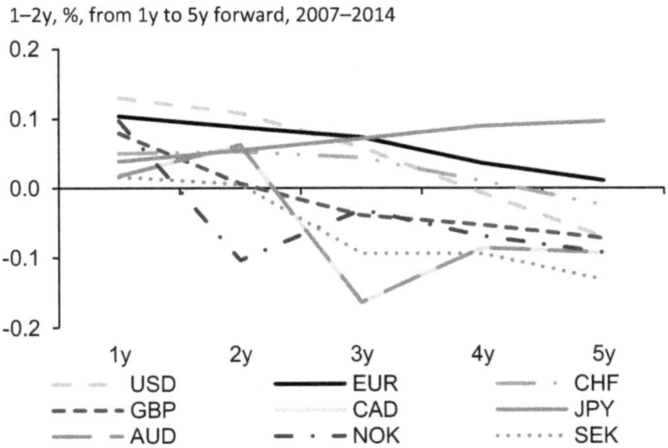

Figure 8.41: Implied slope change (2007–14, 1–2y).
Source: Commerzbank, Bloomberg

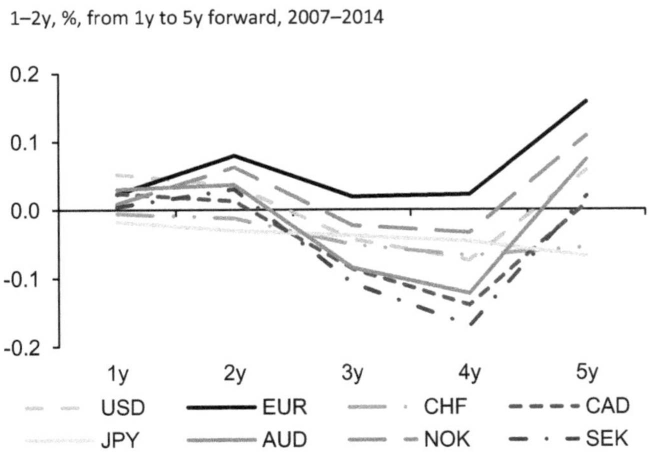

Figure 8.42: Actual slope change (2007–14, 1–2y).
Source: Commerzbank, Bloomberg

2–10y, %, from 1y to 5y forward, 2007–2014

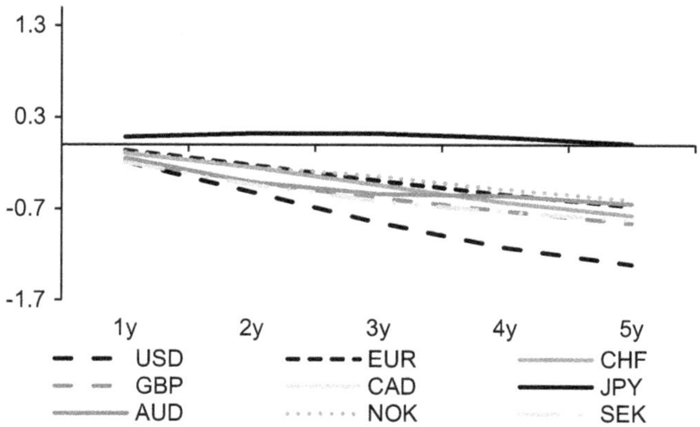

Figure 8.43: Implied slope change (2007–14, 2–10y).
Source: Commerzbank, Bloomberg

2–10y, %, from 1y to 5y forward, 2007–2014

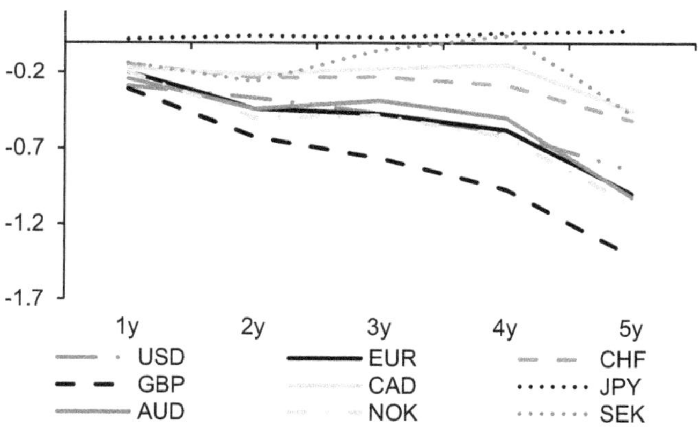

Figure 8.44: Actual slope change (2007–14, 2–10y).
Source: Commerzbank, Bloomberg

10–30y, %, from 1y to 5y forward, 2007–2014

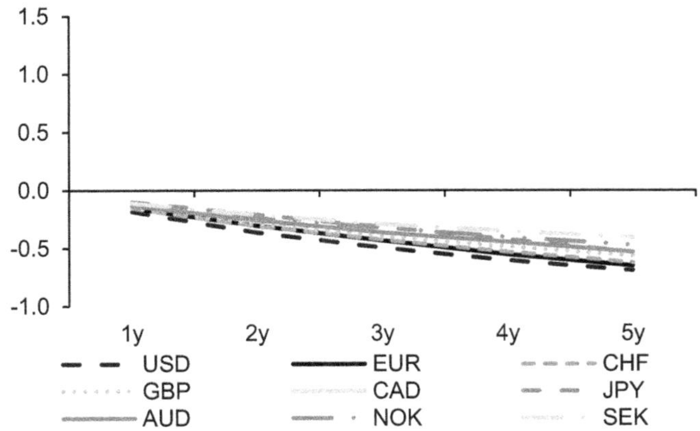

Figure 8.45: Implied slope change (2007–14, 10–30y).
Source: Commerzbank, Bloomberg

10–30y, %, from 1y to 5y forward, 2007–2014

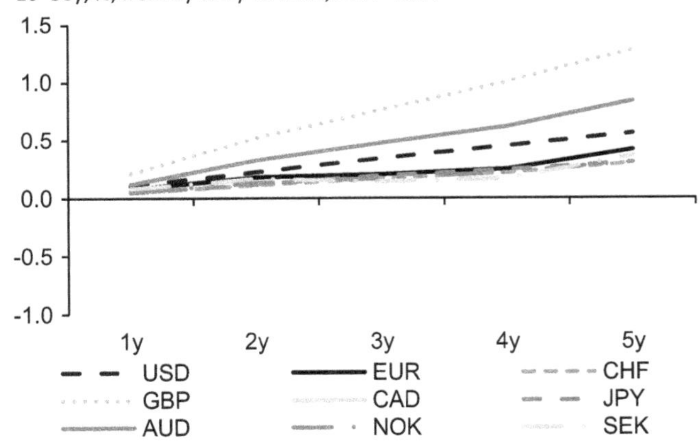

Figure 8.46: Actual slope change (2007–14, 10–30y).
Source: Commerzbank, Bloomberg

Appendix 8.E: Implied vs Actual Slope Changes, 2014–2020

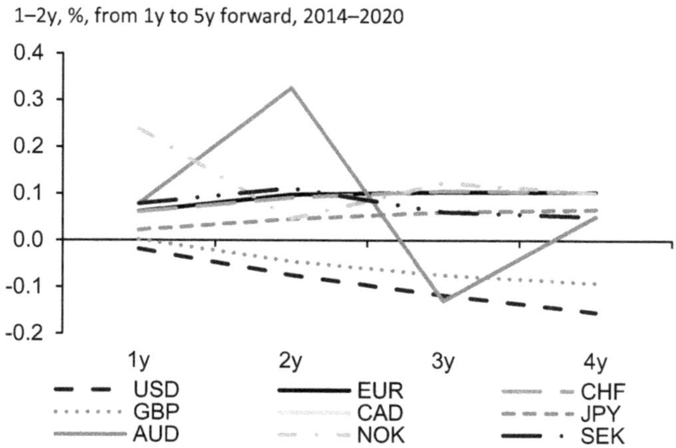

Figure 8.47: Implied slope change (2014–20, 1–2y).
Source: Commerzbank, Bloomberg

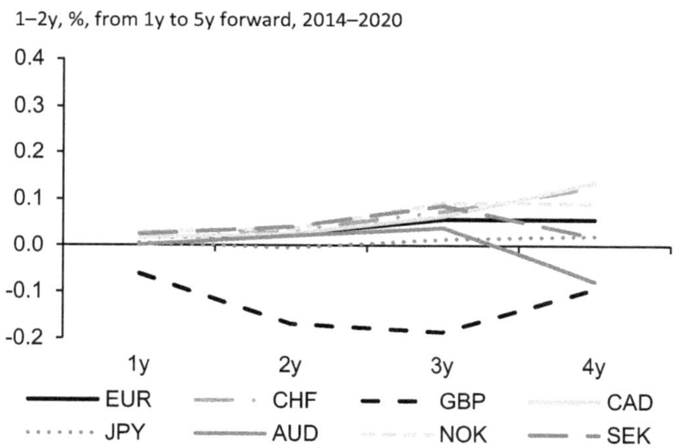

Figure 8.48: Actual slope change (2014–20, 1–2y).
Source: Commerzbank, Bloomberg

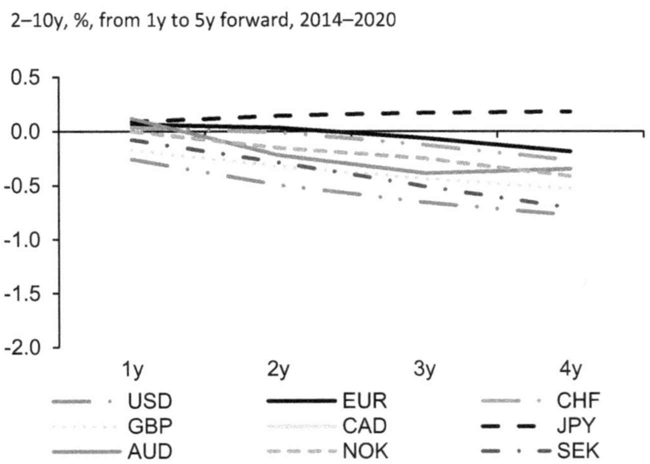

Figure 8.49: Implied slope change (2014–20, 2–10y).
Source: Commerzbank, Bloomberg

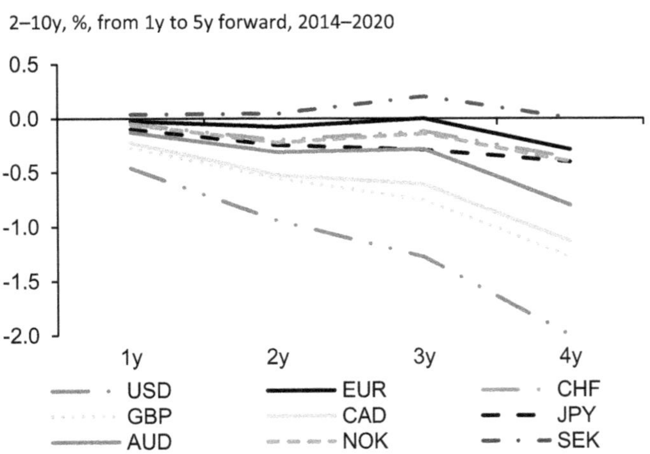

Figure 8.50: Actual slope change (2014–20, 2–10y).
Source: Commerzbank, Bloomberg

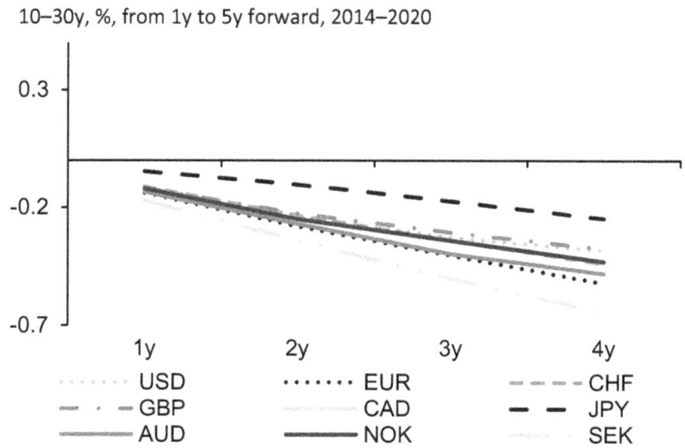

Figure 8.51: Implied slope change (2014–20, 10–30y).
Source: Commerzbank, Bloomberg

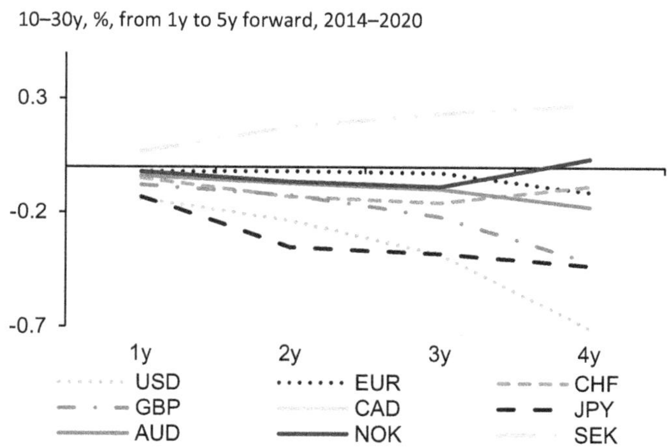

Figure 8.52: Actual slope change (2014–20, 10–30y).
Source: Commerzbank, Bloomberg

Chapter 9
Implied vs Realised Convexity

Chapter 8, when published as a Rates Radar, stirred many interesting discussions. We were motivated to expand our analysis to compare the theoretical or implied convexity value of a bond with the actual realised convexity value over time.[1] We are able to show that this 'implied convexity value' is a good overall estimate of levels of realised convexity value over a 1y horizon. For completeness, we repeat a small part of the derivation of the convexity formulae here, though it is covered more thoroughly in Chapter 8.

Where does convexity value come from? The price of a bond changes with changes in yield. However, this price change is non-linear, with the price being a convex function of the yield. Thus, the bond holder always does a little better under yield change scenarios than a linear approximation would indicate. This non-linearity is the 'convexity', and as longer-dated bonds are more sensitive to yield changes, they exhibit higher convexity than shorter-dated bonds. A bond or other instrument with high convexity is very desirable.

How large is convexity value? Though it's very common to hear that ultra-long bonds are popular due to high convexity, it's rare to see numbers attached to this convexity value. In part, this is because it is a calculation involving a number of assumptions about future yield and volatility levels, so it can only ever be an estimate. Also, the calculation itself is somewhat complex; it can be done using finite differences, or by multiplying the PV of each cashflow by a factor connected with yield and tenor. In Chapter 8, we showed that it is also possible to derive a closed-form solution for convexity, though it is quite long. Thus, it tends to be discussed more qualitatively than quantitatively, which is a pity, as precise comparisons can be useful. In this chapter, we show how the value of convexity has changed over time for instruments of different tenors.

We compare implied and realised convexity. What is also very relevant for bond holders, and also rarely seen, is a measure of how much convexity value a bond turned out to generate. This will of course depend on yield and volatility changes over the period in question, but it is of interest to see how accurate the 'implied' convexity is, relative to the actual value realised over time. We calculate the implied convexity value for EUR instruments using two different methods: (1) using current bond yields, and (2) using Bloomberg consensus forecast yields. We show that the two calculations lead to very similar estimates. We then compare this to the realised convexity value over a 1y period, and show that with some variation, implied and

1 This chapter was first published as Commerzbank's Rates Radar, 'The value of bond convexity', August 2018.

https://doi.org/10.1515/9783110688733-009

realised values certainly fall into the same range. We show that the main drivers of implied and realised convexity value are implied volatility and change in yield, respectively.

Defining Convexity

Convexity is the parameter defining the degree of non-linearity of the price of a bond with respect to yield. The price P of a bond of n years' tenor, yield y and coupon c is given by the following:

$$P = \sum_{i=1}^{n-1} \frac{c}{(1+y)^i} + \frac{c+100\%}{(1+y)^n} \tag{1}$$

If the yield of the bond changes, of course it is possible to recalculate the new price using this expression. However, it's not very intuitive to see how price and yield relate to each other from this. Thus, it is usually expressed as

$$P_t \approx P_0 + D(y_t - y_o) + \frac{1}{2}C(y_t - y_o)^2 \tag{2}$$

where P_t is the price of the bond at time t, D is the duration, and C is the convexity. D and C are of course the first and second derivatives of price with respect to yield, and have closed-form solutions, as follows:

$$D = -\frac{1}{1+y}\left[\frac{1+y}{y} - \frac{1+y+n(c-y)}{c[(1+y)^n - 1] + y}\right]$$

and

$$C = \frac{cV^4}{(1-V)^3}\left[n(1-n)(1-V)^2V^{n-2} - 2nV^{n-1}(1-V) + 2(1-V^n)\right] + \frac{2cV^3}{(1-V)^2}\left[-nV^{n-1}(1-V) + (1-V^n)\right] + (1+c)(n+1)nV^{n+2} \tag{3}$$

where

$$V = \frac{1}{1+y}$$

Thus, if an investor holds a bond, with known duration D and convexity C, they can predict the new price it will have at a future time when the yield has changed from y_o to y_t.

Value of Implied Convexity

Convexity *C*, as defined, is just a coefficient, not a value. What is the value of this nonlinearity? Clearly, the value of the third term in equation (2) depends on the change in yield, and so the expected value of the convexity of a bond – over the next year, for example – will depend upon the expected range of changes of yield over that time.

Suddenly, now we have changed from our fairly deterministic expressions to something more related to averages, forecasts and statistics. Because we don't exactly know the future value of the bond yield, we can't definitively state what the value of the convexity term will be. However, statistics comes to our aid, and if we know the future standard deviation σ_y of the yield, we can say

$$\text{Convexity value} = \frac{1}{2}\sigma_y{}^2 t \times C$$

This makes a number of assumptions, none of which are unassailable. It assumes that the future distribution of the yield is known, stationary and lognormal, all of which may be challenged. Nevertheless, it certainly serves to provide a useful estimate, and additionally, we do have a ready-made market estimate for σ_y in the form of the swaption volatility for the relevant tenor and time forward.

We need also to consider what value to use for the coupon of the bond. This will enter the calculation of convexity value via equation (3). We can do two things here – the first is to use the yield as the coupon, assuming that the curve will retain its current form over the next year, and the second is to use a forecast value. To obtain forecast values through history, we have created a series of 1y ahead forecasts from the Bloomberg consensus forecast series, which updates each quarter. This is only available for the 10y case, but nevertheless is useful.

Using all these assumptions, we can go back through history and extract yields and swaption volatilities to create the graphs in Figures 9.1 and 9.2 of the implied convexity value. Of course, we could also use different volatilities if we felt we could do better than the swaptions, but that starts to become fairly speculative.

Two things are worth noting here. The first is the difference in scale; the 50y instruments indeed have a far greater convexity value than the 10y case. The second is that there is almost no difference in using forecast yields vs assuming constant yields. This is consistent with Chapter 8, in which we also showed that there was little difference if we used forward yields. The reason is that the main driver of implied convexity value is the implied swaption volatility, whose range of variation is vastly larger than the relatively modest adjustment in yields.

This is actually somewhat reassuring. When one realises that the implied convexity relies on so many different assumptions, it could be thought that there is little way to obtain a reliable estimate. But when we realise that a single input, the future yield volatility, dominates, at least we have narrowed the range of uncertainty.

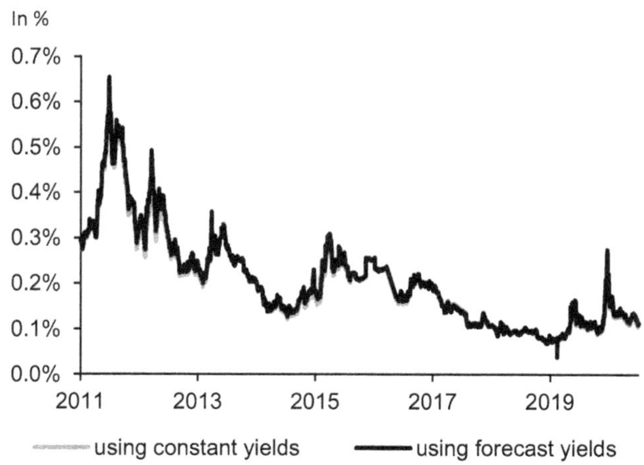

Figure 9.1: Implied convexity value, 10y German bonds.
Source: Commerzbank, Bloomberg

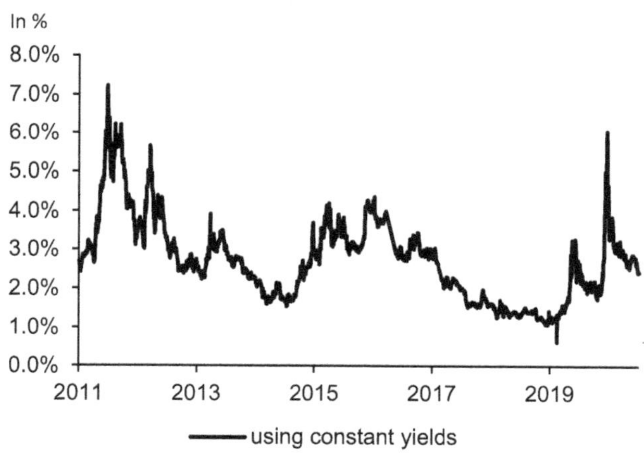

Figure 9.2: Implied convexity value, 50y EUR swaps.
Source: Commerzbank, Bloomberg

Value of Realised Convexity

We can now turn our attention to the actual realised value, which the convexity has supplied in the past. The realised value of convexity is the performance of a bond that occurs when yields change. In other words, it reflects the additional price gain from the duration increase when yields fall, and the reduced price loss from the duration decline when yields rise. This also explains that the realised value of convexity is always greater than zero and is zero when yields stay the same.

In algebraic terms, we use equations (1) and (2), restated here, to compute the realised value of convexity.

$$P = \sum_{i=1}^{n-1} \frac{c}{(1+y)^i} + \frac{c+100\%}{(1+y)^n} \tag{1}$$

$$P_t \approx P_0 + D(y_t - y_o) + \frac{1}{2}C(y_t - y_o)^2 \tag{2}$$

Using equation (1), we find the exact value of the bond price one year ahead. Then we use equation (2), with P_0 taken as the bond price at the start of the year, and D and C the duration and convexity at the start of the year. Using these values, together with the change in yield over the course of the year, we hope to use the price calculated with equation (2) to match up with that calculated with equation (1).

In Figure 9.3, we see the results. The solid grey line, hardly visible, is the full price calculation at the end of the 1y period using equation (1). The black line, again not very visible, is the price calculated using only the first two terms of equation (2). It can be seen that it does not match perfectly to the full calculation. The dashed light grey line is the price calculated using all three terms in equation (2), including the convexity value. It can be seen that the inclusion of this final term is a better approximation to the true price.

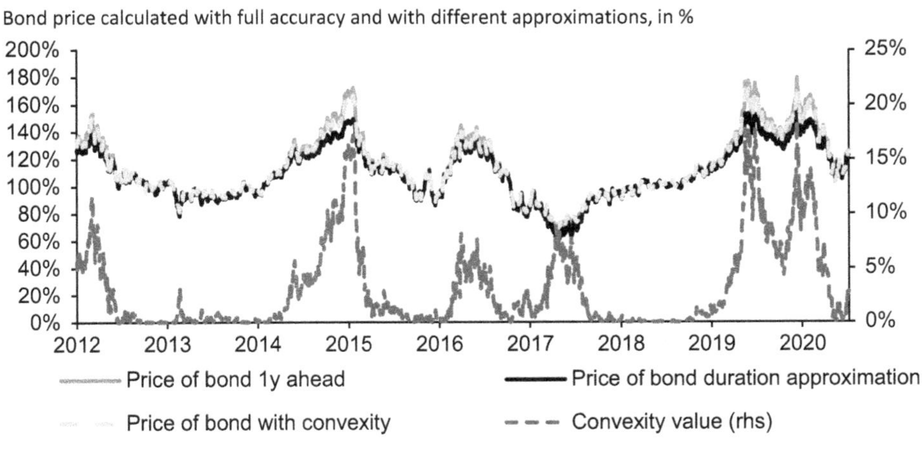

Figure 9.3: History of 50y bond price with convexity value.
Source: Commerzbank, Bloomberg

Finally, the dark grey dashed line at the bottom of the chart, which is charted using the axis on the right, is the convexity value term on its own – that is, just the third term of equation (2).

$$Convexity\ value = \frac{1}{2}C(y_t - y_o)^2$$

This is the realised convexity, and is primarily driven by the change in yield over the course of the year. For this long 50y instrument, it can be seen that it is large, over 10% at times.

Finally, we can graph implied vs realised convexity together, as in Figure 9.4. We see that while we would hardly expect implied convexity to accurately indicate changes in realised convexity, the overall levels of realised convexity oscillate around implied, and on the whole it appears to be a reasonable estimate. Note that the near-zero levels of realised convexity occur when the change in yield over the course of the year is close to zero.

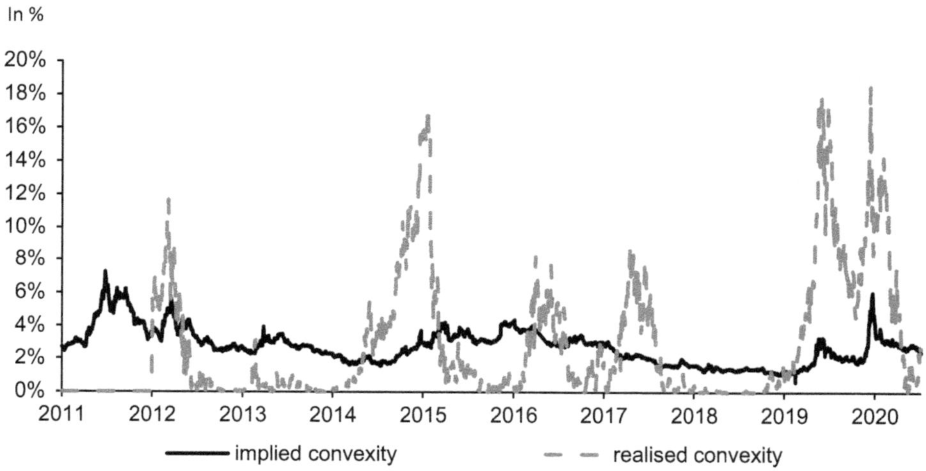

Figure 9.4: Implied vs realised convexity for 50y bond.
Source: Commerzbank, Bloomberg

These calculations emphasise the importance of the ultra-long end of the curve. Our graph in Figure 9.5 shows the realised convexity value for 10, 30 and 50y maturities. While realised convexity for the 10y case peaks at 1.25%, for the 50y case, we see close to 20%, which is very significant.

Finally, we take a look at realised convexity value over different timescales. So far, our analysis has concentrated on a 1y period, but it is also interesting to focus on shorter periods. In Figure 9.6, we plot the realised convexity value over 1y, 6m and 3m periods for a 30y bond. It can be seen that even over shorter periods, the convexity value can be considerable when there is substantial yield variation.

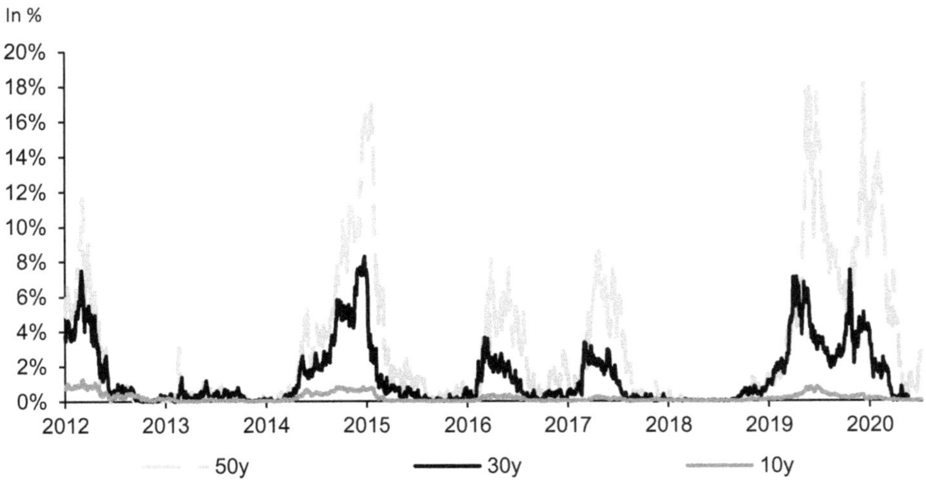

Figure 9.5: History of convexity value for bonds of different tenor.
Source: Commerzbank, Bloomberg

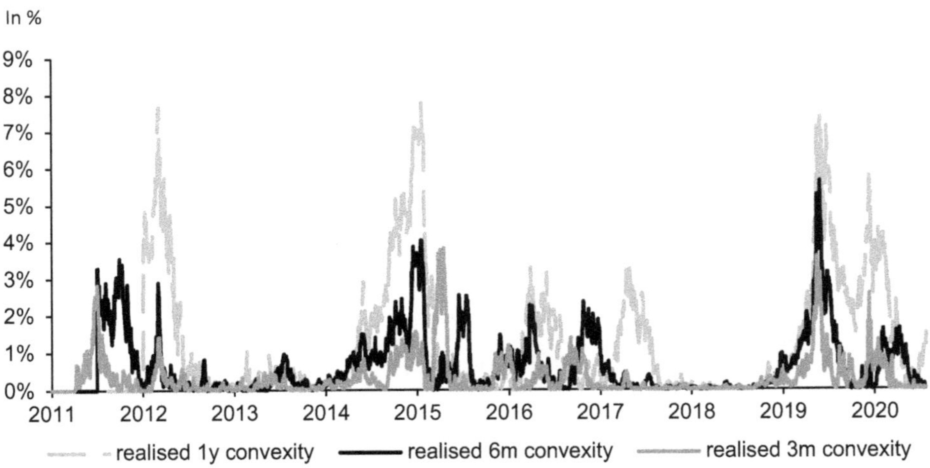

Figure 9.6: Realised convexity of a 30y bond over different periods.
Source: Commerzbank, Bloomberg

List of Figures

https://doi.org/10.1515/9783110688733-010

List of Tables

https://doi.org/10.1515/9783110688733-011

About the Authors

Jessica James is a senior quantitative researcher at Commerzbank in London, and previously was head of the Quantitative Solutions Group. She joined Commerzbank from Citigroup where she held a number of FX roles, latterly as global head of the Quantitative Investor Solutions Group. Prior to this, she was the head of the Risk Advisory and Currency Overlay Team for Bank One. Before her career in finance, James lectured in physics at Trinity College, Oxford. She holds a BSc in physics from Manchester University and a D. Phil. in atomic and nuclear physics from Oxford University.

Her significant publications include the *Handbook of Exchange Rates* (Wiley), *Interest Rate Modelling* (Wiley), and 'Currency Management' (Risk Books). Her latest book *FX Option Performance* came out in 2015. She has been closely associated with the development of currency as an asset class, being one of the first to create overlay and currency alpha products.

Jessica is a visiting professor both at University College London and at Cass Business School. She is a managing editor for *Quantitative Finance*. Apart from her financial appointments, she is a fellow of the Institute of Physics and has been a member of their governing body and of their Industry and Business Board.

Christoph Rieger heads the Rates & Credit Research at Commerzbank. Together with his research teams, he covers the full range of fixed income products, from money markets, government bonds and SSAs to covered bonds, financials and corporates, developing big-picture themes alongside commercial trading and funding strategies.

Prior to this role, Christoph was Head of Rates Strategy at Commerzbank and he worked as senior interest rate strategist at Dresdner Kleinwort with a specific focus on money markets and interest rate derivatives. Before joining Dresdner Kleinwort in 2004, Christoph held various positions in fixed income research, starting in 1998 at Commerzbank as a government bond analyst before moving to London in 2001, where his main focus was on interest rate strategies using derivatives. His academic background is rooted in economics, in which he holds two degrees: an MA from Temple University (Fulbright Scholarship in Philadelphia, PA) and a diploma from the University of Cologne (Germany). Christoph is a member of the ECB Bond Market Contact Group.

Michael Leister is responsible for interest rate strategy at Commerzbank. His research team of four analysts covers the full range of liquid and structured rates products for the major currencies, in cash as well as in derivatives space.

Michael joined Commerzbank London in 2012 with a focus on € rates and global inflation markets, after working as Interest Rate Strategist for WestLB in Düsseldorf and London with a focus on government bonds.

He holds a masters degree in economics from the University of Mannheim and was awarded the CFA charter in 2012. Beyond financial markets he is a frequent participant in city and mountain marathons (PB 2:47).

https://doi.org/10.1515/9783110688733-012

References

Adrian, T., Crump, R. K. and Moench, E. (2008), updated 2013. Pricing the term structure with linear regressions. Federal Reserve Bank of New York Staff Reports, no. 340. https://www.newyorkfed.org/research/data_indicators/term_premia.html.

Arai, F., Makabe, Y., Okawara, Y. and Nagano, T. (2016). Recent trends in cross-currency basis, *Bank of Japan Review*, http://www.boj.or.jp/en/research/wps_rev/rev_2016/data/rev16e07.pdf.

Bernanke, B. S., Boivin, J. and Eliasz, P. (2005). Measuring the effects of monetary policy: A factor-augmented vector autoregressive (FAVAR) approach. *The Quarterly Journal of Economics*, *120*(1), 387–422.

Borio, C., McCauley, R., McGuire, P. and Sushko, V. (2016). Covered interest parity lost: Understanding the cross-currency basis. *BIS Quarterly Review*, http://www.bis.org/publ/qtrpdf/r_qt1609e.pdf.

Christensen, J. H. E. and Rudebusch, G. D. (2019). A new normal for interest rates? Evidence from inflation-indexed debt. Federal Reserve Bank of San Francisco, Working Paper 2017-07. https://doi.org/10.24148/wp2017-07.

Chua, J. H. (1984). A closed-form formula for calculating bond duration. *Financial Analysts Journal*, *40*(3), 76–78.

Cohen, B. H., Hordahl, P. and Xia, D. (2018). Term premia: models and some stylised facts. *BIS Quarterly Review*, September 2018, 79.

Crump, R. K., Eusepi, S. and Moench, E. (2016). The term structure of expectations and bond yields, Federal Reserve Bank of New York Staff Reports, no. 775 May 2016; revised April 2018.

Du, W., Tepper, A. and Verdelhan, A. (2016). Deviations from covered interest rate parity, *SSRN*, https://ssrn.com/abstract=2768207.

Ernst and Young (2014). Applying IFRS 13: Credit valuation adjustments for derivative contracts, http://www.ey.com/Publication/vwLUAssets/ey-applying-ifrs-fair-value-measurement/$FILE/ey-applying-ifrs-fair-value-measurement.pdf.

European Banking Authority (2014). EBA report on CVA, April 2014, https://www.eba.europa.eu/documents/10180/950548/EBA+Report+on+CVA.pdf.

Fama, E.F. (1984). Forward and spot exchange rates. *Journal of Monetary Economics*, *14*(3), 319–338.

Greenwood, R. and Vayanos, D. (2014). Bond supply and excess bond returns. *The Review of Financial Studies*, *27* (3), March 2014, 663–713, https://doi.org/10.1093/rfs/hht133.

Gregory, J. (2011). *Counterparty credit risk.* Wiley Finance.

Haltom, R., Wissuchek, E. and Wolman, A. L. (2018). Have yield curve inversions become more likely? Federal Reserve Bank of Richmond, *18* (12), https://www.richmondfed.org/publications/research/economic_brief/2018/eb_18-12.

Hordahl, P. and Tristani, O. (2014). Inflation risk premia in the Euro area and the United States. *International Journal of Central Banking*, http://www.ijcb.org/journal/ijcb14q3a1.htm.

Hull, J. C. and White, A. (2014). OIS discounting, interest rate derivatives, and the modelling of stochastic interest rate spreads. *Journal of Investment Management*, March 2014.

Ilmanen, A. (1995). *Understanding the yield curve*, United States Fixed-Income Research Portfolio Strategies. Salomon Brothers.

ISDA. (2010), Market review of OTC derivative bilateral collateralisation practices, ISDA Collateral Steering Committee.

James, J., Fullwood, J. and Billington, P. (2015). *FX Option Performance: An Analysis of the Value Delivered by FX Options Since the Start of the Market.* (New York: Wiley).

James, J., Leister, M. and Rieger, C. (2016). Demystifying the term premium, Commerzbank Rates Radar.

https://doi.org/10.1515/9783110688733-013

Kim, D. H. and Wright, J. H. (2005). An arbitrage-free three-factor term structure model and the recent behavior of long-term yields and distant-horizon forward rates. The Federal Reserve Board, Washington.

Kopp, E. and Williams, P. D. (2018). A macroeconomic approach to the term premium. IMF Working Papers, no. 18/140.

Li, C., Meldrum, A. and Rodriguez, M. (2017). Robustness of long-maturity term premium estimates. FEDS Notes, Board of Governors of the Federal Reserve System. https://www.federalreserve.gov/econres/notes/feds-notes/robustness-of-long-maturity-term-premium-estimates-20170403.htm.

Miron, P. and Swannell, P. (1991). *Pricing and hedging swaps*. Euromoney Books.

Rime, D., Schrimpf, A. and Syrstad, O. (2017). Segmented money markets and covered interest parity arbitrage, *Bank for International Settlements*, BIS working papers no. 651, http://www.bis.org/publ/work651.pdf.

Ruiz, I. (2015). *XVA desks: A new era for risk management*. Palgrave Macmillan.

Swanson, E. (2007). What we do and don't know about the term premium. Federal Reserve Bank of San Francisco, FRBSF Economic Letter. http://www.frbsf.org/economic-research/publications/economic-letter/2007/july/term-premium/.

Index

https://doi.org/10.1515/9783110688733-014

The Moorad Choudhry Global Banking Series

Principles of Green Banking: Managing Environmental Risk and Sustainability by Suborna Barua

Bank Asset Liability Management Best Practice: Yesterday, Today and Tomorrow by Polina Bardaeva

Reverse Stress Testing in Banking: A Comprehensive Guide by Michael Eichhorn, Tiziano Bellini, and Daniel Mayenberger (eds.)

Random Walks in Fixed Income and Foreign Exchange: Unexpected Discoveries in Issuance, Investment and Hedging of Yield Curve Instruments by Jessica James, Michael Leister, and Christoph Rieger

www.ingramcontent.com/pod-product-compliance
Lightning Source LLC
Chambersburg PA
CBHW080937240926
51849CB00004BA/482
* 9 7 8 3 1 1 0 6 8 8 6 8 9 *